DATE DUE

DE 16 '98			
AP 29 '99			
MR 2 9 '06			

DEMCO 38-296

DUKE ELLINGTON

BY
BARRY ULANOV

DA CAPO · NEW YORK · 1975

Library of Congress Cataloging in Publication Data

Ulanov, Barry.
  Duke Ellington.

  (The Roots of jazz)
  Reprint of the ed. published by Musicians Press
Ltd., London.
  Discography: p.
  Includes index.
  1. Ellington, Duke, 1899-1974.
ML410.E44U4   1975   785.4'2'0924 [B]   74-31300
ISBN 0-306-70727-6

Published by Da Capo Press, Inc.
A Subsidiary of Plenum Publishing Corporation
227 West 17th Street, New York, N.Y. 10011

DUKE
ELLINGTON

DUKE
ELLINGTON

BY

BARRY ULANOV

LONDON

MUSICIANS PRESS LIMITED
114-116 CHARING CROSS ROAD,
LONDON, W.C.2

PRINTED IN GREAT BRITAIN BY LOWE AND BRYDONE PRINTERS LTD.,
LONDON, N.W.10

TO THE OLD GUARD,
TOBY AND SONNY AND
FREDDIE AND TRICKY
AND HARRY,
FOR THEIR MUSIC
AND THEIR SPIRIT

CONTENTS

(All chapter titles are Ellington song titles)

INTRODUCTION

DUKE ELLINGTON WAS BOTH FLATTERED AND FLATTERING when he first heard I was working on this biography. About six months later he had a second thought about it. "Biographies, like statues, are for dead men, aren't they?" he speculated. But this book is no portrait in stone: it is the picture of a man very much alive, whose achievement, already great, is still growing, shaping, perhaps, the future of American music.

To musicians all over the world, Duke's contribution is enormous; it is reverenced by jazzmen, respected by traditional musicians. His music is adored by millions of fans from Irkutsk to Indianapolis, from Hollywood to The Hague. Unfortunately, in his own country the pressures of prejudice have consistently crushed ultimate commercial achievement: appearances at the top hotels (with one or two exceptions), a fat movie contract, a sponsored radio program. There are those who argue that Duke is successful enough, that any additional traffic with commerce would destroy his musical integrity. But Duke's intense devotion to high standards is not so easily dissipated. The integrity which is at stake is that of the American people, who have been a good deal less than equitable in their recognition of their own colored great. One of the purposes of this book is to call this malfeasance to the attention of my countrymen.

I have tried, here, not only to present the career of Duke Ellington and the collective greatness of the Ellington Orchestra, but to delineate the atmosphere and conditions of the jazz world as well. If I have been at all successful, it is because of the wonderful co-operation I have received from all concerned —from the members of Duke's band and associate organizations, from Duke's family and friends, and from Duke himself, who, despite his morbid speculations, extended every possible aid and comfort.

Special thanks must go to the oldest members of the band, Toby Hardwick, Sonny Greer, Freddie Guy, Joe Nanton, Harry Carney and Rex Stewart, who freely put their memories and their scrapbooks at my disposal. Thanks are also due to Cootie Williams and Barney Bigard, for helpful and revealing conversations; to Duke's family, Mercer, Edna and George Ellington, Florence Walker, Ruth and Daniel James, who were all extremely generous with time and information; to Billy Strayhorn; to the Pinn family; to Henry Grant; to Leonard Feather; to Barbara Hodgkins; to Willie Manning and Richard Bowdoin Jones and Al Celley and, most particularly, to Mildred Dixon and Jerome Rhea, for invaluable aid.

My wife, Joan, is in large measure responsible for the finished condition of this book. Without her, there would have been no index; without her, there would have been some glaring errors. Her loving contribution falls just short of full collaboration.

Barry Ulanov

DUKE
ELLINGTON

CHAPTER ONE

WASHINGTON WOBBLE

"**B**OY," DUKE ELLINGTON'S PHYSICAL EDUCATION TEACHER said to him sternly one day at high school, "you're never going to amount to anything as long as you live." Ed Henderson was complaining about the way young Ellington spent his time, drumming on table tops, running his hands over imaginary keyboards. When class was called to attention, as often as not, Duke wasn't there. And if he was there, he gave very little of the attention called for. "No, boy, you're never going to amount to a damn thing," Ed Henderson said, shaking his head sadly.

The young Duke felt differently about his future. When he was late in getting up for school, his mother or his Aunt Florence would shake him and push him and rush him out of bed into his clothes. Once dressed, Duke's tempo would change. He would come downstairs slowly, with an elegance. At the foot of the stairs he would stop and call to his mother and his aunt.

"Stand over there," he would direct, pointing to the wall. "Now," he would say, "listen. This," he would say slowly, with very careful articulation, "is the great, the grand, the magnificent Duke Ellington." Then he would bow. Looking up at his smiling mother and aunt, he would say, "Now applaud, applaud." And then he would run off to school.

Duke always felt he would be a success. He counted on it as he counted on the charm of his smile and the ease of his personality even as a very little boy in Washington. Ed Henderson was wrong and Duke knew he was, but he just smiled at the high school teacher, who, in later years, telling the story to his students, always left Duke's name out of it until the very end. After admitting that he "really had to eat his words," he got great roars of delighted recognition and approval from the boys as he named the student for whom he had predicted such a bad future.

Duke's childhood was a happy one, a full one, one that was bound to induce a sense of confidence and security. It was a life of much ease, provided by his father—who was first a butler and then a Navy blueprintmaker—balanced by a degree of discipline, provided by his mother, and a sprinkling of strife which arose out of the conflicting temperaments of his parents.

Duke's parents were born in the same year, 1879: James Edward Ellington on April 15, in Lincolntown, North Carolina; Daisy Kennedy Ellington on January 4, in Washington, District of Columbia. Uncle Ed, as everybody, even his children, called him at one time or another, was the second youngest of a family of fourteen. Uncle Ed and his brother George, the youngest of the Ellington children, paired off: they both took up buttling for a profession. But while George accepted tradition and went to work for the oldest, most conservative and best known firm of caterers in Washington, Duke's father, typically, found a very different way to follow his profession. He took a job at fifteen with a very well-known white doctor, M. F. Cuthbert, who lived on a fashionable stretch of Rhode Island Avenue. Within a few years, James Edward was butler, confidant and very close friend. He carried messages between Dr. Cuthbert and his friends and patients and became deeply involved in the confidences of all. Sometimes George spelled him at his job, and sometimes, in exchange, he worked with George or in place of him. They buttled at White House receptions together and at great parties in the Embassies and Ministries throughout Washington. James Edward, however, missed the greatest of all Washington receptions, in 1938, when George went to work at the White House as one of the principal American equerries at the state visit of Their Britannic Majesties,

King George and Queen Elizabeth. He had died just one year earlier.

Duke's father was a perennially happy man who enjoyed all the pleasures life provided him, who relaxed easily and didn't let anything worry him very much. Daisy Kennedy was, in almost every way, his direct opposite, a woman of rigorous moral principle, stiff-lipped and, in direct contradiction of her beautiful face and figure, prim of mien and manner. She frowned upon cosmetics, and only by the application of affectionate family pressure was she persuaded to put on lip-rouge to pose for a photograph shortly after she came to live in New York. Her family wasn't quite so large as her husband's, but with eight brothers and sisters she was used to lots of people in her house. Both she and her husband felt lost without swarms of relatives about them. They had only two children of their own, and those spaced sixteen years apart, so the Ellingtons, J. E. and Daisy K., were always surrounded by sisters and brothers and aunts and uncles and the various progeny thereof. Duke grew up in a house literally filled with dozens of cousins.

Edward Kennedy Ellington was born in his grandfather's house, "old man Kennedy's place," on April 29, 1899, in the twentieth year of both his parents. This was the year of the great blizzard. The snows were so bad that winter that in the last months of Daisy Ellington's pregnancy they were piled up to the second-story windows on 20th Street where her family lived. Shortly after Edward was born, J. E. took his wife and child to live on Ward Place, a very short block just at the beginning of Washington's northwestern section, where the Negroes of the city were gathered in greater numbers than in any other part of the city.

The Ellingtons were colored, in a city which drew as strong and unbreakable a color line as any railroad station, residential section, school, store or place of employment in the states to the south of it. Washington, District of Columbia, the nation's capital, forced its Negroes to live lives of unwanted distinction, physically, intellectually, morally apart from the white inhab-

itants of the hot city by the Potomac. The remarkable thing
about families like the Ellingtons is that they were able to grow
up so completely like the rest of the country, to think, read,
write the same thought patterns, the same verbal formulations;
to use the same symbols, foster the same aspirations and bring
them to fruition in almost exactly the same way that men and
women thought, spoke, fought and achieved in Spokane and
Kalamazoo, New York and New Zion, Santa Fe and Santa Barbara. It is remarkable; it is impressive; it is not accidental.

The inheritance of these people is enormous: it goes back to
Africa, to cotton fields and Mississippi River levees—the popular
symbols of Negro culture. It also goes back to the tightly packed
holds of slave ships, which brought the Negroes to America; to
the exquisitely designed and decorated plantation houses where
they worked after picking cotton; to the ships which plied the
Mississippi and brought them from slave quarries in the South
to schools and more decent, independent lives in the North. It
goes back to twelve million square miles of the continent of
Africa, to a feverish fight for existence against every natural obstacle in the jungles. Africa suggests a primitive culture to the
average white man. Actually, as our anthropologists have proved
clearly, it is a culture of great size and scope and meaning,
which produced human beings of the same physical and intel-
lectual and moral dimensions as the backwoods of the Iberian
peninsula, as the front cities of the Anglo-Saxon isles and the
middle European valleys. It is the culture in which the police
force was first made a public institution, in which cattle were
used to produce milk and iron was smelted, for the first time.
It is a creative culture, in which the brilliant conception of
abstract representation was first projected in art, in which perhaps half of our musical instruments were first developed. All
of this was Duke Ellington's inheritance, Africa, cottonfields,
levees, plantation houses, slave ships, good schooling, everything the Negro had—and a good deal the white man had, as
well. For, like most of our colored population, the Ellingtons
were a strong racial mixture, black and white and bronze and
sepia, brown, yellow and all the other magnificent shades and

The Duke as Master
of Ceremonies : the im-
maculate dress, the
happy smile, the relax-
ed hands are typical.

J. E., Duke's father, proud of his boy's New York success, poses with son in late 1923. Freddie and Uncle Ed were attentive to the same detail—the florid tiepin. All three assumed careful hands-in-pocket informality for the photo, one of the few ever taken of Duke's father.

Mercer Ellington *(above, right)* at ten follows his father's example. The other boy is a friend.

Duke at ten: even then urbane in look and dress.

Just before leaving
Washington for New
York, Duke left this
memento of good
living for his friends
and his family.

First flush of success, first New York apartment, expensive cigar (he no longer smokes them), dressing gown.

Mercer forms his band and he and Father Duke go over his library together, flashing the same smile.

The first successful Ellington concert was given at Colgate University, with Duke playing against the solemn background of the chapel's organ pipes.

Glee and athletic prowess mix in Duke's first movie lot appearance (1930), as the *Check and Double Check* chorus chases the bandleader across RKO's Hollywood acres.

Rex Stewart

The late
Arthur Whetsel

The late
Jimmy Blanton

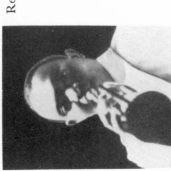

Tricky Sam
(Joe) Nanton

Below: Duke leans across the reeds at a record session to explain a voicing to Johnny Hodges. Al Sears (with glasses) and Jimmy Hamilton (turned from camera) await Johnny's expected variations on Ellington's verbal theme

Cat Anderson *(left)*, whom Duke calls "my phenomenon," hits a seemingly impossible note, in a Yankee Stadium appearance of the band. Cat always points to the note in the air as he makes it. That's Hayes Alvis on bass.

The band jumps; Freddie Guy, Duke, singers Kay Davis, Joya Sherrill, Marie love it.

Ivie Anderson, longtime Ellington vocalist, at the Colgate University Concert, one of the band's first.

The full band, at the 400 Club, 1945 : Lawrence Brown soloing ; saxes, Sears, Hodges, Hamilton, Carney (Toby away) ; trombones, Nanton, Jones ; trumpets, Jordan, Hemphill, Anderson, Nance ; Rex's stand ; Guy behind Duke ; Raglin on bass ; Greer on drums ; vocalists Kay Davis and Marie at Duke's right.

ena Horne finishes her presenta- on of an *Esquire* award to Stray- orn with a kiss.

The 1937 Cotton Club dressing room : Duke, Irving Mills, lyric writer Harry Nemo.

"How's it going?" Duke cups an attentive ear. Strayhorn corrects mss.

"That's it!" Duke okays the ensemble sound at the record studio.

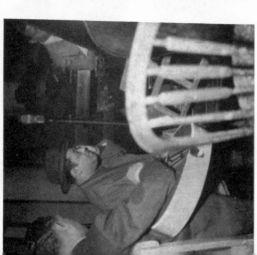

"Get it? See?" Taft Jordan and Ray Nance aren't certain that they do.

Below : Lawrence Brown and Duke trade ideas over the saxes' (Carney, Hardwick, Hamilton, Hodges, Sears) heads.

The first big band. The R.K.O. late, 1930. Jenkins, Whetsel. Tizol, Duke and othe

The same band that made *Check and Double Check*, the Cotton Club and jazz history in the late 1920's. It was almost the end of the tuxedo era.

The 1943 Ellington orchestra assembles for a Pathé short: Raglin on bass; saxes Webster, Jones, Hamilton, Hodges, Carney; Guy; brass men Nance, Jones, Nanton, Williams (Sandy), Tizol, Baker, Jordan: Sonny at back, Duke in front.

Above: Drummer, drink
raconteur and best friend
William "Sonny" Greer
Inset: Joya Sherrill reco
one of Duke's latest arrar
ments.

tints of human pigmentation. With this variegation of epidermal hue went as rich a mixture of cultures.

From his immediate surroundings, from a long line of forebears who had risen to a firm place in American society, young Edward Kennedy Ellington took his immediate interests, those of any young American boy—baseball, the movies, roving in gangs, street games and parlor socials. He was a good baseball player: hard-hitting enough to earn a place high up in the line-up; smart enough as a fielder to play center field; sufficiently flexible and versatile to play second base, besides. He played this latter position so well that for a while he was called Otto, after a leading second-baseman of the day, Otto Williams. By the time Duke got to his teens, he and his gang were dressing in imitation of the movie stars of that day, leaping fences and jumping across Great Divides in the manner of Douglas Fairbanks and Richard Talmadge, smoking cigars and drinking "fire-water" in the manner of Stuart Holmes, racing cars the way Barney Oldfield did. The street games were like a million other American street games, the roving gangs were like most other bands of small boys clustered together by parochial interests arising out of residence on a common street. But the fights were a little different. The fights were quite often with white boys, and almost as often as they were with white boys they were simply because their opponents were white. It didn't matter who started them: the differences of skin produced differences of opinion; differences of opinion produced chips on shoulders quickly, and the altercations began.

Duke grew up with baseball, motion pictures, fights with whites and pride in his ancestry. He grew up with a happy awareness of the strength of families, the length of their affections and the vigorous loyalties which could and often did arise out of these groups. He grew up with a personality so startlingly ambivalent, as a result of the violently crossed influences of his father and mother, that today there are those who think of him only as a reticent man, completely shy and willfully inarticulate; others who regard him as a shameless extrovert; and still others who fancy him as either a hopeless or a delightful combination of both major traits. But whether introspective or exhibitionist, concerned with baseball, the movies, food and family, like any white American, or probing his Negro antecedents, it is of these psychological and sociological facets that Duke Ellington's music consists. From them it takes shape and size and meaning, and we must never lose sight of them if we are to understand, appreciate and enjoy the man and his superb creations.

When Edward Kennedy was four, Daisy Kennedy sat down to the piano to play *The Rosary*, and he wept. "It was so pretty," he said, "so pretty."

When Edward was seven, Mrs. Klingscale was engaged to teach him piano. Mrs. Klingscale has been called, variously, "Chinkscale," "Klinkscale," any number of reproductions of a tinkling sound combined with the name of the octave base of Western music, in a kind of onomatopoetic justice. Edward was a tolerable piano pupil. He played Czerny's five-finger exercises, the ubiquitous pestilence every beginner at the keyboard from Liszt downward has experienced, since Beethoven's pupil devised them for his pupils. He learned something about the basic scale relationships, the diminutions and augmentations which made keys major or minor, the intervals which formed the fundamental chords, the tonic, subdominant and dominant. He was apprised, in sum, of the mechanics of music, but, much as he got of the mathematics of the relationship of A, B and C, of the flat, sharp and natural shapes of a note, of the fractions, whole, half, quarter, eighth, sixteenth, which gave rhythmic value to the measures and phrases, he got correspondingly little of what had made him cry at hearing the maudlin sounds his mother made on the piano when she played *The Rosary*. He played at a church concert given by Mrs. Klingscale and won her compliments and his parents' plaudits, but he himself got so little satisfaction from what he had done that "it all slipped away from me" for six or seven years. Not till he was in high school did music mean much to him again.

For a while, in the later years of grade school and the first of high, his dissatisfaction with the piano was so great that, like thousands of other youngsters the world over, he did everything possible to get out of practicing. Generally, he could be found at the vacant lot behind the YMCA a few blocks away from the house on 13th Street, between R and S, to which the Ellingtons had moved when he was eight years old. He played baseball and football there, in season. But 'though an organized game would often find Duke in the line-up, at second base or in the outfield for baseball, at almost any position in football, he wasn't always playing one of America's two most popular sports when he should have been practicing piano. He was more versatile in his interests and more elusive than that, and there were times when the Northwest streets Q to U, 11th to 16th would ring with "Edward, Edward, where are you?" or "Duke!" —the imperative mood for the young nobleman. His whole family, parents, aunts, cousins, were enlisted, at one time or another, in the hunts for Duke. They almost never found him.

Edward K. became "Duke" Ellington at the very early age of eight. The ennobling was effected by Ralph Green, brother of Mrs. Pinn who lived next door to the Ellingtons when they lived, from 1905 to 1916, just across 13th Street, moving from one red brick Victorian house to another, with similar bays on the fronts and points on the roofs and trees and grass around them. Ralph Green was an incorrigible nicknamer, and his sobriquets always stuck. He called one of his brothers-in-law "Joker"; another, who was a Puerto Rican lawyer, he called "Doc" to that gentleman's considerable pleasure and, upon occasion, embarrassment, when he was called upon to minister to the ailing. "Zeb," as he himself was called, named Edward "Duke" for no reason at all, but simply because that was as good a name as any to give the eight-year-old boy next door with the nice smile and easy disposition. But it was not only by the name which he gave Ellington that Zeb Green contributed to Duke's career. Zeb was a gifted musician, though he couldn't read a note of music. He played piano by ear and improvised upon the rubber-band he stretched about a cigar box. He sang very well in a high tenor voice which elicited tears from his audience when, a few years later, he or they were drunk.

Zeb and Duke's mother were not the only musicians young Ellington heard. J. E., though he, too, didn't know a chord from a piece of string, on paper, was a capable pianist, and a soul-shattering sentimentalist who also made his listeners cry.

Duke went to Armstrong High School, some blocks away from his home, but still in the Northwest neighborhood to which the Washington Negroes had moved when the government moved into the near Northwest, confiscating buildings and erecting new ones. Armstrong was the leading Negro manual training school. Duke went there to study drawing, freehand and mechanical. He was deeply interested in art, interested in little else in the secondary school curriculum, and it was only for those classes that he would show up with regularity. His grades were both sustained and let down by his interests.

It was during the first two years of the little more than three Duke spent at Armstrong—from February, 1914, to June, 1917 —that he showed his greatest interest in drawing, in drawing of all kinds. He was a nimble sketch artist, but he wasn't much interested in sketching for its own sake; he wanted to make money with this gift. When he shifted from Boynton Dodson's class in Freehand to R. I. Vaughn's in Mechanical Drawing, he was assigned to do plaques and linen banners and posters announcing various athletic contests and other school functions. The National Association for the Advancement of Colored People announced a poster contest. Duke entered and won. That was the kind of thing he wanted to do with his drawing. It was fun to make posters, fun to fool around with color and composition, fun to win prizes. Just before he left high school, he was offered a scholarship to the Pratt Institute of Applied Arts in Brooklyn, perhaps the country's outstanding institution in the field. But by then Duke had found other interests. He turned it down.

One of Duke's new interests was Edna Thompson. Without meaning to, really, she seemed to be following him around.

When his family lived at Ward Place, hers did, too. When his family moved to 13th Street, so did hers. She was in a lot of his classes at Armstrong; sometimes she sat right behind him. They went on school picnics together; it was natural to take Edna. They talked a bit together about music. She practiced far more diligently than Duke did and was far better disciplined in the traditional ways of music. She sat down with Duke and made him really work out the intricacies of scoring music. She made a profound impression upon him.

With Ernest Amos, the music teacher at Armstrong, he had regular classes. But that wasn't enough. When Duke became really interested in the ways of the art of music he went after its complexities intensely. He decided to study with Henry Grant, to take private lessons from the music teacher across the street at Dunbar High School. Grant taught a lot of boys whom he knew well and with whom he'd fooled around playing rags and shouts; he was "O-toe" Hardwick's teacher and Arthur Whetsol's; he led the Dunbar High School orchestra in which the boys played, and it was a good school orchestra.

Henry Grant remembers Duke as a very good student, who grasped the intervallic relationships, both chronological and simultaneous—those of melody and harmony—very easily. He remembers him, too, as a creative musician, even in his first attempts at harmony, in his little exercises. Harmonizing a simple melody was always an experiment in color with Duke; it was always important to him to create a sound that "rang," as he put it, either because it was mellifluous, exquisitely concordant, or because it was bizarre, challengingly discordant. But for all his experimental writing, Duke was anxious to learn the fundamentals, and with the encouragement and the painstaking supervision of this happy little musician, he secured a good base in the theory and harmony of music.

Duke, as his interests changed, began to look further into the technique of playing ragtime piano. He spent lots of time in class running his hands up and down the desk as if he were executing difficult glissandi or flashy arpeggios or just rousing chords. Behind him, three of his musical friends would beat out time on the tops of their metal stools. They bent low over their stools; Duke concentrated on his desk, shoulders hunched up, as they still are when he plays piano, little crow's-feet of attention stepping around his eyes. Mr. Dodson, the art teacher, looked at the boys. They seemed to be the nucleus of a rag outfit; they were quite audible above the classroom conversation.

"Well, gentlemen, you ought to charge admission," he said. The boys stopped immediately. At other times, gathering that Duke was the natural leader of the quartet, he asked, "Ellington, what's going on?" Duke didn't answer. He side-stepped the issue with a smile and a bow and an "Excuse me."

One day, the teacher, exasperated, pinned him down. "Come now, Ellington," he said, "what's it all about?"

"Mr. Dodson," Duke blurted out, "we have an outfit."

Mr. Dodson could see that the music and the art were pretty well linked together and he didn't worry much from then on, as long as Duke was really doing something with the hunched shoulders and the flashing hands besides beating his desk.

There were some conversations with Mr. Pinn, the short little man next door with the twinkling eyes and the faint look of mischief which he must have picked up from his Scottish ancestors. Duke was always running in and out of his house, and Mr. Pinn didn't see him very often. But every once in a while he would intercept the boy on a run up or down the grilled-iron front stairs.

"What are you doing?" Mr. Pinn asked Duke in 1914.

"Taking up drawing."

"Gonna be a great artist?"

"Mebbe."

"Gonna drop your drawing?" Mr. Pinn asked Duke in 1916.

"Probably not."

"Gonna be a professional pianist?"

"I think so."

Then Duke started to practice two or three hours at a time, usually at night. He would get on a chord "and plunk and plunk and plunk it out," as Mr. Pinn describes it. "He wasn't a very good pianist then, and two or three hours of plunking out the same chord or a few notes running away from it got to be pretty wearisome." Mr. Pinn hoped he would run into Duke again so he could speak to him about it. One day Duke was running down the front stairs just as Mr. Pinn was leaving his house.

"That's getting to be almost unendurable, Duke," Mr. Pinn said, getting right to the point.

"What, Mr. Pinn?" Duke asked.

"Why, your practicing, Duke."

"Oh," Duke said, "of course." He stopped thoughtfully for a moment on the last step. "I tell you, Mr. Pinn," he explained, "one of these days I'm gonna be famous." And off he ran.

A few days later, Mr. Pinn and Duke met again.

"Mr. Pinn," Duke said, "I'm gonna start a little band. If you know anybody who's gonna want a little orchestra, send them up to see me."

It just so happened that Mr. Pinn ran into some women, a few days after that, who wanted a small colored orchestra for a party. He sent Duke after the job. The women reported back to him on Duke's performance and he in turn told Duke.

"Duke," Mr. Pinn said, "those folks were carried away with your music."

"Really?"

"Yes. Really."

"Well," Duke said, with a sigh of contentment, "that gives me encouragement. I'm gonna go on."

The next time Mr. Pinn saw Duke he was leading a five-piece band. The next time after that, he was in New York. He was going on.

CHAPTER TWO

FLAMING YOUTH

"**H**ERE COMES DUKE!" THEY SHOUTED, WHEN EDWARD EL-
lington strode down the halls of Armstrong High. It
wasn't flashy dress that maintained ducal status for
him; his mother never would have permitted that. It was, rather,
the extraordinary neatness with which his shirt and tie, trousers
and jacket and hat and coat fell into place. The crease in his
pants was always firm; the knot of his tie always well-shaped and
right up to his collar; his shirt clean and well-matched for color
and texture with suit material and tie stuff. His shoes were
shined. He gleamed. And his posture was erect, his shoulders
thrown back. His legs strode ahead almost as if they led a proud
independent existence, a regal gait he has never lost, though
since his thirties his weight has been almost twice that of his
adolescent years, hovering around the 200 mark. His large
bronze head commanded attention; his voice was strong, imperious. At sixteen, he was Duke Ellington by natural entailment.

Otto Hardwick, several years younger than Duke, smaller,
gayer maybe, a close friend because of their close musical interests, lived a block away from him, on T Street. Jerry Rhea
was a neighbor. They were school friends, friends on the street,
but never really deeply attached until they began to play and
sing music together. But it was Otto's older brother, John, who
got most of Duke's time, who lingered over ice cream sodas with
him, gobbling great heaps of the stuff in the lazy Washington
weather. They fell naturally into the hazy, happy lethargy of
the city's spring, summer and autumn, as the sun oozed heat
through the low overhanging trees of old streets circling away

from government buildings. The informal stoops on the red brick and brownstone T Street houses sheltered impromptu parties of youngsters under the austere shadows of Washington's pseudo-classic monuments. The atmosphere was softly, insinuatingly urban; the architecture, mixed ante-bellum South and pre-Christian Greece, imposed a certain dignity upon these colored youngsters which no other group of jazzmen—those from New Orleans, Chicago, Kansas City or New York, to name the principal sources of jazz talent—ever possessed. Duke had it, of course; so had Otto Hardwick, the Miller brothers, Bill Escoffery, Claude Hopkins, Arthur Whetsol, Elmer Snowden, Rex Stewart, all the musicians who were born or bred in the capital; they had it, they have it. There was a Washington pattern: it involved a certain bearing, a respect for education, for the broad principles of the art of music; a desire for order, for design in their professional lives. These things, this pattern, gave to Ellington and his associates, from the very beginning, a line of development, a sense of growth toward a larger and more meaningful expression, that, as much as anything, made the top level of jazz inevitable for them.

Duke was almost always on top. The kids, the Hardwicks, Millers, their boy and girl friends, used to give house parties. They never meant much unless Duke played piano at them. That was partly because Edward Ellington, springing heavily into his teens, was aware once more of the emotional power of music and of some of the means to communicate it. It was just as largely due to the force of his personality. Then, as now, the girls flocked around him, shared his piano stool with him, hovered over his showy hands, angled for his broad smile and his humor-puckered forehead.

They were well-off at these house parties. Soft drinks and ice cream were the fare. Duke's raggy piano was the entertainment. Music and confections kept the kids happy for hours and hours and hours, and even as severe a parent as Otto's father, self-appointed guardian of the morals of all the youngsters in his district, was brought around to smiling approval of the parlor socials. But Jerry Rhea's father could never quite stand to hear

Duke play rag-tail and bobble-scale down the pianos in their houses.

"Get that noise out of here!" Mr. Rhea screamed down at Duke and Jerry.

"They aren't doing anybody any harm," Mrs. Rhea answered for the kids. But the voice of masculine authority was stronger than hers and out it went.

Perhaps Ellington's ragtime was tiresome listening for the generation just before his. The only musical roughness they had experienced had been in the lyrics to such songs as *I Love My Wife, But, Oh, You Kid!* and *Everybody's Doin' It Now.* The polyrhythms of ragtime piano must have sounded strange in 1914 and '15. The strong accents on the usual weak beats, the weak ones where they had been strong, were jarring syncopation for older ears in the younger years of this century. The incessant repetition of the walking bass, going up and down the chords in the same pattern, over and over and over again in the left hand; the percussive sound of the piano, as the hands jumped back and forth in the style that is still a part of jazz, called "stride"—these things jangled the nerves and set heads aching when the nerves and heads were used to the peaceful rhythms and soporific sounds of Victor Herbert and Ethelbert Nevin. It is not without cause that so many of the representative rags were called "shouts."

Duke was really taken with ragtime. "Those ragtime pianists sounded *so* good to me! And they looked so good! Particularly when they flashed their left hands. I noticed that the left hand was the trick of it and that audiences were most impressed by a showy left hand. So I developed a showy left hand. I had little but a vague remembrance of those piano lessons in my mind, but I could see that the rag pianists employed more affected fingering than the concert pianists and that attracted me very much. I hit that fingering very hard and somehow it seemed to come natural to me."

Duke says he "wasn't very smart," and for all the hard-hitting, "I could never catch on to what anyone else played, so I developed my own stuff." He went to rent parties, where the cost of

admission and the price of drinks went to pay the house rent of
the hosts, and at these parties he heard the premier rag pianists
of the Washington day, Clarence Bowser, Lester Dishman,
Louis Brown, Doc Perry, Louis Thomas. Through the shouts of
encouragement from the party-goers, the boom of the piano
crashed. Bowser was "majestic," in Duke's estimation. His
lush style sparkled prettily. Dishman was "fast as they
came, with a humming left hand, and beautiful melodic weav-
ing against it in his right." The parties justified the name of
"house hops": the houses hopped. The music justified the name
of "shout": it roared. And, piecemeal, Duke managed to catch
on, a run here, a chord there, a hum from Dishman, a touch of
Bowser's majesty, and a great scoop of James P. Johnson's technique.

James P. was the great rag pianist of the day. His piano roll
of his own *Carolina Shout* was must listening. Duke slipped the
Swiss-cheese-like paper on his piano's roller, slowed its speed
down and followed every hill and dale its playing made upon
the instrument's keyboard, pressing his fingers down after
J. P.'s, pedaling after Johnson, until he had learned to shout
Carolina. When James P. Johnson came to Washington to sup-
plant the piano roll with his person, Duke was ready. Johnson
sat his barrelly figure down at the piano, flashed his infectious
grin, tossed back his bullfrog face, and, with eyes shining,
hopped, stomped and strutted through the strident figures of
his celebrated composition. It was at a big gathering, and the
large crowd yelled and clapped its approval. Duke followed, addressed the piano in more sedate fashion, as was fitting in the
younger man, the comparative unknown. But he was the local
boy and sentiment was with him, his gang was behind him. He
rolled over a few bars. He strode into it, and with hands leaping from the piano in the impressive manner he had learned
from watching Dishman, Bowser and friends, "he ran him
right out of the joint," as one of the witnesses recalls the event.

From running the great J. P. right out of the joint, it was an
easy step to the confidence necessary to compose his own rag.
Working after school at the Poodle Dog Café, a high ranking

soda fountain "establishment," right around the corner from the Washington Senators' ballground, it was logical to call it the *Soda Fountain Rag*. Now all that was necessary was the opportunity to play it.

One day the heavy-drinking pianist at one of the cafés, a "whiz" of a pianist but even more brilliant a drinker, drank so much he knocked himself right out. Duke sprang to his place, and without a moment's hesitation to clear away the prostrate form of the overcome piano-shouter, he jumped into the opening bars of *Soda Fountain Rag*. He played it as a one-step, two-step, waltz, and as a fox-trot, slow, middle-tempo and up. "They never knew it was the same piece," and "I was established. Not only did I write my own music, but I had a repertory!" Duke became more interested in this repertory, in his piano altogether, than he was in his painting, and in 1917 he left high school just a few months before graduation.

Duke began to get a reputation. His several versions of the *Soda Fountain Rag* pleased waltz, one-step, two-step, fox-trot and tango lovers. Washington was almost the gayest of American cities, in the years from 1916 to 1919, when Duke was coming up. And his piano, even at its raggiest, noisiest, most rhythmically confusing, was a welcome condiment to jaded diners looking for new seasoning.

The embassies of the embattled European countries were seriously interlocked in competition for party honors, and after our entrance into the war removed several of the belligerents from the Washington scene, the gatherings organized by the American ministries and ministers more than made up for their departure. The gaiety was contagious. It spread from diplomatic circles to lower castes of Washington society. It reached out to such centers of organized fun as the True Reformers Hall, plunk in the middle of Northwest Washington. The *true* reformers had long ago left the squat, meandering building, which housed one great hall and many small meeting rooms. In one of these, Room 10, Duke Ellington and various groups of musicians used to rag and shout and make tentative stabs at melancholic musing in the blues form on more Saturdays than

any of them can now remember. In Room 5, at the True Reformers, Duke played his first professional job, from 8:00 P.M.
to 1:00 A.M., for seventy-five cents!

Room 10 it was where Duke's Washingtonians took shape in
'17, '18 and '19. Otto Hardwick was playing bass fiddle then;
William Escoffery was on guitar; the Millers, Bill, Brother and
Felix, who were "sophisticates—they drank corn and gin, but
heavily," filled out the band, with Lloyd Stewart on drums.
Otto was too small to carry his bass, so his father would lug it
for him, taking advantage of the opportunity to check up on
"his boys." Arthur Whetsol, who was a pre-medical student at
Howard University, sometimes blew cornet for Duke. The band
began to take some sort of rough shape, with a regular rhythm
section, Elmer Snowden coming in on banjo, with a large number of good hornmen who would come in, one or all, for the
Saturday nights in Room 10. Duke persuaded O-toe, as they
called Hardwick, to switch to a C melody saxophone, and the
melody line got a break.

Duke began to branch out. He tried his flashy hand (his left,
of course) at one of the five pianos in Russell Wooding's enormous band, one of Washington's most successful colored commercial orchestras. Sitting down at the instrument assigned him
for the first performance with Wooding, Duke, characteristi-
cally, began to dream; he saw "some spots for nice things," to
indulge his musical fancies and his dream-world fantasies, in
the score in front of him; he indulged; Wooding, less indulgent,
sent him on his way.

One of his first jobs, in 1916, had been with Louis Thomas,
the "eminent" ragtime pianist and leader of "gig" bands, the
one-nighter outfits. Thomas told Duke if he could learn to
play *The Siren Song*, he could play piano in his third band, a
watered-down, watered-down version of the society crew which
brought Louis his biggest money. Duke spent a day learning
The Siren Song, and got the job. When he arrived to play it,
he learned, to his consternation, that the job was a "legitimate"
one, that they weren't going to play any "jumps." "The musicians started talking to me about correct chords, and I knew

that in a few minutes I'd be sunk. Then somebody requested *The Siren Song,* and in great relief I started plunking out the number." He threw in the flashy handwork he'd picked up from Washington's rag pianists and from Lucky Roberts, *the* man for the trick of throwing his hands away from the piano, who used to come down from New York to play the Howard Theatre, Washington's number one Negro theater. The familiar figures of *The Siren Song* and the hands jumping impressively from the keys elicited screams of delight from the kids around the stand. Duke knew how to do it.

Duke played with Thomas, with Daniel Doy, another leader of pick-up bands for one-night jobs, in fact with almost all the "gig" bands. His experience grew. Doc Perry—one of the chief leaders of these small jump outfits who played one night in one café, one night in another, Saturdays at lodge halls and Sundays and Fridays, maybe, at house hops—insisted that Duke study hard, refresh his technique and become as alert as the legit musicians. With this experience, the Room 10 sessions and the long nights spent at home working out original compositions, crude, brief, but original, Duke felt it was time to make his band permanent. He had noticed that Thomas, Perry, Meyer Davis all took big ads in the telephone book, advertising their musical catering services. He took one just as big, figuring that if his name were set in type as large as the others most people would consider him equally important and throw lots of work his way. He was right. They did, after a while.

Hardwick and Whetsol, the Millers and Snowden and Escoffery, Jerry Rhea, who sometimes sang with the band, wondered why they got such choice jobs, picking up some of the Embassy work, playing almost exclusively for white folks. It was months before they saw Duke's ad in the phone book and understood.

It's true that Duke and his colleagues got good jobs, but the jobs didn't come overnight, and they continued, for several years, to be mixed with the literally tough ones, roughhouse ones, nasty ones. Those were the evenings which started out as balls and ended as brawls. "We'll give you the five dollars [sometimes it was seven dollars] later," the guy who hired them told Duke. "Fine," Duke said. But somehow, a few minutes before the dance was to end, somebody insulted somebody else and nobody got paid.

Duke was making enough money in the late teens to move his folks a block and a half away from 13th, between R and S, to a new house of their own at 1212 T Street, between 12th and 13th. It was a good house, a larger house, for sister Ruth Dorothea Ellington, who was born in 1915, sixteen years after Duke, to grow up in.

Duke was making enough money even to think about marriage. He thought about it and decided for it and asked the logical girl to be his wife. Edna Thompson, who had skirted his grade and high school days, whose family had moved with his in the short Negro migration from near to farther Northwest Washington, who had taught him a little about music and shared party gaiety and block social life, was his girl. They were married in July, 1918. They produced a child, Mercer Kennedy Ellington, the following year. Another child, born shortly after Mercer, died in infancy.

Edna not only encouraged and stimulated some music. She was right behind his drawing and painting, too. She remembered a masterpiece of pen-and-ink drawing he'd done at high school, an unusually sensitive sketch of that stereotype of high school drawing classes, the head of a Greek god. She remembered the signs at high school and the work he'd started doing for dances and theaters around Washington. They were better than average posters announcing dances, describing new movies and stage shows, and, like his music to come, fitting content with form very well. There was Edna's verbal encouragement and her attractiveness as a subject. Duke painted signs for money and sketched her for kicks. He sketched her playing with Mercer and feeding him, the fair, lissome mother and the blissful, slightly browner son in adored and adoring juxtaposition.

"I was awful shy," Edna says of these drawings, "and so I could hardly look at them and appraise them; they were of me, after all. But Duke said they were art, and so I guess they were."

She concludes ruefully that she "would sure like to be able to judge for myself now. But they've all disappeared."

Duke was faced continually, in those years, with a difficult problem. Should he go on with his art? Should he go on with his music? Which would make more money to take care of his wife and son and contribute to the running expenses of his parents' house and his own, a few blocks away, on T Street? Like the man who picks up everybody's overcoats and the bat-boy who gathers the whole baseball team's bats in his arms, Duke compromised by doing everything at once.

By 1919, the phone book–stimulated business was steady, the income was high, around $150 or $200 a week for Duke himself, with five bands working for him and no end in sight to the lucrative flow. At the parties they played they were meeting "nice white folks," for the first time forgetting differences of skin in similarities of musical interest and temperament. Duke was beyond the *faux pas* stage, or embarrassing moments of the kind he'd had with Doc Perry once, at the British Embassy. "I showed up in a sharp shepherd's plaid suit at a formal. Doc never forgave me."

And the sign-painting business was thriving, too. In combina-tion with a friend, Ewell Conway, Edward Ellington had formed a partnership signified by the combination of their last names. Sign-painting by day, piano-playing by night, Duke was a successful businessman, happy that he had decided against the Pratt Scholarship.

There were great friendships. Differences of age faded away in the camaraderie of music. Duke, Otto, Whetsol, Jerry, Otto's brother, the Millers, and so on, were of different ages, somewhat different in background, a whole range of temperaments among them, but doggedly, fanatically, furiously devoted to their music. Sometimes they played together, sometimes under other gig leaders. But after every job, every night, they'd meet at the late places and talk about the night's work, about the changes they'd worked out on some familiar tune, about tomorrow and tomorrow and three years ago last Wednesday when they were playing more baseball than music.

"That band at the Howard is a whiz," O-toe would say.

"Sure is," Bill Miller would agree.

"Don't say?" Duke would query.

"Yeah," Otto would continue. "Puerto Ricans—Marie Lucas' outfit—great trombonist name of Tizol."

"Uh-huh." Duke would nod, as he crammed the last spoonful of one of the Miller brothers' ice cream sundaes into his mouth. He'd already finished his own.

"Hey," one of them would call out, "look."

"Yeah?" Duke or Otto or Bill or Felix or Snowden would ask. But the uplifted affirmation was rhetorical. They knew what came next.

"Don't they look awfully tired?" the same one would continue, nodding in the direction of the bandstand.

"Sure thing," was the consensus of opinion, and Otto, Duke, et al., would rush to the stand, to relieve the "tired" musicians, having themselves only just come from a night's hard playing.

They loved to play. The Poodle Dog, the Dreamland, the Industrial Café received nightly musical bouquets from them in testament to that love. "A jam session was a jam session then," Duke says today, and so do Otto and Sonny Greer and Rex and any of the musicians in the Ellington organization who go back that far. "We didn't play for money," they continue, "we played for kicks. And they were kicks. You came into a place, say the Dreamland. You noticed a guy on the stand who played your kinda horn. You walked up to him or the leader and you put him on. Oh, either he was tired or what did he think he was anyway, the only C melody in the world, or the only pianist or drummer or cornet, huh? And you finally got to take his place. And you played everything you knew and a hell of a lot you didn't know you knew. And it was murder, for him or for you, but it was kicks, too, and a musical education. That was a jam session." You will very rarely see Ellington musicians in such jam sessions now; without originality but with enough feeling and experience to back up the epithet, they call today's jam sessions "prostitution."

"People talk to me about improvisation," Duke elaborates,

"and how jam sessions are the thing, but after all, there is so little that's really improvised at a jam session. Most of the guys play things they're used to playing over and over again. Tunes suggest certain phrases and those phrases suggest other phrases, a chord suggests an obvious modulation into another key, and you get less that is actually fresh and new and vital at those sessions than you do when we work out an arrangement and leave time and space for a man to stretch himself in his solos."

"Then someone sent for Sonny Greer from New York," says Duke, talking of the old days.

"That's all," Otto Hardwick says.

" 'The sensational Sonny Greer,' I called myself," Sonny intones, "and I was."

"And he was," everybody agrees.

"Little Willie from Long Branch," Jerry Rhea sneers affectionately.

Sonny scowls, but little Willie he was. William Greer was a man of almost medium height, fast on the verbal draw, even faster, amazingly enough, on the drumsticks, in 1919. He was the light tan boy with the personality, from Long Branch, New Jersey. Smart in school in everything but German, he picked up drums to ingratiate himself with the teacher of that language because she doubled as supervisor of the school band. Oh, Sonny was a fast man, a fast boy, a fast drummer.

Long Branch was less than 200 miles up the Atlantic Coast from Washington, but what a difference! Sonny Greer had never played with anything but a white band until he came to the capital city. Up and down the New Jersey coast, with Wilbur Gardner at the Green Gables, four years for Mabel Ross at the famous Ross-Fenton farms following Vincent Lopez's seven-piece band in those formative years for dance music and jazz. He knew Diamond Jim Brady, and talked with as much sparkle as Brady's gems radiated, of those stones, "big as a fist," of that appetite, "big as the man."

"We watched Sonny work in the pit," Duke recalls, "and he

used a lot of tricks. He was flashy, and we were impressed by flash, but our minds still weren't made up. We decided to give him the works, and find out just what sort of a guy he was."

Duke stands on the street corner. He figures he's the natural lead for a conversation with Sonny, for he's a killer in his new shepherd's plaid suit (that was the pattern, those days!) bought on time.

"I'll bet you only passed through New York," Duke says.

"Passed through, all right," Sonny comes back, "stopped off to see Diamond Jim and Lillian Russell, paid my respects to the Hoffman House and the Waldorf, spent a weekend in Central Park. . . ." And he names every place of interest, and many of none, in the big city. He's in.

"We decide you're okay," Duke says. The others nod. Sonny grins.

Willie Greer worked through a few weeks in the Howard Theatre pit band and then quit to join Ellington. He was a decided asset at jam sessions after business hours, a great teller of tales who could always top the last whopper with a ten-minute stopper about a fabulous musician or a girl of prodigious feats or a man who could drink his own weight in corn. When Elmer Snowden's eight-piece combination played one night at the Dreamland, opposite Duke's crew, that night just three men, it was the tricks, flying frantically between drumsticks and piano fingers, worked out by Greer and Ellington, which won them the coveted honors of the evening.

There would be another session. It wouldn't matter much who was playing with whom, as long as Sonny was with Duke. Either one of them could out-talk any other musician; together they could "raise hell with Congress," as a confrere put it.

"You're gonna get cut," Duke would yell to the other musicians.

"Not a chance," Sonny would confirm him.

"It's this way," Duke would offer, "you see, we've got a mess of new stuff from New York that just can't be beat."

"And a trombonist who plays all the trumpet notes," Sonny would add.

"Every number an original"—from Duke.

"Nothing you ever heard before, so how you gonna beat it?"
—from Sonny.

"Give up now, 'tain't worth trying"—together.

Nervously, their musical opponents would mount the stand,
but they were defeated before they began.

With the advent of the 1920's, Duke, O-toe, the Millers, and
their friends and business associates, passed from ice cream to
"fire-water" in earnest. With Sonny's presence for morale, the
boys were "topnotch juicehounds," Duke says. They strutted
after the walks of their favorite movie stars, choked a little over
the stronger drinks, the first experimentations of a nation waltz-
ing weakly and questioningly into Prohibition. They raced
their cars.

The youngest of the Hardwicks was a car fan, as mad for the
fire-eating automobiles as he later was for photography, the
language the French speak and the game of Blackjack. O-toe
had made some brief forays into the $90 suit class, but he found
cars an even better way of wasting money. So he bought one,
a Pullman, probably the most independent, least reliable, most
cantankerous Pullman of a long line of independent, unreliable
and evilly disposed Pullmans. It didn't have a crank handle and
you had to push it to get it started. It always stalled on a hill,
sometimes just a few feet upgrade. They called it the Dupadilly. One day it stalled "in the middle of nowhere" and they
just left it.

After the Dupadilly the Hardwicks bought another car from
the used-car man, who was known by the unexplained and apparently inexplicable name of "Dear-Me." "Dear-Me" sold
O-toe "a honey of a car," and Hardwick's "honey" and Duke's
Chandler, a recent acquisition, and Claude Hopkins' car used
to get mixed up in heats that were anything but dead on Washington's hot streets in the summers of '19, '20 and '21. Claude,
a neighbor, was making some headway as a bandleader and
pianist, too, with occasional jobs in New York and offers from
Europe and Australia. They had much to talk about and drink
about as well as to race about.

Then, one eventful day in 1922, came a wire from bandleader Wilbur Sweatman. He wanted Sonny in New York. Sonny wanted Otto and Duke, and that meant New York for Greer, Ellington and Hardwick. Dissolve Washington into a panorama shot of New York. Skyscrapers gleaming in the twilight sun. Cars "rushing madly" through the canyons of Wall Street, Broadway and Fifth Avenue. People drinking, eating, living madly. Where "everybody" was rich and stayed high all the time and Duke Ellington, Sonny Greer, Otto Hardwick, Arthur Whetsol and Elmer Snowden had to split a hot dog five ways to stay alive.

CHAPTER THREE

DROP ME OFF
IN HARLEM

THERE WERE TWO KINDS OF BANDS, IN 1922. ONE WAS THE production outfit, lots of saxes, pianos, banjos, and as many brass as the leader could get to play together—twenty, thirty, forty men. The other was the small unit, five, six men, piano, banjo, tuba, drums, cornet and C melody sax, or clarinet; it played jazz. The Original Dixieland Jass Band, which no longer sounded quite so original in 1922, was one of the latter; so were the New Orleans Rhythm Kings and the best little band of them all, then, King Oliver's Sunset Café gang in Chicago, with Louis Armstrong on second trumpet. In New York, Harlem was shifting noisily, happily, with rather bleary eyes, from a center of faded white respectability into the city's Negro quarter. The shift was made to the tune of James P. Johnson's piano and Willie Smith's, to Count Basie and Fats Waller striding lushly along their keyboards. Joe Nanton's barrelhouse trombone at the Bucket of Blood blew brazen notes through the uptown mist, and Bubber Miley and Sidney Bechet were playing their style-setting horns (trumpet and clarinet) with Mamie Smith at the Garden of Joy, atop a rock at 140th and Seventh. Glasses clinked and liquor gurgled at the Green Cat and Connor's, where Bubber sometimes played and topers wandered unevenly up the steps from Mexico's. Rhythmic inebriation was the order of the day, jazz was on its way in. And Duke, Sonny and O-toe went to work for Wilbur Sweatman, whose band was emphatically of the first type mentioned, large and unrhythmic, where

26

the day's order was order itself and happiness was a thing called after-work drunks.

The Washingtonians did not last very long with Sweatman. A few theater dates, the Lafayette, then Harlem's biggest and most important house, at 135th and Seventh, and a Staten Island spot, which was, as Sonny put it, "a weekend of grief." But the real "grievin'" was still to come. With the end of their brief career with Wilbur, the gentlemen from T Street and Long Branch were stranded. Wilbur was still performing every night with his three clarinets, but the Washington boys were on a catch-as-catch-can diet, and they didn't catch very much. At night it didn't matter a great deal whether or not you had any money, you made the rounds. If you had your instrument with you, or could play piano, you were admitted, and everybody bought you drinks.

The Capitol, at 140th and Lenox, featured a pianist called Willie the Lion. His surname was Smith, but they called him the Lion because, during the war, then recently ended, he had volunteered to go up to the front to fire a French 75. Others volunteered, too, but few stayed with it so long: for 33 days and nights Willie fired the cannon at the Germans and when it was over he was famous as the Lion. Famous during the war for his bravery, afterward for his piano playing, the Lion played a delicate style, with lots of pretty little runs, or a rambunctious one, but whichever it was, the tempo was almost always the same. "Belly-laugh tempo," Duke calls it.

When you came into the Capitol you either were in step with the Lion, literally, or you had to stop and get into it. It was a middle tempo, just like a belly laugh, hah-hah-hah-hah, hah-hah-hah-hah. "The world's greatest atmosphere," Duke recalls. "The Lion would growl at you, 'Well, all right, take it from there,' and with the aid of some crude red liquor, you would." Willie's florid style made an enormous impression on Duke, and to this day they still play alike. Duke never copied the Lion's physical approach to the piano, cigar clenched hard between his teeth, back sharply angled against the chair-back, stomach rising stubbornly between him and the piano, knees, often as not, crossed; but he did imitate his fluttering arpeggios, his charming chordal commentaries.

The Lion would play at the Capitol for a living and at a lot of other places for kicks. Then, maybe, Duke would sit down at the piano, or Fats Waller would. Fats was following his mentor, James P. Johnson, around town. The Lion said of Fats, "Yeah, a yearling; he's coming along, I guess he'll do all right." Piano duels were as much the thing in New York as they had been in Washington.

Rent parties were big, too. And the big man, James P., got to play them. But he couldn't play them all, so he turned a lot of his business over to Lippy, a professional character "who had heard so much piano he couldn't play any more. He only thought piano." Lippy gave work to a lot of piano-players. In the course of spreading it around, Duke got a small share, and even Sonny, who had lots of New York contacts, picked up some piano work. (There has never been a man in the Ellington band who couldn't play some piano.)

Lippy knew where every piano, pianist and player-piano in town was located. He and James P., Fats, the Lion and Duke ("I was one of the main hangers-on") would cruise together. Lippy would walk up to any house at any hour of night. He'd ring the doorbell. Somebody would wake up after a half-hour's inescapable ringing and shout out the window, "Who the hell is making all that noise?" "It's me," said Lippy, "and James P. is here with me." It was magic, open sesame. They were in and the evening was on. Those evenings lasted through many mornings. The Washingtonians' introduction to New York showed them a glamorous city which came most thoroughly alive at night, one that produced an unending supply of golden sound, if not the metal itself in any considerable quantity.

The sound and the taste, of music and liquor, were enough to keep Duke, Sonny and O-toe in kicks and without kicks for some weeks, but there came a time when shoes losing soles tried these men's souls, when the lack of steady work crippled their ambition, when they looked as down-at-the-mouth as their footgear was down-at-the-heel. They were ready to quit.

One day Duke was kicking his heels disconsolately along the Lenox Avenue sidewalk, his regal stride suspended temporarily for a subdued pace, his eyes on the ground instead of attached imperiously to the horizon ahead of him. "Flop!" He stopped. A flashing white envelope twinkled ahead of him in the Harlem sun. Something about it. He stooped down laboriously to pick it up. Who knows? He opened it. Fifteen dollars!

Duke bought himself a new pair of shoes and three coach tickets back to Washington. Sonny, whose fortunes were now firmly linked with Duke's and Otto's, entrained with them to their native city, to regular meals again, real home cooking, money in the pocket and a generally easier if less romantic life.

Duke was occupied, when he got home, with his wife, Edna, and his son, Mercer, who was now four years old and being looked after by his grandmother; with the remnants of his sign-painting business, and with the possibilities of his old band-booking business in Washington. Otto, reunited with his family, was just having fun, blowing a little horn and eating, drinking, balling with his old friends. Sonny was being absorbed into the Ellington family household.

"I've got some rare whisky for you, ole man," Duke's father told Sonny.

"No kidding?"

"Look at that dusty decanter," said Uncle Ed, as Sonny, like almost everybody else, called him.

"Sure is dusty."

"Been around, this stuff has."

"So I see."

"Drink up."

Sonny took a long quaff and exclaimed at the richness of the old whisky.

"Food for the head," he said. "Lo-o-vely!"

Next week, Uncle Ed greeted Sonny again.

"Found another rare bottle." He talked it up big, trotted out another fine-looking piece of cut glass, sometimes covered with mold or dust, sometimes polished to a shining surface, with the amber or nutmeg-brown contents shining through the pris-

matic glass, cutting salivary patterns across Sonny's mouth as his
eye caught the gleam.

"Don't say?"

"Do indeed."

"Food for the head, food for the brain, nourishes the nerves,"
Sonny said.

"Quite right," J. E. Ellington agreed and offered him the
bottle.

Sonny never discovered that old Uncle Ed, delighted with the
drummer's unceasing lust for liquor, was giving him a wide
sampling of the Ellington collection of wine and whisky bottles but just one liquor, straight corn. Oh, there was some
variety of vintage. Some of it was a rare two-month-old corn,
some of it all of four, some of it just distilled, but always corn.
And Sonny, coming from the North, hadn't ever tasted corn.

Another distinguished drinker was Thomas Waller, just a
kid then, but very much at home across the mahogany of a bar
or the ivory of a piano. He passed through town, playing in a
burlesque show, that Spring of 1923, and stopped off at all the
places to battle a little piano and tip a few crocks. He and Duke
got to playing and talking, and before many chords and drinks
had passed, Fats was invited up to the Ellington house to break
chicken legs and wings with the family. Over the fast-disap-
pearing birds, which Aunt Daisy fried to such a delectable
brown, Fats told Duke about the troubles of his band. The
money wasn't bad, but it was so damn boring.

"Hey, Duke," he said, "we're all gonna quit. Whyn't you
come to New York and grab our jobs? Huh?" As always, he
rolled his eyes and tipped his head back for interrogative emphasis.

"Not a bad idea," Duke assented. But with big-city-bred cau-
tion, with the tone of a man who has once been burned but
hasn't lost his appetite for fire, he said, "Yes, yes, Fats, but I'm
not taking any chances. Wire me when you get to New York
if there are openings for me 'n' Otto 'n' Sonny, and maybe
Snowden and Whetsol, and then when we know we've got the
job, we'll come right up."

"Good enough," Thomas Waller agreed, and sealed it with a bone.

Some weeks later a wire arrived: "FATS STAYING. OTHER JOBS OPEN."

Sonny, Otto, Whetsol and Snowden went up ahead. A few weeks of silence and they sent a wire. "EVERYTHING FIXED. JOB CINCH FOR YOU." Duke followed.

This time there had been wires, no chance for anything to go wrong, so Duke left some money with Aunt Day (as his mother was often called), took a good pocketful himself and came up in style. He hired a drawing room, ate his way through a couple of the Pennsylvania Railroad's most expensive meals and arrived at Penn Station in New York with little more than a dollar.

But Ellington's traveling in style. He hires a cab and goes uptown on his last few pennies.

He comes to 135th and Lenox, 136th, 138th, 140th. There they stand, in front of the Capitol. All four of them, Sonny, Hardwick, Artie, Snowden.

"Well, whatd'ya know?" Otto asks.

"How's things?" Sonny wants to know.

"Good to see you," the more restrained Whetsol acknowledges.

Greetings exchanged, but before there is time for news, the four chorus: "Give us some gold!"

"Gold?" Duke squeaks, his voice rising in the way of teen-age boys which has never left him.

The story comes out. Wire or no, there isn't any job yet. Promises, yes. Job, no. It'll come soon, but meanwhile they've got to live.

Gigging began again, but only half-heartedly, because the burleycue sinecure was in the offing. It never materialized, however.

Fortunately, the Washingtonians stuck together, and when Ada Smith, whose mop of red hair had already won her the name of Bricktop, met the boys and learned of their sad situation, she got to work. Duke had worked with her, accompanying

her singing, at the Oriental in Washington. The others had
either played for her or partied with her.

"Work you need, work is for you, and work you shall have,"
she said.

She went right up to Barron Wilkins and told him what was
what, who these kids were and what was to be done for them.
Barron Wilkins was an important man in Harlem, a politician,
a Boniface. "Barron's," one of the brightest spots in Harlem,
was the successor to a similar club downtown which Wilkins
had run. In the changing course of night-life fortunes, which
made one place the favorite one month, another the next, and
spared few clubs and owners from a frantic existence tottering
between the edges of bankruptcy and a million-dollar success,
Barron's remained *the* uptown place. It was Harlem headquarters for Bert Williams, the great colored comic, for Jack Johnson, the Negro heavyweight champion of the world, for Frank
Fay and his theater associates, for Al Jolson and up-and-
coming chorus girls like Lucille La Sueur (Joan Crawford).
That was the spot, Bricktop decided, for Duke and the Washingtonians. She was persuasive enough to convince Wilkins, and
he let his regular band go and hired Ellington, Hardwick,
Whetsol, Greer and Snowden.

People who had come to 134th Street and Seventh Avenue
just to feel some of the atmosphere, to read political futures or
just to get drunk, began to listen to the music. There were lots
of small combinations in Harlem, but none quite like this one.
The little basement-café with the distinguished clientele took
on an added atmosphere from the soft music of the Washingtonians. Elmer Snowden acted as leader and business representative, but Duke set the moods. He organized rehearsal sessions
at which both "head" and scored arrangements were set, almost everything was planned. The music was planned, planned
to serve as background for bar babble and table talk—"conversation music." It was also designed to move hips, lift feet and put
just a slight edge, a kind of cerebral aphrodisia, on the eaters
and topers.

The jazz which had come to New York in 1923, via New

Orleans, Chicago and points in between, was a crude one, limited to blues for the most part, blues, blues singers and rough little bands backing them up. The Original Dixieland Jazz Band (the double s had become a double z) had caused a little excitement with its driving but helter-skelter ensembles at Reisenweber's Restaurant downtown. Fletcher Henderson had just moved into the Club Alabam' for the beginning of his epochal New York stay, but his band was still nothing special. The biggest kicks in town were still being provided by the pianists, James P. Johnson, Tom Waller, Willie the Lion, William Basie, and others. Just emerging from the raggedy shout stage, their keyboard formulations were the richest harmonically and the least constricted melodically, tonally. Duke's band, though only five pieces, was something of a revolutionary change, both for Harlem, the district, and New York, the big city. The great innovations in growl were still to come, but Duke mixed soft volume and organized voicings with traditional gutbucket sounds, never losing the vitality of true jazz, never without the sense of color, of texture, which distinguishes his writing and playing and leading above all other composers and bandsmen in the medium.

After a few months at Barron's, Ellington, Hardwick, Snowden, Greer and Whetsol were household names, at least from 125th to 145th streets among musicians. There was a momentary uneasiness in the band when they discovered that Elmer, business representative, and thus nominal leader, had paid himself a little more than they were getting, in recognition of his extra services. They decided to dispense with all his services, regular and extra. That's when Freddie Guy came in.

Freddie was Virginia-born but New York–bred. He came to New York in his mother's arms and was a thorough New Yorker by the time he met Duke, Otto, Sonny, and Artie Whetsol. His musical background was much like theirs, gigging around the city, working with John Smith's bands, which varied from ten to fifty pieces, with three or four nights' work guaranteed him every week. He'd been taught a little music at elementary school, the do-re-mi version of the diatonic scale, and a few

names for the pleasant sounds the instruments of the orchestra
made. The rest he picked up himself. In early 1923, he was
the banjo player in his own band at Earl Dancer's Oriental
Café, which was upstairs next door to a poolroom not far from
Barron's. Fats played piano in the band; Angelina Rivers sang
and played fiddle with them. It was a good tonky spot, but
Earl Dancer was shooting for higher stakes. He moved on, leaving Guy in possession of the premises. Freddie was in demand:
his steady playing was a rhythmic bulwark in those small combinations; his reliable character was an emotional base. Barron
Wilkins told the leader of the orchestra which followed Duke
that he could have the job at his place if he got Freddie Guy.
But Freddie elected to leave the Oriental, Barron's and Harlem
with Ellington, when, six months after beginning their run,
the Washingtonians cut out.

Leonard Harper was a dancer and a producer uptown, who,
like most of the other professionals in Harlem, had noticed the
boys from T Street. He came in often, sat around, talked. One
night he offered Duke, once more the leader of the band, a
proposition. He, Harper, was producing the shows that season
of '23-'24 at Connie's Inn, run by the brothers Immerman—
Connie and George—and at the Hollywood. Connie's Inn
was uptown, right next to the Lafayette Theatre; the Hollywood was downtown, 49th and Broadway. Would the Washingtonians like a crack at either job?

"Would we? We're there now," Duke answered.

The Hollywood was another basement-café, rather small, turgid with alcoholic vapor and cigarette smoke. Barron's had been
patronized by a small number of "Mr. Gunions." These men
overran the Hollywood. "Mr. Gunions" were spenders, in the
language of musicians of the times, men with money, "gunions"
of dollars to their name. At the uptown place, the regular earnings of the Washingtonians had been $30 a week supplemented
by about $20 a night made from these liberal "gunionaires."
The tips were even bigger at the downtown spot, and became,
in effect, the real earnings of the musicians; they looked upon
their salary checks as supererogatory and all but threw them

away. Sometimes, in the orgies of wild spending these war-made
money men indulged in, a "Mr. Gunions" would throw halves
of $10 and $50 bills on the dance floor for the privilege of
watching the waiters and entertainers scramble for the matching pieces.

The Hollywood Café, 49th and Broadway. The Washingtonians had arrived. Duke, still slender, was a sharper dresser
than ever before. Otto, who described himself as "a sportsman—
not a musician," was the smartest-looking bald-headed man on
Broadway: he'd lost all his hair but a kind of reverse beard on
the back of his skull, at seventeen, yet his natural good
looks, fresh young face and good dress made him almost as much
of an attraction for women as the more flashy Ellington. Sonny
was the patter-man, ingenuous as a Little Willie from Long
Branch, ingenious as Sonny Greer, drummer at the Hollywood.
Freddie Guy was New York all over, as quietly self-assured as
Sonny had been loud and honest in his proclamation of knowledge of persons and places in the big town. Arthur Whetsol
was as he always had been and would be, a quiet, studious musician, who, having relinquished the medical career he had begun
at Howard University, was determined, now that he had put
valve to finger, mute to bell of his horn, to be as good a trumpeter as one could be.

Sharp dressers, self-assured men of the fast world of 1923, they
were, nonetheless, making their first downtown appearance in
New York, their debut in the big time, and they were nervous.

"Make it good, fellows," Duke said, as he fingered the faille
silk of his dress tie, clearly nervous.

"We do it, Daddy," Sonny promised, and the others nodded
in vigorous confirmation. But they were all nervous, too.

Duke strode out to the tiny self-enclosed bandstand, sat down
at the piano. The others followed, in solemn procession. Duke
turned around to look at the well-dressed crowd, still reflecting
the touch of a hot summer in their dress, which wasn't entirely
formal. The men wore the blue serge jackets and cream flannels
of the period, the women the flat-chested, low-waisted, low-
backed, high-kneed evening gowns of the flappery times. Otto,

Sonny, Freddie, Artie seated themselves. Sonny fooled with his drum equipment, making mental reservations about its shabbiness, promising himself a gaudy replacement very soon.

Duke turned to the musicians. "It's time, fellows, let's go."

They went, but he didn't. He put his finger on his mouth, his right index finger, and tried to think what came next, what came first, what came at all. Freddie plucked harder at his banjo strings. Artie and Otto blew louder, but it was still a blank to Duke. He looked inquiringly at the faces of his friends, then past them, his eyes blanking as completely as his mind.

Before the evening was over, Duke had played many more imaginary tunes on his lips, with his finger, than upon the piano keyboard. But it was only a one-night stand his lips played: next night he was ready for work; the scare was over; everybody fell in together.

The manager of the Hollywood, manager and owner and close friend of everybody who worked for him, was a bright-looking little man named Leo Bernstein. His clothes gleamed prosperity; his countenance was perpetually light-struck, as if a new idea were always being shaped in his head. His big new idea for the Hollywood was that it had had enough name changes in the past few years, sometimes as many as a dozen in a season. Therefore, the thing to do was to change the name from the Hollywood to the Kentucky Club, but this time with finality, this time for good, for keeps. Somehow Leo and a providential freedom from fires, which had closed down the 49th Street *boîte* so many times before, made the new name stick. The Ellington band and the dogged attachment of the owner to his new name kept "Kentucky" shining on the sign outside the club; the brilliance of the new band made "Kentucky" a by-word for good jazz, first in the minds of showfolk, finally among a huge number of night-clubbers in New York.

Showfolk, with that astonishing acumen for spotting talent in showfolk, were the first to recognize Duke and Otto and Sonny and Artie and Freddie for the remarkable combination they were. Al Jolson, not yet on his knee to his *Sonny Boy* but already similarly posed in devotion to his *Mammy;*

Jimmy Durante, and his raucous, ribald associates, Lou Clayton and Eddie Jackson, were devotees of the band. Jolson was playing at the Winter Garden; Clayton, Jackson and Durante were just a block away at the Silver Slipper. Harry Richman, who was playing piano in a basement cabaret around the corner, accompanying the Dolly Sisters, sat between his sets listening to the Washingtonians.

Bernstein was quickly impressed with his musicians, but not only with their music. He had other problems than that of providing music for his patrons; he was greatly helped in the solution of some of these by the musicians.

"You know how it is, Sonny," Leo told the drummer.

"No, Leo," Sonny replied. "How is it?"

"Well, it is Prohibition," Bernstein explained, "and there are Federal Agents."

"Uh-huh."

"And, on the other hand—"

"I'm ahead of you—the good people will not be prohibited."

"You're right, Sonny."

"Damn right I am, Leo."

"So we'll serve the people. But we gotta know who is and who ain't a Federal," Leo said, somewhat sadly.

"That's my job," Sonny replied, "that's my job."

"Hmm?"

"Just leave it to me. I'll okay 'em for drinks. If I say no—no! If I nod my head—they drink."

And so it was arranged. Sonny Greer grappled with the complicated problem of dealing or not dealing drinks under the tables of the Kentucky Club. For four-and-a-half years, he nodded or shook his head at the waiters, after quick perusals of those who requested whisky, or what passed for it. And in four-and-a-half years, he never made a mistake. The Kentucky was never raided; no hatchet-wielding, cop-surrounded, subpoena-carrying representative of the Treasury Department or the Department of Justice ever chopped, invaded or sued the Club. Leo's easily yielded faith in the sensational drummer from Long Branch was completely justified.

C

Leo had more than faith in Sonny and the boys: he had great affection for them; he was as relaxed an employer with his employees as this very informal business has ever seen. Breakfast dances were the big after-hours entertainment in Harlem in '23 and '24 and on through the early thirties. They were very big, very attractive, and the musicians couldn't wait to get through a breakfast dance night, to hotfoot it uptown.

One night Leo was out front watching the band. He noted a haste in their playing, rushed tempos, missed notes, lack of interest in solos.

"Bored?" he asked Otto. Otto smiled.

"Can't get through fast enough?" he asked Duke. Duke shook his head.

"All right," he said, "get through with that set and come in my office." They looked nervously at him and went quickly back to the business of playing their music. They took longer than they usually did on a set of numbers. Then the five of them filed into Leo's office looking a little sheepish, grinning by starts and turns.

"What took you so long?" Leo said.

They looked at each other. What was coming?

"Longer you take, later you get uptown," Leo said.

"Huh?"

"Now you, Otto," Leo said, "you can't wear that dirty old shirt at a breakfast dance. Take it off."

"That's the only shirt I got on the job."

"Take it off and take mine," and he stripped off his own.

"And you, Sonny," Leo said, "put on this ring." He gave Greer a five-karat diamond ring taken from his own finger. He straightened ties, pulled down jackets, gave Guy a handkerchief, then lined them up in front of him.

"Now then, gentlemen," he said, "you look as if you worked for me! Get the hell out of here and don't get home until you're good and plastered."

Getting plastered was a cinch, but the boys didn't go to the breakfast dances simply to loosen their spines or spill their nerves. They also went to watch and be watched. Jeff Blunt's was *the* breakfast dance place, 143rd and Lenox, next to the Cotton Club. Around four or five in the morning they'd start to troop in, the city's famous entertainers, little known show people, beer runners and their overlords, and a throng of colored citizens, Harlem inhabitants, who always knew where to go for a good time.

Lots of noise at these dances. Lots of heat, generated by closely packed crowds. Drinking. Much corking and uncorking of hip flasks. An occasional fight. A great sense of high life. Pulses seemed to double time. You floated rather than danced. The Washingtonians mixed well with the luminaries: they were readily accepted by them, particularly by the musicians. Paul Whiteman, having ascended the jazz throne, was a very welcome friend, a flush nightclubber, a lush patron. He would come down to the Kentucky, bringing his own home brew with him ("much better'n your stuff"). He'd plunk a century note on the piano ("just a note of appreciation"), sit down and grin all night with pleasure ("That's our Pops," his musicians said).

The Whiteman organization, deep in strings and brass and singers, a behemoth of a musical family, was a block away at the Palais Royal, 48th and Broadway. The guys came over to the Kentucky all the time. These white musicians, at the top of their profession, liked good jazz and good jazzmen. They drew no color line. They were "ofays," but "ofays" who were friends, not enemies.

"Ofay" is the colored man's word for white; it is Pig Latin for "foe." The use of this word is of deadly significance; it indicates just how strongly the Negro feels about his white brother, whose own feelings, and actions, have been so far from fraternal toward the darker-hued fellow. The Ellington musicians, all but Sonny Greer, had had every reason to hate white people, coming, as they did, from Washington, as restrictive a city, along color lines, as any in the deep South, with a few more employment opportunities, perhaps, a few less Jim Crow divisions, but with a general conception of race as bigoted, as pathologically twisted as a lynch mob's. The Ellington musicians had, nonetheless, only a fatalistic acceptance of race differences. To them, when they arrived in New York, it was simply a matter of slight readjustment, of a freer life but one still organized along racial lines, with their own ghetto, a gay ghetto, but a district apart, with more mixing permitted downtown, but watch your place, black man, in restaurants and night clubs and theaters, and woe unto you if you entered the wrong one, where the Fourteenth and Fifteenth Amendments to the Constitution were unheard of and colored people "simply did not belong." You could be asked to leave, politely. You could be told to leave, rudely. You could be thrown out. In any one of a dozen ways you could be embarrassed, shocked, humiliated. New York was like that. But the Washingtonians didn't hate: they were fatalistic, sad when they thought about it, more often blank to skin pigments, lost in the wider range of musical colors.

The entrance of people like Leo Bernstein and Paul Whiteman made a difference, counteracted their fatalism, brought them all the way from a numbness about themselves as Negroes to a new appreciation of the goodness and decency, the fairness, consideration and real understanding of some whites. In spite of its name, the Kentucky Club was the scene of tolerance and appreciation, of the breaking down of many racial barriers for Ellington and company. Distinctions could be forgotten: there didn't have to be a Mr. Eddie or a Mr. Charlie (one set of names for the two races), a black or a white, a Negro or an ofay. In many, many cases, foe became friend in Bernstein's Kentucky at 49th Street and Broadway in the middle nineteen-twenties.

CHAPTER FOUR

ECHOES OF THE JUNGLE

THE NINETEEN-TWENTIES WERE THE TIMES FOR THE NEGRO, the times for the "New Negro." African sculpture had not yet made its bowlegged entry into the homes of the smart, the chic, the wealthy, but the jaded appetites of that postwar generation had found new salivation in the "African" entertainments. The Negro, the New Negro was encouraged to develop African and pseudo-African themes because they were exotic, oh so bizarre! The noise of jungle drums and their jazz equivalents was such a pleasant change from the concord of salon orchestras, tea ensembles and large dance bands featuring fiddles! The colors of the jungle, great swoops of brilliant hue, were such a diverting novelty! And the frank attitude toward sex of those "Africans," the free indulgence, how tempting that was, too, how tempting!

Carl Van Vechten, a quondam music critic, an unquestionably sincere apostle of this neo-African cult, gave parties for his colored friends, talked the movement up, wrote about it. He wrote a novel, *Nigger Heaven,* a pathetic narration of Negroes and Negro traits; but more important than its narrative or characters was its demonstration of a brazenness which passed for courage, a surface insight which many thought profound. Van Vechten, and others in rabid imitation, bandied about the hateful term, "Nigger."

Negro poets flourished. Claude McKay came from Jamaica, absorbed American Negro culture in Kansas and New York, courted and was courted by radicals, and wrote about *Harlem*

Shadows, in 1922, after preliminary skirmishes with the *Springs of New Hampshire.* Later, in 1925, he wrote a novel about the Harlem of the mid-twenties, *Home to Harlem.* A background in Jamaica, where such discrimination as existed was sotto voce, made McKay a revolutionary pamphleteer in his poems:

> Like men we'll face the murderous, cowardly pack,
> Pressed to the wall, dying, but—fighting back!

Countee Cullen, a New York University student, wrote a searing, saddening lyric, *Color,* and built a large audience for his verses. In 1929, at the end of this era, he sent his publishers a poem from Paris, *The Black Christ,* "hopefully dedicated," he said, "to white America." In it he anticipated the consciously nasty, brutally shocking imagery of Lewis Allan's song, *Strange Fruit,* and Lillian Smith's novel which borrowed Allan's title. But this was ten years before the song, fifteen before the book:

> Somewhere the Southland rears a tree,
> And many others there may be
> Like unto it, that are unknown,
> Whereon as costly fruit has grown.

James Weldon Johnson, lyric writer for his brother Rosamund's spirituals and secular songs, United States consul, lawyer, propagandist and poet, wrote *Fifty Years,* a review in verse form of his people's achievements after the Civil War. This was in 1917, before the big times for the cultured Negro began. Five years earlier he had written a book moderately successful commercially but altogether effective as a testament of a Negro's faith in people and progress, *The Autobiography of an Ex-Colored Man.* In this new era, James Weldon Johnson had his biggest success, with a collection of Negro sermons in verse, *God's Trombones.* This was 1927, height of the zealous, near-fanatic devotion of certain whites to Negroes and their arts. The book was the announcement, not only of a writer's religion and racial identification, but of the identification of music, of jazz instruments in particular, with his race. It was an association of Negroes and jazz which was to continue for a long time through the writing of younger Negroes, such as Langston Hughes, and older white poets, such as Vachel Lindsay. Lindsay wrote *The Congo, A Study of the Negro Race* and *The Booker Washington Trilogy*, essaying jazz meter and speaking straightforwardly about Negroes and Negro problems, straightforwardly and also rather naïvely. In *Daniel Jazz* he named the name of the music which was influencing him, and again caught some of the rhythm of jazz, some of the feeling of the Negro himself and more of the feeling of others about him.

Naïveté about Negroes was not confined to whites. Negroes themselves were caught up in the Africanism which swept New York and most of the other big cities in the early twenties and stayed with this country's intellectuals and pseudo-intellectuals until the fourth decade of this century. In the war year of 1917, another Jamaica Negro came to the United States, one Marcus Garvey. He and a friend, Amy Ashwood, had founded the Universal Negro Improvement Association in 1914, in Kingston, Jamaica. He was President; she was Secretary. They didn't have anyone under them at first; few later on—in Jamaica. But the American Negro was more receptive. The first year in the United States—only seventeen members. One more year, 1919, and there were 5,000. Then, bang! Garvey was arrested for libeling the Assistant District Attorney of New York. He became a popular figure among his people, a wronged Negro. Colored soldiers returning from overseas, with a determination to implement their constitutional and statutory freedom with action to guarantee it, rallied round him. One year later, 1920, it was the biggest mass movement the Negroes had ever known. There were three million Garveyites!

What did Garvey preach, in his wheedling, haranguing accents? Back to Africa! All of Africa for the Negro! The Negro must have, in Africa, a home like the white man's Europe and America. If the imperialists of the world wouldn't give them Africa, they would take it! Take it! Take it! Back to Africa! The Negro's home! He organized with thoroughness. There were uniformed Garvey troops. Color guards at meetings. Marches through the streets of Harlem and Chicago's South

Side and other Negro quarters. From all over the United States, the West Indies and Central America, money poured in, as Negroes parted with furniture and clothing and last savings to support Marcus Garvey and gain a continent for themselves. He declared himself Africa's Emperor and President, appointed nobles under him, distributed legislative committee chairmanships as lavishly as he did his phony titles. He sent delegations to Liberia and the League of Nations, bargaining for Africa. He bought a couple of steamships, put them into operation between New York and Africa and called them the Black Star Line. "The Black Star Line," he said, "will sail to Africa if it sails in seas of blood." He stood up in Madison Square Garden and defied the police, who were after him, to arrest him. He was a romantic hero, a blood-and-thunder orator, a handsomer, darker but not much more scrupulous Hitler.

He never indited a program, never offered to his millions of followers more than dreams and steerage passage to Africa, which was not his Empire, and he not its Emperor. He was not above plotting with the Ku Klux Klan, the most vigilant and virulent and violent detractors of his people, to move the Negro population from their southern precincts to African vale and veldt. He was not above using the United States mails to defraud, according to the United States Government. He was convicted of this serious charge in 1926, imprisoned, deported to Jamaica and ended up in London, where negotiations, begun in the West Indies, to effect a peace between him and the British Empire, finally succeeded. Stanch supporter of the Lion, he was last heard of (and heard) in Hyde Park, advocating the highly unrevolutionary program of Africa for the English, who already have so much of it.

Ellington was not untouched by the Negro revival, by Van Vechten's party world, Cullen's and McKay's and Johnson's versified broadsides, Garvey's marching men. Neither he nor any of the men who played with him was a Garveyite, but they were affected by this neo-Africanism, by the rise in the Negroes' consciousness of their ethnology. Whether it was an accident, a charming trick of fate, or simply Ellington's sly, innocent-ap-pearing way of doing things, shortly after the band moved into the Kentucky (née Hollywood), the first of the "jungle" sounds moved onto the bandstand with them, the first of the growls which have typified Duke's music ever since.

Charlie Irvis joined the band. Charlie Irvis was a New York boy; he'd played at all the Harlem spots. But the sounds he made with his trombone were, as Duke says, "jungle-istic." He used the cap of a bottle for a mute and played all around the bottom of his horn, growling elfishly, oafishly, suggestively, jungle-istically at the Kentucky customers. He tried to make the trombone sound like a saxophone and rolled off long cadences of clear notes, broken by those exquisite shivers of sound, a bleat, a brump, a yawp, which European visitors would call *echt Afrikanisch, vraiment Africaine,* and in which the wealthy cultist could indulge his wildest fantasies about "the primitive Negro arts."

Ellington's consciousness of the value of these sounds took shape slowly. He certainly was not going to accept the cultists' appraisal at face value: he had too little respect for movements of any kind, and superficial racist doctrine left him unimpressed. But he was strongly aware of the mechanical sounds of the world around him and determined to reproduce them in his music. It was still a few years early, in 1923, for his reproduction of the echoes of the jungle, of the sonorities of the colored man's dreams, his black and tan fantasies; many years later he sought to capture the nervous rhythms of a crowded Harlem tenement's airshaft, the crescendos and diminuendos of a railroad train, the Daybreak Express. Like the Lion, who painted tone pictures of *The Boy in the Boat, Morning Air* and *Rippling Waters,* Duke's palette was committed to a pale impressionism in the first years of his stay at the Kentucky. But Charlie Irvis ruffled the placid surface of Ellington's "conversation music" with a series of doo-wa's and rrrr-ump's which were like injections of a nasty word, a saucy phrase, wonderful touches of musical innuendo. They added a fillip to the Washingtonians' music which made an already out-of-the-way band unique.

The musicians themselves, far from recognizing their inim-

itable qualities, were joyfully settling down into their new routine. Sonny never made a mistake in okaying customers for
drinks, and the customers saw to it that he got plenty himself.
Among the customers were gangsters, beer-runners, bootleggers,
the aristocracy of the underworld, men who lived hard and
drank harder. Around various parts of their persons, they carried pint bottles of New York's "Red Likker" or corn or, if they
were more finicky, brandy or Scotch. One of these notables
would lift a trouser leg and reveal a bottle strapped to his left
calf; another had moved his gun to a specially built pants
pocket and ensconced his bottle in his under-arm holster;
others, less ingenious, carried their liquid spirits in hip pockets
or strapped to their waists. When they came to the Kentucky,
grateful for Sonny's kindnesses or the quality of Ellington's
music, they would leave a tip. Out from hip or side pocket,
shoulder holster or leg, would come a pint bottle. In fraternity
the tipping man would drink half the bottle, in fraternity and
one gulp, leaving the rest to be quaffed similarly by Sonny,
Otto, Duke, Freddie, Charlie or Artie.

The drinking got serious. A musician who made time, who
arrived at seven o'clock for a seven o'clock job, was a punk. No
musician considered himself a jazzman if he didn't get drunk
often and thoroughly. He would go up to "the Mexican's" place.
Gomez, who had never seen Mexico, was an affable Carolinian
of Latin ancestry, whose "cave" had atmosphere. There the musician would mix his liquor one night—combine the raw alcohol
and some mild flavoring—drink it the next night. He would
come down to work rolling but not even slightly affected on his
instrument: the keys were still in the same place, the mouthpiece exactly where it had been the night before, the music
still came out of the bell of the horn. It was occasionally dis-
turbing that, when everything else in the immediate vicinity
had changed so much, keys, mouthpiece and bell should remain
fixed. But music was the fixed value in these musicians' lives
and they easily adjusted themselves to this one fact in their
world of fantasies.

The routine was established; this was the way they lived after they hit the Kentucky. With characters like Irvis and Bubber Miley to implement the pattern, it was inevitable.

Bubber turned up in late 1924, cut musically, emotionally, from Irvis' cloth. Like Charlie, he didn't worry much, played what he wanted to, when he wanted to. Like Charlie, he growled. Like Charlie, he was a New Yorker. James Miley was a graduate, *summa cum laude*, of the West 62nd Street gang, the kids who lived at the edge of Hell's Kitchen on New York's West Side. These kids out-roughed the gangs just south of them, in the fifties and forties and thirties. They also out-played them; a number of great colored jazzmen grew up in the so-called 62nd Street "Jungles." Bobby Stark, who played fine trumpet with Fletcher Henderson and Chick Webb; Freddy Jenkins, who joined Duke in 1928 on trumpet and novelty vocals; Benny Carter, from Henderson through McKinney's Cotton Pickers, and the Chocolate Dandies, to his own excellent band, a brilliant trumpeter and alto saxist—these were Miley sidekicks. Miley taught them much of what they learned of the fundamentals of their horns and the art of music. "Bubber" (the nickname is an extension of "Bub," which he picked up as a young boy) gigged around New York, played all the Harlem places and found his way downtown to Reisenweber's, where the Original Dixieland Band had made its stand.

Slim, with a face as round as the sun, bright brown in the cheeks, brilliant gold in the mouth, his sparkling fillings spreading rays before him, Bubber laughed a lot, and had strong lines of laughter cut across his face. His eyes danced when he smiled, and as they pirouetted, so did his music. "He was completely uninhibited, irrepressible," Otto Hardwick recalls. "Nothing at all for him to stop in the middle of a chorus, remembering some nonsense, double up in hysterics, nothing coming out of his horn but wind!"

Whetsol was all for going back to Howard, to resume his medical career, which still hadn't reached the primary stage of Hippocratic oath and doctor's degree. Duke pleaded with him, but Arthur wanted to go, so Arthur went and Bubber was marked as the man to succeed him.

"Let's go up after him," someone suggested.

"Why not just send for him?" Otto asked.

"Done it," Duke explained, "but he won't come."

"Why not?"

"Happy where he is. Says when Whetsol gets back, we'll let him go."

"Oh."

"Let's get him," Sonny says. And off they go.

When the Washingtonians arrive at the little uptown spot at which Bubber's playing, they sit down with him as if it's just a regular visit.

"How's tricks? Things? Music?" they ask.

"Fine, fine," Bubber replies.

They take a couple of drinks together. Because there are several of them, just one of him, they are able to spread their liquor around, make it look good, but stay well on their feet. Bubber gets juiced. When he's really stiff, they lead him out.

"Needs fresh air," Sonny explains.

"That's our pal," Otto tells the bartender, "we'll take care of him."

They take care of him. When Bubber Miley comes to, he's playing trumpet at the Kentucky Club, with Duke Ellington's Washingtonians.

They tell how Bubber got his ideas.

He'd walk along the street with Duke. He'd see a sign. Advertising a cleaning and dyeing service, say, Phil Cooper's cleaning and dyeing service. Cooper the Cleaner. Or Cooper the Dyer. Or Cooper, cleaning and dyeing, holes rewoven, spots removed, etc. Bubber would look at it. Then he'd say it. Then he'd sing it.

"Cooper the cleaner," Bubber'd say.

"Uh-huh," Duke would affirm.

"Cooooo-puh the cleannnnn-uh!" Bubber'd sing.

"Huh?" Duke would ask.

From simple signs, Bubber would construct "riffs," two- and four-bar phrases, which he would hum over in his mind, getting the rhythmic accents from the rise and fall of the syllables in

the signs, constructing the melody from the way his voice leaped
over the vowels and consonants. Thus an interval of a fourth,
a third, a seventh. Thus a Miley melody, riff, figure. Thus much
music for Ellington.

Or maybe it would be in church, hearing the organist play
a familiar hymn. Invert the second four measures and you get
a great jazz tune, Bubber thinks, and he does, and he gets a
fine jump figure. From the sound of organ and choir at church,
he got some of his most famous solos. His twenty-four-bar
masterpiece, the improvisation he tacked on to his own *Black
and Tan Fantasy,* was based, he said, on a Spiritual his mother
used to sing, *Hosanna.* Actually, there are other hymn materials
in his solo, but the whole is permeated with the melodic sub-
stance of the Spiritual and helps to give to *Black and Tan* that
overtone of nave and apse, or ramshackle crossroads church,
which is perhaps its greatest effect.

The sources of Bubber's music are important: they indicate
how broad the sources of Ellington's music are, and how large,
how profound are the dimensions of jazz at this level. These
men—strongly addicted to "partying," to long, stiff drinking
bouts, to making music in such helter-skelter surroundings as
an after-hours joint, a blowzy speakeasy, somebody's "buffet
flat" rent parties and their regular jobs of work—culled solos,
arrangements and combinations of both from everything around
them and reflected, as nobody before, the sound and tempo and
mood of their country.

The growl, to Bubber, was a fabulous tool. He could use it
to intone the tragic sounds of graveyard cities, the late night
calls of slow freight trains or the simple crying of a deserted
woman, some of the inspirations of solos like *Black and Tan*
and *East St. Louis Toodle-Oo,* which became the Ellington
band's theme. He could laugh at you and set you laughing with
him, as in *Got Everything but You* and *Flaming Youth.* His device wasn't complicated, a mute that filled the bell of the horn,
the bottom of a plumber's rubber plunger, which he would hold
in the palm of his right hand and pull to and from the trumpet.
But, easy as it seems, other trumpeters couldn't imitate it until,

five years later, Charles Williams, "Cootie," took his place, and, after some months of study, mastered the technique. Tricky Sam picked it up from him, when he replaced little Charlie Irvis in 1926, and was called upon to reproduce the lowings of Irvis' 'bone, its ululations in definite pitch, its wit and wisdom, comedy and high tragedy of sound. Irvis' growling, blown with bottle aid, with cap and sometimes with bucket over the trombone's bell, was familiar to Tricky; they were close friends. But Tricky didn't think he was up to Charlie.

Tricky, as small as Charlie, was then just Joe Nanton, proud possessor of a surname which only his family owned ("No other Nanton in the phone book or any place else"). He felt like "just Joe Nanton." He and Charlie would wander around the uptown spots together. Charlie would suggest going in someplace and playing a "cutting session," the name they had for jam get-togethers in the twenties.

"No, man, you don't get me in there," Tricky protested, in his soft, husky but high-pitched voice.

"Why not, boy?" Irvis inquired.

"Ain' good enough."

"What you mean?"

"Well," Tricky would explain, "just listen to that guy blowing trombone now. He's too good, man. I'm nowhere. I can't blow before, after or beside him."

"Before, after or beside that guy, you're great," Irvis would reply. "Why, he's nothin' . . . he's just full of tricks. You can play so much better than him. We're goin' in." And in they went.

Joe Nanton was close to Charlie Irvis and close to Bubber Miley. He had met Bubber for the first time when the trumpeter was playing at the Waltz Dream Dance Hall on 53d Street, just after leaving Mamie Smith's Jazz Hounds (the little band that brought Coleman Hawkins and Joe Smith, tenor and trumpet greats, to New York), just before going to work at Reisenweber's. Bubber and Joe Nanton hit it right off. They built a "beautiful friendship" on the basis of similar tastes in the playing of music, the drinking of liquor and the disposition of their leisure time in those vital pursuits.

Tricky joined the band under protest, but not the same sort as Bubber's. Joe just didn't want to take his friend's place.

Duke came to him with an offer.

"Joe," Duke said, "Charlie Irvis is leaving."

"Damn shame," Tricky said. "Good man."

"So are you."

"Not as good as Charlie."

"We want you to take his place."

"Charlie'll be back next week," Tricky said.

"No, he won't," Duke assured him.

"I can't take a job away from my friend," Tricky protested again.

"He took himself away," Duke insisted. "The job's open. Somebody's got to fill it. You're the right man. So—"

Tricky promised to come up and join the band that night.

All night the band sat around, waiting for their new trombonist. Without Irvis or the new man, there were big holes in the set arrangements. Otto and Bubber got tired of alternating on solo choruses. But holes, fatigue be damned; Tricky didn't show.

Next night, Duke went down and got him.

"You're coming with me," he told the reluctant little trombonist with the sliding-pine nose and the tubby build.

"Guess I am," Tricky said.

Duke waited "on" him until he got dressed, and then, as Tricky says, "He TOOK me with him." (The capitals are Tricky's.)

The band was playing at the Plantation then, at 50th Street and Broadway, a short time-out from their regular endeavors at the Kentucky that spring of 1926. But the Plantation wasn't paying off, so, after a delay on the first week's pay, and no pay at all the second, the Washingtonians left. They went up to New England, to Salem, Massachusetts, which, since the summer of 1924, had been their hot weather home.

They played in Salem at the Charleshurst Ballroom. Sometimes you could find them, before or after hours. More often you could not. Duke was usually out with the police force's Lieutenant Bates, who later became Salem's Mayor, and then its Representative in Congress. Or, with the other Washingtonians, he was over at the Coast Guard barracks, or being whisked around the Salem-Marblehead Harbor. All of Salem followed the band, felt as if these boys from Washington, New York and New Jersey were natives, almost as much a part of the tradition of their town as Nathaniel Hawthorne and the House of Seven Gables.

The band returned to the Kentucky Club, after turning down a booking in West Virginia. "The South! God damn, no!" was the consensus of opinion, and the band was still being run, pretty much, by a consensus of opinion. The return was a happy one, not only because everybody loved coming back to New York, but because interest in the band had deepened, intensified, and the depth and intensity of that interest had been successfully channelized. They were to make records!

A record-making session, in those days, was almost comparable to a colored band playing the Waldorf (which never happened, of course): it was a sensational event. Ellington, Hardwick, Irvis, Guy and Greer had, with the addition of a man on wind bass, Bass Edwards, been approached earlier in the year to make records. This they had done, with two trumpets, Harry Cooper and LeRoy Rutledge, Jimmy Harrison on trombone, Don Redman, George Thomas and Prince Robinson on reeds, added for the date. They had made that date for Gennett, a big "race record" company, which sold most of its discs in the South and the Negro quarters of the North. Gennett wanted blues and Gennett got blues, but only two of the four sides seemed like best-seller material to the record company and so two were never issued. And the two that did come out, *If You Can't Hold That Man* and *You've Got Those Wanna Go Back Again Blues,* disappeared so fast from the market that nobody seems to have a copy of this first record of Ellington's.

Another date for Gennett produced *Animal Crackers* and *Lil'*

Farina, with Charlie Johnson on trumpet and Prince Robinson on clarinet the only additions. And then records for Buddy, Perfect, Harmony and Cameo followed. Obscure labels today, not the biggest then, these did have a following and helped add to the reputation of the band, billed on records as the Duke Ellington Washingtonians, or simply the Washingtonians. They made mostly blues for those labels, eight sides of stuff like *Stack O' Lee* and *Bugle Call Rag, Trombone Blues* and *Georgia Grind.* Then, on their last date for Cameo, they trotted out standard repertory, three of the great Ellingtonian or Washingtonian numbers of the day, *East St. Louis Toodle-Oo, Jubilee Stomp* and *Take It Easy.* And with the introduction of these tunes came the introduction of the Ellington band to important recording activity, to important broadcasting and to a countrywide reception which would permit expansion of the organization, a larger personnel, a broader instrumentation.

Bass Edwards was the band's first wind bass man. They really wanted a string bass, but where could you put a string bass at the Kentucky? The ceiling was too low over the bandstand. But Bass Edwards, who looked like a cross between the two instruments, played "a hell of a wind bass." He played five G's on the horn, a phenomenal five-octave range; most men bothered with less than half that. He would run over intricate arpeggios on the instrument, tough lipping and accurate fingering of the valves demanded. Then he would remove his fingers from the valves and play the same stuff with only his lips to form and hold the notes, and he gave them perfect valuation and precise pitch. Bass, who has since banged around with half a dozen colored bands, didn't stay more than a year with the Washingtonians, but he left a strong impression. "He could cut rings around symphony men on tuba," his colleagues said, still say, and they offer his range, flawless technique and stunning lip control as proof.

Max Shaw, who succeeded Bass when the band went into the Plantation Club over the Winter Garden for its ill-fated two-week run, was another phenomenon. "He scared us," the musicians recall. Max had a broken jaw-bone. He took quanti-

ties of aspirin (mixed with whisky) to keep the excruciating
pain from felling him. But he continued to blow horn, to out-
blow anybody else's horn. The band would come into a studio,
a theater or a big ballroom, and Max was ready.

"See that?" he would say, pointing at the rafters of the hall,
the supports under the balcony of the theater, the beams across
the studio's ceiling.

"Do indeed," Otto might say, or Sonny, knowing what was
coming next, and still wondering.

"Look strong, don't they? Watch me," Max continued, "just
watch me. I'll jar those rafters; I'll make 'em shake."

Shattered jaw-bone quivering as he set the tuba mouthpiece
against his teeth, Max would blow. Once, twice, three times.
And the rafters shook, the beams rattled, the notes shook the
hall.

"Jarred 'em, didn't I?"

"Did indeed." And Otto or Sonny or Duke or anybody
around would be as amazed the tenth time or the fiftieth as the
first. Tough enough for a well man, with perfectly shaped and
healthy jaws and teeth; impossible for a musician with a broken
jaw. But, impossible as it seemed, he did it. "Did indeed."

Shortly after returning from Salem, in 1926, the band got an
offer to go into the Flamingo Club, down Broadway from the
Kentucky. Duke had written the score for *The Chocolate Kid-
dies*, in 1924, and though the show never got to Broadway
(it did get to Berlin, Germany, where it ran two years), Jack
Robbins' one-room publishing firm spread some of its numbers
around and they earned something of a reputation as a show-
tune writer for Ellington. The Flamingo Club wanted a band
that could play show tunes—straight. With the band's reputation as a purveyor of conversation music, Duke's background as
a writer of show tunes, the Washingtonians were a natural for
the Flamingo. In they went.

"Now look, fellows," Duke explained, "we play straight, see?
No faking. No ad lib. Strictly as written."

"Yeah," the boss corroborated, "we wanna hear the melodies."

"Getcha," the boys assented.

The first night they managed. Somehow, by great self-control, superlative attention to the tunes called out by Duke, will-power in their desire to make good at the distinguished Flamingo Club, somehow they managed.

The second night they managed. But you could see that Bubber was uncomfortable. He pulled at his collar a lot, straightened his neck in its stiff starched brace often.

"I'm sick of this stuff," Bubber said.

"I know, Bub," Duke comforted him, "but look at the class we're getting."

"Class!" Bubber sniffed.

The third night, Bubber struck. In the middle of a slobbery slow tune, everybody expiring gracelessly over its dull figurations, but playing it straight, Bubber lifted horn to mouth and blew. The band lifted right with him. Tempo came up, they began to go. Hell with the tune, hell with the tempo. Go! Boom, the jitterbugs fell right in. They weren't called jitterbugs then, but jitter they did, that night, to the suddenly reinspired Ellington band.

Next night they came on the job, Bubber arrived with gloves on, spats, elegant cane, hat in his hand, in imitation of the manager's "natty" dress. The band straggled in after Bubber. A few minutes later, they heard some music coming from the environs of the bandstand.

"Look and see what it is," Duke called out to Bubber.

Bubber walked out, still in elegant attire. He ran back, his elegance gone.

"It's another band, Duke. There's another band on the stand." He stopped and looked around at the other guys. "Hey, that's great, isn't it?" He smiled broadly.

A few minutes later, the manager came in, walked silently over to each of the boys with a pay envelope. Two weeks' salary and a pink slip.

Bubber left immediately, got out of the elevator at the street level, walked into his tiny Oakland, a car almost as small as a Bantam or Austin, which had cost him $50, and rapped the back of his chauffeur's head with his knees, which couldn't help bumping the driver.

"Home, James," he said.

Fortunately, Leo Bernstein was fresh out of a band at the Kentucky. Hearing of the Ellington crew's plight, he offered them their old job back. They went gladly.

Then the additions to the band really started coming fast, but not till the most important single change in Duke's life took place. Whether you judge it as good or bad, hate him or admire him, the advent of Irving Mills is pivotal in the life of Edward Kennedy Ellington and all those associated with him. When Mills stepped in, accident and chance stepped out; big business took over and the rise of the Ellington orchestra was made inevitable. That with this rise should also come serious disillusionment for the men in the band, a deepening sense of personal and collective tragedy which has never left these brilliant musicians, that, too, was inevitable.

CHAPTER FIVE

THE DUKE STEPS OUT

RVING MILLS WAS A DAPPER LITTLE MAN, SLEEK IN HIS DRESS, slick in his manner. In the late twenties, he was a successful song publisher and a band manager beginning to come up with the expanding band business. He was building a business, a family, a fortune. When he found Duke, the size of the first and last, the comfort of the second, were assured.

Irving walked into the Kentucky Club one night in 1926. There they were on the stand: three horns, Hardwick, Miley and Nanton; four rhythm, Ellington, Guy, Edwards and Greer. They were playing W. C. Handy's *St. Louis Blues,* which, almost from the day it was written in 1914, had become a jazz classic, *the* jazz classic. The Washingtonians put their individual stamp on the performance. The tango introduction was pretty much as Handy had written it, but from there, try to find St. Louis, Kansas City or any other Missouri town. It was simply the blues, with a couple of progressions here and there which followed the original. But, close to or far from William Christopher Handy's tune, the sound the seven men built up was impressive.

"What's that you're playing, Duke?" Irving Mills asked the leader.

"*St. Louis Blues,* of course," the leader answered.

"You don't say?"

"But I do."

"Hmm."

Mills was impressed and a few days later was down to see Duke again. He had some ideas.

"How about doing records, Duke?" Irving asked.

"We've done records.'

"For whom?"

"Gennett. Buddy. Perfect."

"Small fry. How about Columbia?"

"Well, how about it?"

"We'll arrange it," Irving Mills promised.

Mills arranged that, and almost everything else Ellington did from then on for thirteen years. A contract was later set between the two men, giving each 45 per cent of a new corporation, Ellington, Inc., and giving lawyer Sam Buzzell the remaining 10 per cent. Duke, in turn, was given a share of some other Mills properties.

Irving, whose meteoric career almost justified the assumption that he was the Mills of the Gods, changed things pretty fast. The band now had a real leader. Ellington was front man, not merely arranger, pianist and business representative of the Washingtonians. The idea that Freddie Guy had advanced several times in '23, '24 and '25, that the guys should incorporate as a co-operative band, was certainly dead now. This was a business, not big yet, but growing, with Edward Kennedy Ellington as President and Irving Mills as Treasurer.

In June of 1927 the band went up to New England to do some one-nighters and play another summer at the Charleshurst Ballroom at Salem Willows. Harry Carney joined them at a single stand they were making at Nodding-on-Charles, Waltham, Mass., a suburb of Boston.

Harry Carney was a Boston boy, and just a boy, too, when he joined Ellington, seventeen years old. He'd been playing professionally only two years in 1927, having kicked around with a few local bands. A high-school colleague of Harry's was Toots Mondello, the brilliant alto saxophonist in later years with Benny Goodman and various radio studio orchestras and, briefly, leader of his own outfit. Harry had heard the Ellington band a couple of times on its one-nighters in and around Boston. His instrument was the alto sax then, so he paid particular attention to Otto's deft manipulation of the keys of his horn.

Carney, young, fresh-looking and kind of cocky, looked up at the bandstand. Otto, only five years older, looked ancient to Harry because of his baldness. But his glittering technique didn't escape the youngster. He was amazed at Hardwick's ease on the alto horn, his negotiation of fast runs, his creamy tone. Harry turned to his companion.

"Listen to that old man play all that alto," he said.

"I know," said his companion.

"Damn," said Harry, "that's a lot of horn, that really is.

Harry particularly remembered hearing Otto play *Jig Walk*. Very fancy stuff. When Harry Carney was hired, he was expected to play just that fancy stuff with Duke. Otto was out on one of his escapades, "very temporary," he called them, but he was out, and a replacement was needed. Harry had built a reputation playing around Boston with Bobby Sawyer and Henry Sapro's bands and his name made sense to the Washingtonians. He was hired.

The Ellington band had another sax-playing admirer in their Boston audiences whom they remembered very well when they left New England. A short little boy still in knee-pants, he used to stand around listening intently, sometimes with his growing excitement apparent, but more often with almost somber mien. He'd also kicked around Boston with local bands; he'd played with Bobby Sawyer the same year Carney had, 1925, but he was littler than Harry, younger-looking, less conspicuous, though four years older. This was Cornelius Hodges, "Johnny" to his friends.

Johnny was a Cambridge boy who got some of his music in school, some more in private study. He cut out the same year Harry did, reaching New York in 1927 and joining Chick Webb for his first crack at the big time. He looked so much like Chick that all of the famous little drummer's friends and associates called them cousins, and until today many assume that relationship between Hodges and the late leader, though actually there was no tie other than that of friendship.

Harry Carney was in, Otto was out (temporarily, "very temporarily"). Harry joined in time to play Salem Willows with the band that summer, and he was just fresh-looking enough, just enough of a strutter, so that it was inevitable he would be invited out for an evening with May. Being invited out for an evening with May was a regular routine for new musicians who played Salem. It was quite a routine.

Some of the members of the Ellington band proposed an evening's entertainment to Carney.

"Let's have a time," Bubber suggested.

"I'm on," Harry assented, "but this is my territory, I should be the host and name the places and the people and get the liquor."

"No, no," Sonny insisted, "we know Salem, and besides, you're new. This is on us."

"That's right," Bubber added, "and furthermore, we know just the place and just the party. Good corn liquor, a great person, a wonderful time."

"That sounds wonderful," Harry agreed.

"May is her name," Bubber explained, "and she is really fun."

"Fun indeed," Sonny corroborated.

"But don't forget," Bubber admonished, "she expects us to bring the groceries, lots of them, and some gin for her if we can find it and some pop soda, you know, 'n' everything."

And so they set out for May's laden with packages, food, drink, meat sandwiches, gin and soda. And somehow the bulk of the packages was in Carney's hands. They walked over to May's through Salem's old back streets, through narrow lanes crowded with weathered frame houses, dark even in the moonlit night because they were huddled so close to each other. Finally, one last back street brought them to a gloomy old place, something right out of the seventeenth century and apparently uncared-for since then. Clapboards loose in the mild breeze sawed against each other, making a sad, complaining noise, a wail in the early morning air. A few window shutters flapped back and forth across the ancient windows, adding another disconsolate tone. The doorway was dark; only one weak light shone from the whole house, up in the second story.

"Brrrr," said Carney, "scary-looking."

"Beautiful inside," Sonny assured him.

"May's wonderful," Bubber said, "just don't worry. We're gonna have a time."

"Let's go," Harry said, gathering strength.

They opened the door, which squeaked noisily.

"Who's there?" a woman's voice called.

"It's me, May," Sonny replied.

A lightly clad woman came to the head of the stairs, but before she could open her mouth, a heavy-set man rushed past her. He looked down angrily at Carney, who, of course, was leading the way, bundles in hand.

"So you're the guy who's been fooling around with my wife," he told Carney. "I've been waiting to get a hold of you." And with that he dashed down the stairs after Harry, pistol in hand, firing in the air.

Carney took rapid flight, clutching the bundles, which he was too nervous and scared and bewildered to put down. The man gave good chase, firing as he went. When they got to a principal street, the outraged husband yelled something about a murder, about this man (Carney) shooting his wife or his friend, or something. Passing policemen joined in. They fired their guns, too, and not until Carney had run better than a mile was he entirely free of husband, cops and frightening gunshots. He put down his bundles at last. Winded, he leaned against a tree, puffing, sighing, still frightened. Suddenly, Sonny and Bubber showed up, a good deal less than winded, and really not frightened at all. They allowed Harry to worry a little longer and then explained the gag to him. Thus was he initiated into the good graces of both the musicians and the members of the Salem police department, who, of course, had co-operated with the bandsmen in putting on the horror show.

Almost every band which has ever played Salem, or Salem Willows, or near-by territory, has had the gag pulled on it. Just say, "Oh, May," to a musician who's played Salem and watch him fall out. They all think it's funny; they all like to remember either their own or a colleague's experience with the pistol-packing papa and the police.

Otto returned to the Ellington band shortly after Harry joined, and the Washingtonians had a reed section. They began doubling, Otto playing clarinet—which he had done only upon occasion in the past—with more regularity, and Carney making first overtures on the baritone, which Otto had played earlier. When Rudy Jackson joined shortly after, playing tenor saxophone, as well as alto and clarinet, the saxes seemed enormous to the old-timers. It was possible really to arrange for them, to get depth and breadth of tone and range, a whole variety of three-part harmonies, and, with trumpet, trombone and piano, to get four-, five- and six-part writing. Very exciting.

The additions were made, the band was bigger, its one-nighter pay better. That was a beginning, as far as Irving Mills was concerned. Next, radio.

In radio, there was no need for anybody's interference. It just happened, happened naturally and wonderfully. Ted Husing, who'd come down from Boston a couple of years earlier to make his start at CBS, the Columbia Broadcasting System, was a night-club habitué, a ringsider at Broadway's top spots. He followed Duke's progress with more than ordinary interest. This was his band. He was for it and he was going to do everything possible for it. He did: he gave the band its big radio break when it moved to the Cotton Club a year later. In the meantime, he talked it up big and with the aid of small station broadcasts on WHN, WMCA, managed to get some network time for them out of the Kentucky Club.

The Kentucky Club tag was good enough, well enough known, so that on the series of records Duke and the boys made for Columbia and its cheaper label, Vocalion, that fall of 1927, the billing read "Duke Ellington and His Kentucky Club Orchestra." There'd been just enough broadcasts to get the name around and make the association of club and band a glamorous one.

The band made one Columbia record, *East St. Louis Toodle-Oo,* its theme, and *Hop Head,* then made another side

for that label, *Down in Your Alley Blues,* before moving to the
Vocalion label. On Vocalion, they made *East St. Louis* again,
Birmingham Breakdown and half a dozen sides not so well
known. *East St. Louis* is the brilliant Bubber Miley piece, a profound excursion into the recherché sounds of the rubber
plunger over muted trumpet, with added atmosphere lent by
the heavy bass figure, played by Carney on baritone, Wellman
Braud (newly added) bowing on string bass, and low trombone
notes from Tricky Sam. The *Breakdown* is a negligible stomp,
not comparable in importance to the *Toodle-Oo,* which has
hardly dated after eighteen years, but it does afford the opportunity to hear Duke's "party" piano as it sounded in those days,
and earlier, romping through the sketchy melodic phrase, with
brief solos followed by Otto Hardwick on alto, Bubber on
trumpet and Carney on baritone. This record is important for
many, many reasons. It is the earliest Ellington record still available today (in the Decca-Brunswick album of *Ellingtonia,*
Volume 1); both pieces stayed in the Ellington repertory until
fifteen years later, when *Take the A Train* replaced the first as
Duke's theme and the second was clearly and pathetically dated.

After the Columbia-Vocalion dates, the needs, interests and
offers of the record companies in New York were by no means
satisfied. From other companies, Melotone, Oriole, Cameo,
came offers to do record sessions. The money was too good; it
couldn't be turned down. But, on the other hand, there were
contractual obligations to Columbia. These were easily overcome: for Melotone, Duke used the noms-de-danse of Georgia
Syncopators and Earl Jackson and His Musical Champions; for
Oriole, he led the Whoopee Makers; on another label, the
band became the Lumberjacks.

It was on Melotone that the most famous of all of Duke's early
performances was first recorded and released: *The Black and
Tan Fantasy,* which Bubber Miley did with Ellington assistance,
upon which Bubber and Tricky play so compellingly in their
plunger styles and which ends with the exquisitely apposite in-
terpolation of the Funeral March from Chopin's B flat minor
Sonata, Opus 35. When the band was shifted by Columbia to its

OKeh label, it made its first widely released version of the number. Two different masters of this performance reached England and France; both were released abroad with the orchestra credited as Louis Armstrong and His Washboard Beaters. This extraordinary confusion has caused extraordinary merriment since among jazz musicians and collectors because of the patent absence on the record of a) Louis Armstrong, who never growled on a trumpet in his life; b) Washboard Beaters, whose rub-a-dub-dubbery has never been combined with the beautiful sounds of either Louis's horn or the Ellington band.

Just before the band left the Kentucky Club for good, Victor, biggest by far of the record companies, made a good offer to Duke and Mills which they accepted. On October 26, 1927, the Ellington Orchestra made its first date for Victor, four sides: *Creole Love Call, Black and Tan Fantasy* (again), *The Blues I Love to Sing* and *Washington Wobble*. On the first and third, Adelaide Hall made her first appearance. Her lyric soprano wailings and hummings and glissando calls served subsequently on several Ellington records as vocal obbligatos for instrumental solos, in a neat casting against type. In those days, Paul Whiteman was the only leader who carried singers with him apart from instrumentalists who might take an occasional vocal. Other bands used only doubling instrumentalists (Duke used Sonny Greer) and hired guests to sing with them on records. At night clubs, the vocals were usually taken by the shows' stars, the Dolly Sisters or Charles King or John Steele, or, in later years, by the singing bandleaders, Sleepy Hall, Rudy Vallee, Will Osborne, and so on.

Duke, of course, had never heard a Creole Love Call, or anything like it, in the Louisiana country where you might hear Creoles in love call to each other; he'd never been South. But the title seemed to fit the soft, lazy mood of the music. *Black and Tan* is much like the earlier versions, of which the very first can be compared with this one, since both are still listed in the catalogues and occasionally pressed. On the Victor record the chief advantage is better recording and more incisive growling by the Messrs. Miley and Nanton.

The record sessions were Mills' greatest achievements for Duke. They put Ellington within reach of everybody with a phonograph. Records became Duke's greatest means of expression, the medium in which his band was always at its best. He was one of the very first jazz bandleaders to take advantage of phonograph records, and he very soon became the ablest at getting a balance of microphones and providing a seating arrangement which was most effective for the presentation of jazz instruments. From the very beginning, the Ellington musicians "knocked themselves out" in the record studios. They were well aware that this was their commitment to posterity, the only permanent reproduction of their music, since notation could not possibly duplicate the sounds they made. Irving Mills was pleased at the financial results of Duke's first records. He knew that they would open the way for bookings of greater prestige and lots more money. He was also aware of the musical contribution he had helped to make.

CHAPTER SIX

COTTON CLUB STOMP

MUSICIANS AND EARLY JAZZ AMATEURS AND A GOOD SPRIN-
kling of more ordinary night-club goers had come
down to the Kentucky Club in summer and winter
and spring and fall to hear Duke. They had even braved the
torturing humidity of the early summer of '26, one of the worst
ever in a city infamous for its stifling July heat, to sit in the
cellar at 49th and Broadway, where there was nothing even re-
sembling air-conditioning, to hear the Ellington band. Song
pluggers and music publishers had followed Irving Mills' lead
to the spot. It was very flattering, but it wasn't equally reward-
ing financially. That was important. It was even more important that there was a clear limit to the size of the band and
the scope of the music one could have at the Kentucky. It was
time to leave.

Out of the Kentucky the band went in the fall of 1927. It
played some one-nighters and some theaters. It was at a theater
in Philadelphia in late November that Duke received word that
Mills had signed a contract for the Cotton Club. The band was
to open with the new show on December 4. King Oliver had
been offered the spot first and had turned it down: not enough
money. Money was no obstacle to Duke, who wanted good bookings more than gold, but his contract with the Philadelphia
theater was. It was set to go another week, one week beyond the
Cotton Club opening. Jimmy McHugh, the songwriter who had
written the score for the show, who had persuaded the owners of
the Club (ex-heavyweight champion Jack Johnson among them)
to hire the Duke when the King said no, was terribly saddened

by this new difficulty. Can't you do something, he asked the syndicate which ran the Club. They could.

A very good friend, indeed—a friend of the Cotton Club syndicate—was a well-known Philadelphia gangster. He sent one of his boys over to see the theater owner. His boy didn't say very much. He covered the facts of the situation briefly, then summed up.

"Be big," the boy suggested. "Be big," he pleaded, "or you'll be dead." The theater man was big.

The band arrived in New York the very day of the Cotton Club opening, having rehearsed the new score as best it could in Philly. In New York, there were some hasty run-throughs with the dancers and singers and a quick retreat to the band members' several homes to freshen up for the opening.

Openings in 1927 were like openings today. Nobody knew the music, cues were missed, expected high spots fell through and little-suspected lines and songs and dances turned into sensations. The main point was that the costumes and props were new, the band was being introduced to the big time, the score was attractive, the people were receptive.

The band went into the Cotton Club with a limited understanding of the big-time show world. Duke was not a leader in the sense that Paul Whiteman or Ted Lewis or Vincent Lopez was; on his feet or at the piano, he wasn't that kind of showman. He wasn't a fast-talking Master of Ceremonies or a slick baton-waver; he didn't wear a battered hat or boast of playing more notes per minute than any other pianist. Nobody in the band wore funny hats or clowned. The music had to speak for itself.

Before the Ellington band went into the Cotton Club, the band there had been the Missourians. Not a great outfit, it is chiefly remembered today as the organization Cabell Calloway took over when he quit forever the church-singing of his youth and of his cantor father's mature years, dropped the -ell from his Christian name and made "Hi-de-ho" almost as much of a household phrase as "Oh, yeah?" and "Sez you?" But great or not, most of the Missourians had played in and around Chicago or came from there, and most of the entertainers at the Cotton Club came from there, too. The busboys, the waiters, the cooks, the various workers for the syndicate, the hangers-on came from Chicago. The Cotton Club at 143rd and Lenox in New York's Harlem might just as well have been located at 47th and South Parkway in Chicago's South Side. This was a Chicago spot and Chicagoans alone were welcome to work there. When word came that King Oliver was coming in, the Cotton Club crowd was pleased. Joe Oliver and his boys were just finishing up better than six years in the Windy City and were practically natives of the place. They were welcome. But when the Cotton Club crowd learned that Duke Ellington and the Washingtonians, most recently of the Kentucky Club in New York, Charleshurst Ballroom in Salem and theaters at points just briefly north, south, east but hardly west of those spots, were next, they were annoyed. Washingtonians! they scoffed. Easterners! Ugh! The band found little co-operation at the Cotton Club. It ran into whispered conversations about their supposed ineptness and the ridiculousness of booking them into the place, about their undoubted failure and why had anyone bothered about them, anyway?

Well, Jimmy McHugh had bothered about them because he was a smart songwriter and a keen observer of the values of dance bands. It was his score that was going to be butchered or aided by the band at the CC, and he was determined to get what he considered the best. His sponsorship of Ellington was not the first time a musician had spoken up for the band, nor the last. The first contacts the Washingtonians had made in New York were with musicians uptown, and musicians never lost sight of the band. It was in some part due to the loyalty of these people, the initiates of jazz, that Ellington came through so quickly and so impressively once the opportunities were made for him and his colleagues. Musicians talked the band up, followed everything it did, bought its records religiously. They've never lost their interest and never ceased to be a source of inspiration to the band. Word went around Harlem that Duke was opening at the Cotton Club and the musicians stepped up. There wasn't much they could do: there was a pretty strict color line at the Cotton Club. A very prominent colored entertainer or sportsman or businessman could get a back table somewhere, but, in general, the people of Harlem were conspicuous by their absence from Harlem's number one night club. Although fellow musicians couldn't give the band support in the form of an enthusiastic claque, they could talk about the opening up and down the uptown bars for days and weeks to come and make this band the subject of just enough conversation so the talk would get downtown. And downtown, the white musicians could pick it up, come uptown to hear for themselves and start talking up Ellington themselves. And before very long, in the manner of jazz fairy tales, there could be more and more requests to make records, contracts to double at theaters in and around New York, publicity wherever you turned in the colored press and a good deal in the white. There could be these things; there were.

Ellington, Hardwick, Greer, Guy, Miley, Nanton, the originals, formed the real center of the band, its musical and social focus. Rudy Jackson and Louis Metcalf on tenor sax and trumpet, respectively, and Wellman Braud, the bass man, were additions of some consequence only in that they added to the band's scoring potentialities, but Harry Carney was in from the first note he booted with the band. Shifted to baritone, his mastery of the lower register horn was obvious from the start and his personality, that of a sweet young kid, was a natural for this organization.

The transition from a seven-piece band to a ten, from a free-swinging little outfit which was on its dignity only in the recording studio to one which was required to look staid, play show scores, appear dignified all the time, was made without any enormous difficulties. The change was made without any formal ceremony, and nobody, except Duke, perhaps, was especially aware of it. But change it was, the ineluctable growth from music for its own sake to music for big business, from booking one's own jobs to booking through Irving Mills, from seven pieces to ten, eleven, twelve and fifteen, from wildcat recording for a dozen companies under as many pseudonyms to a contract with Victor, then with Brunswick, from appearances in late spots on their own volition for the kicks of playing to paid jam sessions and tony benefits.

First evidence of the change, apart from the increased numbers in the reed and brass sections, was the remarkable difference in the attitude of the CCC, the Cotton Club Chicagoans. They soon became the greatest of Ellington fans, their firmest supporters.

"Said so all the time," they said.

"Knew it," they said, "had to be. Damnedest band I ever heard."

"The best," they said, "that's it!"

In the manner and mode of speaking of one of Harlem's best known "queens," they chorused, "Love it!"

The big tunes in that first Cotton Club show, which Duke opened on December 4, 1927, were *Dancemania* and *Jazzmania*. They were Jimmy McHugh's, of course, not Ellington's. Duke and his men were not composers of any standing then, and who had ever heard of a bandleader writing the show for a leading night-club revue? Just not done. *Dancemania* and *Jazzmania*, the titles, are tipoffs to the attitude of the day toward popular music, popular dancing and jazz. Mania, madness: people who danced like *that* and listened to music like *that* were psychotic, troubled in mind and likely to go farther, possibly blow their brains out (in 4/4 time, of course, with the drums beating madly, the saxes screeching madly, the trumpets screaming madly). The difference between the attitude of the disparagers of jazz in those days and that of later musical purists, who called jazz a decoy for juvenile delinquency, is very great. Then, it was madness and madness was the thing, the fashion. Later, it was regarded as an invitation to waywardness and it had to go. Of course, neither its madness in the early years nor the beckoning finger to adolescent delinquents later, sent any more of its practitioners to the lunatic asylums and jails than any other profession.

Paul Rosenfeld, leading critic of the 1920's and early thirties, summed up the first sneers and jeers at jazz very well in his book, *An Hour with American Music* (J. B. Lippincott, 1929):

> American music is not jazz. Jazz is not music. Jazz remains a striking indigenous product, a small-sounding folk-chaos, counterpart of other national developments. What we call *music,* however, is a force, adjusted to the stream of the world in which materials float and elements play, and active like them upon the human situation; and, bold and debonair as it is, seductive with woodwind in minor thirds and fuller of bells than a bayadere, our characteristic "dance-music" is cheerfully quiescent. . . .
>
> . . . The typical jazz composition offers mere beat; mechanic iteration, duplication, conformation to pre-established pattern. Its alternation of bars of three and four and five units, the so-called jazz polyrhythm, is sheer willful contrast and change. The chief excitement in it proceeds from a series of jerks, systematic anticipations and retardations of the arbitrary, regular, unfailing beat. . . . We have here to do with an extraordinarily popular drug-like use of the materials of sound. . . . It is smart; superficially alert, good humoured, and cynical. Essentially, nonetheless, it is just another means of escape. . . .

You might ask, first of all, what jazz is an escape from. Rosenfeld makes that clear, in a muddy sort of way. It is an escape from "reality," from "an acceptance of the conditions of existence, of inevitable tragedy and extinction, so abhorrent to the jazz-artist and the jazz public." This is an extraordinarily willful presumption on Rosenfeld's part which others have made since. The jazz musician finds no place in their hieratical metaphysic. The jazz musician remains a superficial entertainer, the administrator of a narcotic. However "alert, good-humoured" he may be, he is also "cynical," too "small-sounding" in his music to produce "a force adjusted to the stream of the world in which materials float and elements play."

How could the jazz musician be anything but cynical in a world which treats him with such arbitrary, patronizing, unknowing presumption? Those quickest to make judgments about jazz have always been outsiders, men who have neither lived with jazz nor loved it, who never apprehended its terms, never reached for its rich metaphysic and theology. From the very beginning, the Ellington band spoke about "the conditions of existence," though not necessarily with acceptance, and knew more "of inevitable tragedy and extinction" than any of their "long-haired" contemporaries. They came from a world of social subtleties such as Rosenfeld and his associates never dreamed, in which the customs and castes and moral strictures of white society were inextricably mixed with an entirely different set of values, based in part on variations in pigmentation, in part on slave or free antecedents, on considerations that a white man couldn't know or understand and didn't try to appreciate very often. From the very beginning, the music of the Ellington organization reflected the Negro's sense of tragedy, his own society and participation in others', his dramatic life, closer to "the stream of the world in which materials float and elements play" than the average white man's.

Consider the names of the early Ellington records, *Black and Tan Fantasy, What Can a Poor Fellow Do, Song of the Cotton Field, Creole Love Call, Black Beauty* and *Jubilee Stomp*. Duke and Bubber and the others were talking of their lives and their people, speaking with mordant wit and controlled anguish, with sadness and with gladness, with an acceptance of what they might call original sin or the accident of color or simply the way of God's world, and with a degree of anger which they rarely permitted expression. The anger had to wait world-wide acceptance of the joy and the sorrow; there would be time enough then to lash out at inequity and injustice, if ever such protest could mean anything.

It is not necessary to listen for the story in Duke's pieces, though most of them are brief narratives, songs of hope or joy or melancholy reflection. It is not necessary to search for the meaning of this music as an expression of Negroes, though it is surely that. This probing and informed listening are not necessary because, from its beginning, the Ellington band has spoken in universal terms as well as the particular, has made a ubiquitous appeal that had to reach out to listeners and dancers all over the world. Sometimes it was just a catchy little tune that caught a listener's fancy and made happy whistling on the way to work. Sometimes, a four-bar phrase struck such a sprightly syncopation that dancing to it was inevitable and utterly captivating for two people in love. Sometimes, the grace of a particular growl, or the bitter humor, the peculiar organization of sounds just short of noise, caught in the listener's mind and gave new order to the clangy, confused obstrepor in the everyday world about him. Always, there was something that Negroes especially could understand, some theme or development thereof, some voicing or voice that caught with moving exactness and delicacy some feeling they had experienced, emotional swirls or cerebral toils or just the mixed pleasure and pain of their hopelessly jumbled world.

The form of Duke's music was loose in those days, looser than it is today, less inspired harmonically, not as driving rhythmically, the melodies not so rich either. But the characteristic colors were there, the variety of growls, the loping saxophone sounds, the heavy beat. There was, from the very beginning, a brilliant contrast of soft, mellifluous sound and crunchy noises like a gravel-throated human talking or laughing or crying.

Louis Armstrong's record, *Laughing Louie,* sold by the hundreds of thousands for OKeh; it was one of the biggest records of that or any other time. Jazzmen of the time were deeply interested in the verisimilitude with which they could reproduce human sounds, and Louis's accompaniment to laughter was one of the most successful attempts to anthropomorphize notes and phrases. In the same way, Tricky Sam and Bubber Miley laughed and cried on their horns and gave human form and personality to their solos.

Sonny Greer had fulfilled an old ambition: he'd bought up all the drum equipment he could find, snares and tom-toms and high-hats, even a couple of kettle-drums. Surrounded by this veritable battery of hide-topped barrels and cylinders, Sonny could make all possible drum sounds; he could convince listeners they were hearing what Mills advertised, Primitive Rhythms. In a time when at least the sophisticated Ellington audiences were convinced that Africa strode almost unhampered beneath the tan skins of his musicians, those sturdy Primitive Rhythms conjured up true jungles, warriors on the forest march, lions and tigers and panthers and their tribal enemies among the humans.

When these audiences went up to the Cotton Club and found "shake" dancers performing incredible gyrations and undulations of their naked bellies, Snake-hips Tucker twisting his thigh joints and haunches as his name suggested, like a boa constrictor or rattler, they were certain they were looking at the direct descendants of the jungle tribes. Ellington's music lent further credence to this picture; Africa spoke in Harlem in the late twenties.

When Ellington got to theaters in the Bronx, Brooklyn and Manhattan, he capitalized on this impression, not consciously perhaps, but it was that which remained with his audiences. He used a "scrim," a transparent screen of gauze-like material, which obscured the band when it first appeared after the heavy outer curtains had been lifted. With soft blue lights giving the stage an eerie atmosphere and with the scrim to reduce the figures of the men to shadows, the first impact of the band was that of a group of men from a world beyond. Duke, who liked to indulge in fantasies all the time about himself, his associates, his music, brought some of the dreams to hazy life on the stages of outlying vaudeville theaters in New York. It all added to his appeal.

Money was pouring in from theaters, special one-night ballroom appearances and records, more money than the Washingtonians had ever seen before. The band shifted to the OKeh label and made its standbys, its good old surefire numbers, again. This time, *East St. Louis Toodle-Oo* was called *Harlem Twist*, to avoid confusion and competition with the Victor and Columbia versions. *Take It Easy* (no relation to the later movie tune of the same name) and *Jubilee Stomp* were back. Then, in their first records for Brunswick, the Ellington musicians recorded that pair again and the *Yellow Dog* and *Tishomingo Blues,* in which the exoticism of W. C. Handy's and Spencer Williams' titles was easily matched by the strange sounds made by Bubber and Tricky Sam. On the first three sides for OKeh a new clarinet was heard: Barney Bigard had joined the band. On the last two there was a new alto: the little Boston boy in short pants, though no taller, had donned his longies and come to New York; Johnny Hodges was in. Before very long he had a new nickname, even as every other Ellington musician. "Rabbit" they called him—because he looked like one.

Barney was an addition to the bald-headed row, not as clean on top as Otto Hardwick, but a well-set young man of twenty-two with sufficiently thin hair to fit his self-assured look and neat dress, to round out a figure that looked like a prosperous lawyer's. Barney was from New Orleans; his personal antecedents were Creole, his skin was white. His jazz antecedents were New Orleans: his tone was big and round, he played the Albert clarinet, which had greater spans to cover than the newer, easier Boehm clarinet. He'd played with the Tios and with Octave Gaspard in the Crescent City and had made enough of a reputation down there to get a call from King Oliver in 1925. He replaced Johnny Dodds with King Joe, made records with Jelly Roll Morton as well as with Oliver and built a fine reputation as a clarinetist of liquid tone and fluent technique. Just before coming with Ellington, he had passed a year with Luis Russell's band of New Orleans émigrés. You can hear the effect he had upon the sound of the band in his impressive entrance and his obbligato back of Tricky in *Tishomingo*. Barney was far more than a replacement for Rudy Jackson; he was an addition of real stature, of the heroic size which long-staying Ellington musicians sooner or later achieved.

Johnny, like Harry Carney, came in as a substitute for Otto Hardwick. Like Harry, too, he came to stay for a little while and remained permanent possessor of his chair. Otto was out this time for more than a little while. He wandered off to various places to have him some fun and was gone three years. Atlantic City, Paris and back to New York.

In Atlantic City, Otto got himself a new name, Toby. Toby followed naturally enough from the last syllable of his Christian name. From 1928 on, it was Toby Hardwick.

In Paris, Toby got himself new kicks. He went abroad on the S. S. *Hamburg* with a steamship ticket and seven cents, all that was left after buying the ticket. But Toby was a friendly guy, a good musician and a remarkable drinker; he ate all right and drank all right and lived all right on the S.S. *Hamburg*. When he arrived in Paris, he made quick contacts. First there was Bricktop, the same Ada Smith from Washington who had secured the Washingtonians their first big job in New York at Barron's. Bricktop was a reigning *reine des boîtes* in Paris. Her club, Bricktop's, at 52 Rue Pigalle, was one of Montmartre's most successful. Handsome red and blue heralds proclaimed in English the virtues of her establishment:

> at
> BRICKTOP'S
> 52 rue pigalle
>
> one can
> drink what you want
> eat the best of food
> dance to good music
> hear your favorite songs
>
> open all night   american bar

For a few months, Toby helped produce the good music for the good Smith. Then he moved over to Les Ambassadeurs, a much larger spot than Bricktop's, a theater-restaurant where Noble Sissle, who'd made his reputation as co-author of the Negro revue, *Shuffle Along*, and composer of the song, *I'm Just Wild about Harry*, led the *Orchestre de Jazz*. Toby played with Sissle another two months and then left for New York, having balled from one end of Paris to the other, learned the fine points of all the world's liquors, met a fascinating variety of people and been accepted without social restrictions and personal prejudices as the first-rate musician and human being he is.

Back in New York, Toby got himself a new reputation. He became a bandleader, not on the gigging basis on which he'd earned some of his first money in Washington, but as a full-time front man for a full-time band. His outfit finally landed a first-rate engagement at the Hot Feet Club, 142 West Houston Street, the pride of Greenwich Village. Its name recalled the club across the street from Bricktop's, Le "Hot Feet," where Toby had played briefly with *la célèbre artiste fantaisiste, Neeka Shaw, et son orchestre,* which was also *ouvert toute la nuit.* The personnel of Toby's band anticipated some of the great music still to come: Fats Waller was on piano; Chu Berry was on tenor saxophone; Wayman Carver, who could never get over his early classical training, doubled most impressively from alto to hot flute, as he later did with Chick Webb; Garvin Bushell was the other alto and Theodore McCoy was on baritone. With Toby up front on alto, too, the band had a four-man reed section in a day when sax quartets were still rare. It jumped like mad, played tricky arrangements and featured as fine a range of soloists as could be heard in New York. The club did well with Toby's band (he was still billed as Otto Hardwick), four girls and four singing waiters. Tips were so big that when they were divided each night among the nineteen musicians, girls and waiters, they yielded $50 to $60 apiece. Toby had to hunt for the guys each week to give them their $35 paycheck. All was well, the jazz was "hell, man" until the end of 1931. Things had been going so well that the owner of Houston Street's Hot Feet went to Chicago to start a similar club there. But he reckoned without Chicago's territorial divisions and dividers: in the carefully organized city of Chicago there was no night-club territory available to men from New York. The man from New York arrived in Chicago early one week and later that same week departed this earth. He could have none of Chicago; the Chicago gangs would have none of him. Toby's career as a bandleader was over.

Before Toby quit as a bandleader, however, he had the satisfaction of knowing he had "cut" Duke, one of the few bands, if not the only one, ever to beat Ellington in a battle of music, official or unofficial. Both bands were playing a benefit at the Hotel Astor for one of the New York columnists who ran such affairs every week. Duke's band was bigger, and better, than it had been when Toby left in '28. This was three years later and

D*

there were three first-rate saxists, Carney, Barney and Johnny. Duke had three trumpets (Whetsol, Miley and Metcalf); Toby had no trumpets. Duke had Tricky Sam; Toby had no trombone. Toby was one rhythm man short: no banjo. But Toby's drummer doubled on vibes; he had five saxes (Chu Berry, Wayman Carver, McCoy, Bushell and himself); and he had Fats Waller.

Both bands blew everything they had in the books. The Ellington organization showed off its plethora of brass. Toby retaliated with rich, round saxophone sounds, wide voicings in the reeds, and a bevy of charging solos by Chu, Carver and Toby, and Fats. After the evening was over, Carney came over to Toby.

"How are you, fellow?" he asked Toby.

"How's my man?"

"Good."

Silence.

"You know, Tobe, you ran us off that stage?"

"No kidding?"

"No kidding!"

In later years, almost everybody in that band was ready to admit that that had been Toby Hardwick's night. The seven-cent trip to Europe had produced great results. A brilliantly equipped saxophonist had come back a full-sized leader. But times and gang killings being what they were, Toby decided to go back to being a sideman. He wound up at Small's, Lenox and 135th, late in 1931. Jerry Rhea, childhood friend of Duke's, later private secretary, confidant, good friend, press agent, anything and everything he could be, ran into Small's to "catch" Toby. He saw lots of other musicians of the period; it was their hangout. Claude Jones and John Nesbitt from McKinney's Cotton Pickers. Don Redman, who ran McKinney's band for him. Fletcher Henderson and lots of his boys. Benny Carter. Coleman Hawkins. Chick Webb and Bobby Stark. Jimmy Harrison. Rex Stewart, who'd just joined McKinney.

"Hey, Rex," Jerry yelled.

"How are you, man?" Rex returned, "Ain't seen you in years."

"Fine, Daddy, fine." They smiled and exchanged handclasps. Jerry continued on his way.

"Where's Toby Hardwick?" he asked one of the busboys.

"At the bar, Pops," the busboy answered.

Jerry found Toby at the bar.

"Toby," he said.

"Rhea, damn it," Toby answered, and one of his face-covering smiles followed, slow but complete.

"It's me, all right, you old bastard," Jerry admitted. "What you been doing, Daddy-o? Never mind, don't tell me, I know."

But Toby did tell him and they exchanged reminiscences, the one of Atlantic City and Paris, the two Hot Feet Clubs and Bricktop.

"How's old Ada?" Jerry inquired.

"Great. What parties she threw! I can't tell you." But he did.

The other told of Hodges and Bigard, of the four brass-men, of Louis Metcalf's temperament.

"He wants to be a star," Jerry told Toby.

"And why not, everybody wants to be a star; why not Metcalf?" Toby, who always sympathized with the underdog, replied.

"Because he just isn't," Jerry explained.

"Well, I am," Toby asserted.

"Bet you are."

"And I play where I'm recognized, if only as a great drinker."

"And where were you better recognized than with Duke?" Jerry asked.

"How's old Duke?"

"Great. But he misses you."

"The hell he does," Toby said.

"Certainly does. Always has, O-toe."

Brief pause for drink identification. Toby downed his rum; Jerry took a long sip of his double Bourbon.

"Do you remember the Dupadilly?" Jerry asked.

"Room 10?"

"The Miller brothers?"

"All that ice cream?"

"And the house hops?"

"And my father?"

"And *my* father?"

"And Duke?"

"And Duke!" Jerry emphasized the name of their boyhood friend.

"Wait'll you see all the drums Sonny has bought."

"Seen 'em," Toby acknowledged.

"I know you have. When you coming back, Tobe?"

"Soon. Very soon. Too soon."

Toby rejoined the band early in 1932. He'd been gone well over three years. He found a very different outfit from the one he had left, one that was never like the old days, one in which there was a clear demarcation between the leader and the men in the band. He had a lot to learn.

CHAPTER SEVEN

REMINISCING IN TEMPO

TOBY SAT DOWN WITH SOME OF THE BOYS. SONNY, HARRY, Barney. They were taking their ease between one-nighters in May, 1932. They knew it would be some time before they could again stretch their legs, talk uninterruptedly, not be jostled and jolted by a lurching train. Even with side trips in the Midwest and Southwest to play locations and theaters, full weeks, split weeks and one-nighters, the dominant impression would be of traveling in a train. They'd see more of trains than of any other domicile. Talk and drink, then, was the order of the day.

"What's happened?" Toby asked of no one in particular.

"While you were gone?" Carney asked Toby.

"While I was gone," Toby answered.

"That's a big order," Barney laughed.

"Can do," Sonny interrupted.

"Well, then?" Toby asked.

"Everything," Sonny answered, "everything. Been everywhere and seen everything." He suddenly remembered Toby had been in Paris, been farther, seen more, maybe, than he and the other members of the Ellington band. "Well, maybe not everywhere, but seen everything to be seen where we were."

"I know you have. Elucidate," Toby encouraged.

"Tell you, man, there was, first of all, and last of all, the Cotton Club. We've seen so much of the Cotton Club we seem a part of the wall decoration. Played there every year since '28 and expect we'll play there till we die."

"Well, I hope not," Toby said.

"What's the matter with the Cotton Club?" Sonny asked.

"Don't answer him," Carney cautioned. "He knows as well as you what's the matter with the Cotton Club. It's a night club and it shows off Willie Tucker and the line of girls very well. It's made a reputation for us, but I'd like to hear us someplace where you could hear us. Less show. More music."

"You're right," Sonny admitted, "right as Millicent." Millicent Cook was Sonny's wife, a dancer at the Cotton Club, whom he married soon after the band went into the spot.

"Well, keep talking, *mon vieux,*" Toby said.

"Catch that parley-voo," Sonny said, winking at Carney.

"Indeed, indeed," Carney acknowledged.

Sonny got on with the story.

"First of all, there was the Follies. You remember before you left, Toby, they were talking about the band for a Follies. Well, we didn't get to play the Follies, but we did get into a Ziegfeld show. *Show Girl* it was; Gershwin score. Nothing special about it either, except one tune, *Liza.*"

"What did the band do? Something of your own?"

"No Ellington. We did Gershwin. The critics, some of them, anyhow, commented on the foolishness, Ellington playing Gershwin, not Ellington. But it wasn't so bad."

"What'd you do?"

"Concerto in F. Some of it. Duke played the piano part."

"They were really talking Concerto in F and *Rhapsody in Blue* and Gershwin, when I was in Paris," Toby volunteered. "They made the *Rhapsody* into a ballet and they were playing it at all the symphony concerts. And the Concerto was done at the Paris Opera. Gershwin's a big name in Europe. He was over in '28 when I was and you should have seen the reams of space devoted to him. Sure is a white-haired boy in Europe, George is." Toby thought a moment. "So are we."

"We?" Carney and Barney chorused.

"Ellington and all. They talk about the band. Some of the records had just got over. By now, it ought to be big talk, talk about Duke and Tricky and Bubber and all."

"Oh, yeah, Bubber," Sonny said, kind of slowly. "He died. You knew that?"

"I did. What happened?"

"Just keeled over and died. Left us in '29, January, I think, shortly after you did. He hung out with a lot of different musicians, made some records with various people. Jelly Roll Morton, I think. Then he made a date himself. Bubber Miley and his Mileage-Makers. He made about a half-dozen sides for Victor. Let's see, I should remember the titles. Well, I remember two of 'em anyway, because they were such good titles, *Black Maria* and *Chinnin' and Chattin'*."

"James Miley sure was a chinner and a chatterer," Toby commented.

"He was, he was," Carney agreed. "Good thing he was with us so long. Gave us something. And fortunately, before he left the band, we made that *Black and Tan* movie short."

"Saw it," Toby said. "Very good, too."

"Won some kind of prize," Sonny said, swelling out his chest as if he were the prize-winning film.

"Yes, it did," Carney seconded. "And it deserved it, I think. The soft lights, the slow close-ups, even slower dissolves. That's good movie-making. And good *Black and Tan*. Ever see Duke look sadder, Toby?"

"Never. Never did see a sadder sight. But it was good sad stuff. Really like a wake."

"Hope RKO wants to make some more," Barney said.

"Hope they want to make some more big movies," Sonny said.

"You mean Amos 'n' Andy's *Check and Double Check?*" Carney asked.

"I do, I do. Sorry you missed that, Toby."

"Understand you drove around Hollywood in a knocked-out old taxicab," Toby said.

"Yeah, 'Fresh Air Taxicab Company Incorpulated.' We became characters. Summer, 1930. I won't forget it."

"What irony!" Toby commented. "Couple of ofays put on blackface and win popularity for Negroes, give Negroes jobs. What irony!"

"Hollywood was fun, ole man," Sonny went on. "Fun." He

took a couple of drinks and resumed. "We went out to that
Cotton Club, Sebastien's. Very different from this one. It's
right near the MGM lot; it's big as hell and filled with people."

"Land around it is funny, too," Carney commented. "Looks
like a Western movie. Dingy streets. Wide-open bars. Cowboys
wandering in and out of 'em, real and fake ones, from the
movies."

"Culver City." Barney identified the site of Sebastien's Cotton Club.

"Remember Eddie Anderson out there?" Sonny asked the
assembled musicians, speaking of the comedian who adopted
the name of Rochester when he joined Jack Benny's radio program some years later.

They nodded. "Doing pretty well. Got some movie jobs."

"Part of a pretty good song and dance team," Barney identified.

"The whole show was good," Barney said. "We had fun on
the Coast. Heard some good music, too. That Elkins band ain't
bad. Good trombonist. Good drummer, a kid named Lionel
Hampton. Louis took over the band when he got out there."

"The movie was a good deal, too," Sonny continued. "One
good song, *Three Little Words,* and we got a fair break in the
footage. Almost could tell us from Amos 'n' Andy."

And then they reminisced some more. About their first season at the Lincoln Gardens Café in Evanston, swank North
Chicago. About the lingering traces of gangsterism in the big
town and the wide open South Side, the colored section, where
you could drink almost as much as in the old days, before Prohibition. Though you might find that one of Big Jim Colosimo's
boys had spilled blood on the front stoop of the place at which
you were drinking, or Al Capone's private secretary might have
plugged a few holes in the ceiling over the bar at which you
were stealthily downing a healthy gulp of Bourbon, the main
point was you could drink in Chicago, the "chicks" were slick
and friendly, the town was good.

Toby told them about the sad fate in that same good town
of the kindly man who ran Houston Street's Hot Feet and they

all shook their heads in friendly condolence and extended great sympathy to the bereaved ex-bandleader. "But we're awfully glad to have you back, ole man," they assured him.

They compared notes on the new guys, talking over the respective merits of Freddy Jenkins and Cootie Williams, the two new trumpeters, and of Johnny Hodges, who got all the alto solos.

"You know Freddy's left-handed," Carney pointed out.

"Funniest thing I ever saw," Toby said. "Particularly when the trumpets stand up and you see the difference in handling the instrument, in fingering the valves."

"Posiest man in the whole business, too," Barney said, in mock anger, a smile crossing his face as he thought of the cocky little man who sat at the end of the brass row.

"Remember him and Bubber?" Sonny asked. "How they used to fight?" He explained. "Bubber couldn't stand seeing Freddy pose when he took a solo. He sets himself, you know, throws his head back, always dances down front. Well, Bubber told Freddy to stop posing so much. 'Cut it,' he said, 'behave like a grown-up horn-man.' He was boss of the section, so he could tell Freddy. Well, Jenkins didn't cut the posing. So Bubber moved him from the middle to the end, where he thought you wouldn't see Freddy so well. Freddy showed better'n ever; he thought up more ways of being seen. Watch him flash those hand cymbals. Whatta man!"

"I like his playing," Toby commented. "Especially his soft muted stuff. Pretty!"

"Talking about Posey's hand-cymbals," Carney talked, "how 'bout Tizol's maracas?"

"How 'bout them?"

"Man, we're a Latin band now. Nothing we can't do. Rhumbas, tangos. You name it. We play it. Tizol's the boy. A real Latin. Comes from Puerto Rico. A very bright boy, a very quiet boy. But, seriously, he writes some good stuff and he handles that valve trombone like a symphony man."

"Hell, I remember Tizol," Toby said. "He played in the pit at the Howard. Played with you, Sonny, didn't he?"

"Sure. And he was flashing those maracas and claves and things then, too. That was a big P.R. delegation in that pit and they all played a little hot wood on the side."

"What about Cootie?" Toby asked.

They told him about Cootie. Told him how Charles Williams had come to New York in '28 with the Alonzo Ross band from his native South. Told him that Cootie Williams was strictly an Alabama boy, Mobile, to be exact, hadn't lost his Southern accent and didn't give signs of losing it. Had played a little drums as a boy, kicked around in school bands and switched to trumpet while in high school. He'd played in Florida and other Southern states and was thrilled to death to hit New York with Ross. But New York hit Ross back. The weather was so damn freezing, after the South, that half the band came down with very bad colds. Six or seven sick. That left only a seven-piece band. The band opened at the Brooklyn Roseland Ballroom with only seven pieces, though fourteen had been hired. That same night the Alonzo Ross band received its two-week notice from the Roseland boss.

The lady at whose house the Ross bandsmen were staying in Brooklyn wanted the rent. They kept promising her; she kept nagging them. Finally, when Cootie couldn't stand the routine of nagging and promising, he sent down to his father in Mobile for $50, paid back rent and distributed the rest among the fellows in the band, those with colds and those without. That didn't leave very much for any of them, but these Southern boys were used to a difficult professional life as musicians. They found a bakery at Cumberland and Fulton where they could get their breakfasts for a nickel, their dinners for a dime. Breakfast: sweet rolls and coffee. Dinner: a bowl of soup and a roll. Cootie tried to stick with the band, but soon there was nothing to stick with. A fly-by-night manager got them a week's work way out on Fulton Street, then ran away with the week's pay. Cootie and a couple of the other Ross musicians found him at his rooming house and, hungry guys that they were, didn't hesitate to use strong methods of persuasion; they got every cent he had left of their pay, but he had already spent a lot of it.

Edmond Hall had come up from New Orleans with the Ross band, and he and Cootie used to cross the bridge into Manhattan to attend the jam sessions uptown. The Bandbox was the place in 1928 and Ed Hall unleashed his Albert-system fingering on his clarinet, Cootie his huge trumpet tone, at sessions there. Everybody used to come in; like Mexico's, it was a Harlem must, if you were a jamming musician. In a few weeks, Cootie heard them all: Fats, J. P. and the Duke still combing glissandi out of the piano keyboard, Fletcher Henderson's men, Benny Carter, Coleman Hawkins, Rex Stewart, Jimmy Harrison, all blowing like inspired madmen.

One "trumpet night," when only practitioners of that instrument jammed at the Bandbox, Cootie was heard by Chick Webb. Chick was a fiery little hunchback from Baltimore, one of the great drummers and bandleaders of his time. It was from his band that Johnny Hodges had come to Ellington earlier that same year, 1928. Lots of brilliant jazzmen had played with him, were still to play with him, for Chick had a fine ear, picked his men with great acumen and from his high drum seat drove them to jazz heights. Chick heard Cootie; that was enough.

"Get your trunk," Chick told Cootie, after he had heard his story, "get your trunk and come live with me."

Cootie was the talk of New York after that trumpet night at the Bandbox, but Chick wasn't working and there was nothing he could do about taking advantage of the powerful young trumpeter's reputation. Chick took Cootie into his rooms, but he was so flat broke himself, he had to go around with his new roommate to his sister's and get $1 or 50¢ for each of them from her. With almost all the spare bucks and halves, the two boys would go to Rose's on Lenox Avenue. Rose specialized in Southern dishes, black-eyed peas, ham hots and rice, the food Cootie was used to. All very thrilling to a Southerner and to a musician. Musicians ate as lustily as they drank and played in the 1920's; still do.

Finally, Chick landed another stretch at the Savoy Ballroom, Harlem's premier dancery. Cootie played with him for three weeks, until the musicians' union delegate walked in.

"Chick, you should know better," the union delegate told Webb. "You know he can't work with you with a Mobile card. Get him out of there."

Chick spoke back to the delegate, Minton, who later opened one of Harlem's leading jam-session spots and eating places. Jimmy Harrison, the trombonist, Bobby Stark, the trumpeter, and the other guys in the band tried to restrain Chick; the little man was all for hitting Minton then and there. Minton told him to get the hell over to the union on the following Tuesday. Trial board.

Chick showed up at the trial board mad as he'd been the previous week when Cootie had been plucked from his band. He told them all off, told them he would use anyone he damned pleased in his band, it was his band, after all. The trial board members, like almost every musician in New York, had tremendous affection for the little four-footer; the more his fists clenched and unclenched, the more his hands flailed in the air, the more their indignation and displeasure decreased. When Chick turned to Minton and told him, "I want to see you as soon as we get out of here," they laughed and told Chick to "git."

For all his brave words, Chick knew the union rules. You couldn't play with a New York band unless you had a New York union card. He didn't put Cootie back on the stand at the Savoy. But he wouldn't let Cootie work with anyone else either, with traveling bands (non–Local 802, non–New York bands) with whom he could have worked. He gave the trumpeter money and stubbornly kept him home idle. He never let Cootie answer the phone, made sure that he wouldn't accept another offer in a weak moment.

But one day Chick had to go out. And that day Fletcher Henderson got into town. He'd heard of Cootie and was interested in getting him to replace Russell Smith, longtime first man in Henderson's brass section. "Smack" (Fletcher) called Cootie. Cootie answered.

"Where you at?" Cootie asked Fletcher.

"Gin mill at 131st Street, Big John's," Smack answered. It

was the place after which the Henderson brothers, Fletcher and Horace, named their famous *Big John Special.*

Cootie played trumpet with Fletcher accompanying him in the back of Big John's place.

"You're on," Fletcher said in his quiet, unemphatic voice. "I'd like for you to go to Philly with me to play an engagement there."

Cootie went along for that engagement. He never had a rehearsal, not one, just ran the first book right down and satisfied such tough musicians as Coleman Hawkins. Smack wanted him to stay; he fitted the band well. But Cootie really wasn't interested in anyone but Chick, and when the band returned to New York after two weeks on the road, to open at the Roseland, its Manhattan home, he just didn't show up. The band couldn't play without him. No one else knew the whole first book, all the lead (melody) trumpet parts. Smack called Cootie up at Chick's. Chick said no go. Smack, pretty frantic now, told his brother Horace to run up to Chick's "and get Cootie, somehow, anyhow!" Horace, in his best persuasive manner, talked long and logically and softly to Chick. He convinced him, and Chick told Cootie to go ahead.

"That was some band," Carney commented, after this long recital of Cootie's background. "Great outfit, all right, Hawk, Stark, Benny Carter, 'Big' Green, Rex."

"Sure was," Cootie agreed. The big trumpeter with the very dark face and brilliantly white smile joined the discussion.

"You and Rex made quite a team," Carney said.

"That Rex really is a character," Cootie agreed. "Good trumpeter, better character. Did I ever tell you about the whisky?" Shouts of "No, no, go on." Cootie told them about the whisky. "Well, Rex had a bottle, a big bottle of whisky, in his locker. And some of the rest of the guys cottoned to it. They raided his locker when he was out of the room and when he returned he found his bottle was drained dry. Turned it over and not a drop left in it. Rex said nothing, told nobody he'd discovered the loss of his liquor. He replaced the bottle next night with another. Only this time, he mixed castor oil with the whisky. The guys found this bottle, too. Oh, what a time on the stand that night!" Cootie laughed, he laughed that low growl-like laugh, so much like his trumpet growl.

"You should have seen Cootie laugh when he joined us in '29," Sonny told Toby. "He never stopped. Right on the stand, too."

"What was so funny?" Toby asked Cootie.

"I used to laugh at Tricky Sam, and Freddy Jenkins, who was doing the growl stuff Bubber used to play. I thought it was very funny. See, I never played anything but open trumpet till I joined Duke in '29. But he hired me to replace Bubber. So, after laughing a lot, I says to myself, this is what the man hired me to do, I'll do it. He never did show me, you know. He just said, 'Listen, just listen.' I listened and made some kinda attempts for two months and finally reached the point where I didn't think it was funny."

"How'd you compare the two bands—Smack's and Duke's?" Toby asked Cootie.

"Well," he answered, slowly, deliberately, "Smack's always got a fast band. Maybe too fast. Band never relaxed. Never a swing to it. Really it was an awful lot of fast music. Duke gets a groove. This is my kind of music." Cootie thought a moment. "Besides," he said, "where else can you get your kicks like you can in this band? Oh, that Palace opening," he said, "oh, that Palace!" The other guys, except Toby, who hadn't been there, of course, started to laugh.

"What about the Palace?" Toby asked. They were still laughing. "Come on, now, what about the Palace?"

"Very funny to us, anyhow," Cootie explained. "We were at Proctor's 58th Street that same first year in the band for me, 1929, when we heard that Mills'd booked us into the Palace. Great. We were all set. The top vaudeville theater. Great. Opening day. Opened with *Dear Old Southland*. Duke had written down some brass parts, to be played in our derbies, which opened *Southland*. We hadn't memorized them. But the show opened with one of those Duke openings. No lights. Black house. Duke brought his hand down. And nothing happened, not a damn thing. Duke turned to us, he said, 'Please fellows, please. Please! Please!' Not a note. Not one note. We couldn't see a damn note. Opening day at the Palace, and not a note. Oh, it was funny. We fell out."

The guys fell out again, thinking of that dead opening. But, as Cootie explained, somebody had had sense enough to yell for lights, and with the coming of light, the show went on. Duke's Palace debut was made without further incident and the band went over.

"Hey," said Sonny, "here comes the man you named, Tobe."

"The Trickster!" Toby exclaimed, as the roly-poly trombonist hove into sight. Toby had named him Tricky Sam because he always did with one hand what somebody else did with two, anything to save himself trouble; he was tricky that way, a regular Tricky Sam.

"Mr. Hardwick, I do believe," Tricky said, and bowed slightly, the bow all but cutting off his voice, that gentle breeze of sound.

"What's been happening, old man?" Toby asked.

"This and that," Tricky said, noncommittal.

"Give me a little data on the thisa and thata."

"Well, one story, anyhow. Anybody tell him about Father White?" Tricky asked the assembled musicians.

"No, no," they chorused. "Tell him." Sonny finished the chorus with a coda of delight. "What a character! What a character!" he mumbled.

"You remember ole Harry White?" Tricky said. Toby nodded. "Trombonist who used to play with all the bands uptown?" Toby nodded again. "Of the famous White Brothers' Orchestra of Washington? He was with us in 1929. Briefly." The guys laughed. "He started a word in his four or five weeks with us. Father White originated the word 'jitterbug,' don't let anybody tell you differently! He had a pet name for musician friends, used to call them 'my bug,' 'my bug this' and 'my bug that.' He had another favorite name for his favorite liquid. Whenever Father White had a solo to play, he always stepped off into the wings of the stage or back of the bandstand and took himself a big snort of what he called 'jitter sauce.' And he always had some 'jitter sauce' around. One day, some practical joker hid Father's bottle, and in his agitation to get it back and into the spot for his solo, he hollered, 'Whoinhell took my jitter, bug?' Somehow that name floated around and finally got fastened onto the Lindy-hoppers, I guess because they hopped around as if they'd been plenty 'jitter-sauced.' But Father White's the guy who said it first."

"Tizol took *his* place," Carney commented.

"Father White, Father White," Toby said, thinking about the lovable trombonist, "Father White."

The talk turned to records. The band had made lots of them while Toby was away. For Victor, Columbia, OKeh, Cameo, Oriole, Perfect.

"Yeah," Toby said. "You guys were making records! I even picked up one of those cardboard records."

"Hit of the Week," Barney identified. "We were 'The Harlem Hot Shots' on that record. *Sing You Sinners* and *St. James Infirmary Blues.*"

"That's right." Toby nodded his head.

"And we were Mills' Ten Blackberries."

"And the Washingtonians."

"Both those were on Velvetone records," Barney identified.

"And the Memphis Hot Shots on Harmony."

"You boys were hot all over," Toby commented. "Harlem, Memphis."

"Oh, we were hot," Barney admitted. "We were Mills' Hot Shots, too."

"We were jolly, too," Carney said. "The Six Jolly Jesters on one record."

"And from Dixie," Sonny pointed out. "On Oriole, we were the Dixie Jazz Band."

"I remember," Toby said. "Remember, I made some of those records with you."

"So you did. So you did. Did you make whoopee with us?"

"Always." Toby laughed. "Quite a whoopee-maker, I." The others laughed.

"I know," Sonny acknowledged. "But were you a Whoopee Maker on records?"

"Don't remember."

"You know. Eddie Cantor was making whoopee for Ziegfeld. Some record man or Mills or Duke, somebody thought up the name for us. Figured it was a great idea. The Whoopee Makers!" Sonny's voice had great scorn.

"Don't forget the Harlem Footwarmers," Barney admonished. "We warmed our feet in Harlem, it said on OKeh. And Lonnie Johnson, the blues singer, was our leader!"

"Heard some of those things," Toby said. "Cotton Club stuff. *Snake Hips Dance* and *Jungle Jamboree. Louisiana. Cotton Club Stomp.*"

"Don't forget my number," Carney said. *"Rockin' in Rhythm."*

"Who could forget your number?" Barney asked.

"The Jungle Band," Sonny said, scornful again. "The Jungle Band."

"Accordion," Toby said. "I remember an accordion on one record and a couple of vocals."

"Baby Cox," Sonny explained. "A kinda stand-in for me."

Sonny had done all the Ellington band's vocals until the Cotton Club and even after that continued to take some. But the Club provided singers for their shows, so there Sonny just sang Ellington specialties. At the Kentucky, he'd sung a lot of things and was featured on Ellington broadcasts.

It was the band on Brunswick, under the name of the Jungle Band, which had first elicited great critical enthusiasm. The two-part *Tiger Rag, Rockin' in Rhythm, Rent Party Blues, Double Check Stomp* and *Awful Sad* were tremendously impressive for their time and still make very good listening. On the two-part *Tiger Rag* you hear a fast band, more like Henderson's kind of flag-waving outfit than Ellington, but full of good solos: Freddy Jenkins, Barney, Carney, Hodges and Bubber and Tricky Sam. *Rockin' in Rhythm* was originally music to accompany Snakehips Tucker, the dancer at the Cotton Club. The band kicks the first figure across, Cootie plays his famous solo, Barney and Tricky Sam and Duke share the rest of the record. These are the most famous of that early group on Brunswick, but there is much to listen to on the other records of the period, the others that are still available, that is. Barney and Whetsol and Carney, sounding just like Toby, whom he idolized, on alto, on *Awful Sad*. And Cootie on *Jazz Convulsions*, recorded very soon after he had mastered the growl style of Bubber Miley and believed in it and gave it conviction. And *The Mooche*, which the band recorded for half a dozen different labels, with its lovely three-clarinet voicing and the Hodges-Miley chase stuff in a kind of jazz stretto.

This was the period when the band marched in and out of record studios with the same frequency with which they packed and unpacked their instruments for work. They made so many records that, even as early as 1932, thinking back over what Toby had missed, they couldn't remember everything they had done. Actually, they had made 138 record sides in the three-year interim between Hardwick's leaving and rejoining the band, and Duke had made a coupling of piano solos, *Black Beauty*, Bubber's lovely melody originally written for the big band, and *Swampy River*, a raggy kind of virtuoso showpiece. The band was under contract to Victor and the bulk of its sides were made at the sign of the phonograph speaker and the listening dog. But there were also all the dates made under different names for the different companies flourishing in New York during those years, all the names cited by the musicians and a few others as well, notably Joe Turner and his Memphis Men and Sonny Greer's Memphis Men, pseudonyms used on Columbia.

To this period belong *Flaming Youth*, another masterpiece, and *Doin' the Voom Voom*, a celebration of one of the hundreds of short-lived dance steps which mushroomed in that time in hope of reaping some of the glory and the dough which the Charleston had garnered. There was *Harlemania*, with its dazzling brass triplets, and *The Dicty Glide*, like its adjective, a "dicty" piece, very flashy, very sophisticatedly aware of all the tricks of the time. Mood pieces suggestive of faraway places, *Japanese Dream* and *Arabian Lover*, and others suggestive only of moods, *Misty Mornin'* and *When a Black Man's Blue,* and *Mood Indigo,* in which, with a combination of trumpet and trombone, muted, and clarinet in chalumeau register, Duke and Barney collaborated to produce one of the ten-inch, three min-ute tone poems irrevocably associated with Ellington.

There were show tunes, like Gershwin's *Sam and Delilah* and Jimmy McHugh's *I Must Have That Man* and *Diga Diga Doo,* from *The Blackbirds of 1928.* There were the two big numbers from *Check and Double-Check, Three Little Words,* which Bert Kalmar and Harry Ruby wrote for the movie, and *Ring Dem Bells,* which Duke wrote for it, in which Sonny rang dem bells. There were the "jungle-istic" numbers, *Echoes of the Jungle* and *Jungle Blues,* and the two-sided *Creole Rhapsody,* one of the first attempts at large-scale writing. For this ambitious work, Duke was granted the annual award of the New York Schools of Music to an American composer in 1932. There were just plain pretty little tunes, like *Sweet Dreams of Love,* and a couple on which Sonny sang, *Sloppy Joe* and *Beggar's Blues.*

In this three-year period, Duke recorded more of the work of composers other than himself and his bandsmen than ever again in his life. But everything had the Ellington touch, the sound of his remarkable band, one great soloist after another, wide voicings and close ones, stinging brass and tingling, every possible dynamic, rich combinations of instruments outside the dance band convention of brass lead, sax counter-melody, or vice versa. Somehow, Duke managed to catch the atmosphere of his world on his records, right from the beginning, and he built up an audience as fast as he could make the records, and Victor, Brunswick, Oriole, and the rest could get the records to the stores. He had a few records which would have sold for anyone, tunes like *Dinah* and *Diga Diga Doo:* they were natu-rals, immediate hits. He had a few others which were pretty certain successes, *Three Little Words, Hittin' the Bottle.* But so had hundreds of other bands, now completely forgotten. Duke also had his own compositions, and those of his associates; very few of these tunes are forgotten. Ellington compositions which never sold more than a few tens of thousands of records are still around, still listened to. The records, when they are out of print, are collector's items, highly treasured, worth extraordinary prices. When they are reissued, they sell out. These were good years, 1928–1931: look at the record(s).

"It's been a good few years," Sonny said.

"So I see," Toby said.

"Future should be good," Carney said.

"May-be," Barney hoped.

CHAPTER EIGHT

PYRAMID

NINETEEN HUNDRED AND THIRTY-TWO WAS A BIG YEAR FOR Duke, though it was one of the worst for his country plunging deeper into its ravaging Depression. It was big for Duke not only because the band made more money and played better locations, but because he entered what might be called the Second Phase in that year. Lawrence Brown joined the band, Toby rejoined, filling the saxes to quartet size, and Ivie Anderson made her first records with Ellington. Duke's scorings, novel and exciting heretofore, became really ambitious as he began to take advantage of the widened and deepened and heightened resources of his organization.

Lawrence had just joined the band when Toby came back. He traveled with Ellington from the West Coast but didn't add his horn to the trombone section until they were back East again. When he did, the effect was revolutionary for jazz. Not only were trombones used in a three-man section for the first time in a bona fide jazz band (hitherto, one and two had been the custom), but Lawrence's instrument, with Ellington, was now employed to project soft and sweet sounds. The trombone was no longer just a barrelhouse horn: it was every kind of horn at once, and Lawrence Brown, indubitably the most versatile of jazz trombonists, could play them all.

Lawrence joined the band as a result of a sudden flash of inspiration and an accompanying thunder of desire. After playing the Paramount Theatre in New York, first colored band to play that movie palace, the Ellington band was finishing a week at its sister theater, the Brooklyn Paramount, in February, '32.

"I want to go to California," Duke said to Irving Mills, who was visiting him in his dressing-room.

"Okay," Mills assented.

And so they were on their way, on the long train trip to the Coast, with stop-offs on the way out. Though the band had just completed thirteen months of one-nighters, Duke was not dismayed at the thought of so much more train travel. He loved trains. He loved stopping off and seeing friends he'd made in Chicago and Cleveland and Milwaukee and a flock of smaller towns he had played during those months. In Ohio, for example, there was that run at the Castle Farms, a suburban spot which provided great luxury for himself and his musicians. There were ballrooms and theaters and friends he had made at each. It was fun to see all these people, to play a few of the better spots again. And besides, the Ellington band traveled in style; it even did one-nighters in comfort in 1932. It traveled in two cars especially detailed for it, a sleeper and a baggage car. No bus for the Ellington musicians, no bumping over back roads, no piling in at the last minute, squeezed into tiny bunks or sleeping sitting up. They had Pullman berths, lowers assigned in order of seniority, Toby, Sonny, Whetsol, Freddie Guy, Carney, Barney, etc. Duke was usually quartered in a roomette or drawing room. Style.

There wasn't much trouble about getting good bookings for the band, either on the Coast or on the way out there. There was a great demand for it. Steady broadcasting from the Cotton Club had done it, with good plugging from announcer Ted Husing over the Columbia Broadcasting System. For a while the band was on at the same time as Amos 'n' Andy, 7 to 7:15 P.M., Eastern time. It was a choice between voices in blackface or great jazz played by a Negro orchestra. Ellington won thousands of listeners in that competition. And then there was that special events broadcast, when Husing, up in a plane over Manhattan, announced an Ellington "remote" from the Cotton Club, in a two-way broadcast.

Theater bookers had been impressed by the band's performance with Maurice Chevalier, when the straw-hatted French comedian had made his New York debut at the Fulton Theatre in 1930. Duke was booked in as a dual attraction and as accompanist for Chevalier. The Frenchman was scared of American audiences, terribly nervous about facing his first. Duke went on before him and received solid applause for his work, so much applause that Chevalier looked up from his dressing-room mirror and asked what had happened. But there was no one around to satisfy his curiosity, so he came down to see for himself He had almost poked himself beyond the wings into full view of the audience when some of the guys in the band reached for him and pulled him back.

"You have nothing on but your longies, old man," Sonny told him.

"*Mon Dieu*, you are right," Chevalier affirmed. "*Alors,*" he said, after thanking Sonny and the others for saving him from a burlesque appearance, "what about thees audience? Will they be for me?" The musicians assured him they would. They cited the applause the band had received and took him back to his dressing room, comforting and reassuring him as they went. Toby's French would have helped then, but a genuine rapport was established between Chevalier and the band, and from the very first appearance, the show was a success. It helped Chevalier. It helped Ellington.

The good notices the band had received, its consistent airtime and its fine work in theaters resulted in excellent bookings all the way out and six top weeks in California. Duke played three at the Golden Gate Theater in San Francisco and three at the Paramount in Los Angeles and came right back East again. He stayed in L. A. just long enough to pick up Lawrence Brown.

Lawrence and Lionel Hampton, who played drums with the Les Hite band fronted by Louis Armstrong, were particular favorites of Frank Sebastian, who ran the Culver City Cotton Club. They were regulars there, regardless of the band or bandleader who came in; their contracts were with Sebastian. Lionel had come out to Los Angeles from Chicago a couple of years earlier, soon after his seventeenth birthday. Lawrence was a Californian.

Irving Mills went out to the Cotton Club to catch the show. He listened to the great Louis and then was amazed to hear a young trombonist, a handsome young man with more dignity than anyone that age had a right to, get up and play just as much fine music on his horn. His tone was beautiful, his technique impeccable. He played ballads with captivating straightforwardness. He played jazz like a trombone version of Armstrong, giving his melodic variations jazz inflection by his short slides, which added a gutty sound and a rhythmic lift.

"You're for us," Mills said to himself.

"He's for us," Mills told Ellington.

Duke went to hear Lawrence Brown play and was as impressed with him as Mills had been. He asked Lawrence to join his band.

"Gladly," Lawrence said. He was delighted to get out of the Armstrong-Hite band, not because of any grievance he had against Louis or Les, but because of their manager. This character had demanded that all the guys in the band come out to the Cotton Club, which was far out of L. A., to take publicity pictures on Easter Sunday. "Just to take publicity pictures? I quit!" Lawrence said, and he joined Duke.

Lawrence was born in Topeka, Kansas, but, from infancy, brought up in California. Educated in the public school system of Pasadena, he still makes grateful reference to that education. "Learned piano, violin, tuba, alto, trombone. What could be more wonderful for a kid with musical ambition? Every school in the nation should place that much emphasis on music, maybe more. Music does something for the soul. A youngster interested in music hasn't any time for gang wars and such demoralizing ways of spending his time."

Lawrence had been a church-going youngster; he played in churches and on the air, as a boy. His first "spectacular musical appearance" was before a Mother's Day crowd of 6000 at the late Aimee Semple McPherson's Temple in L. A. "I was scared stiff, so scared I've never gotten over it. I hadn't seen that many people ever before in my life."

After school, the churches and radio, Lawrence graduated to

professional bands, playing with Charlie Echols in a dance hall in Los Angeles and with the bands at Sebastian's. He worked with Curtis Moseby's Blue Blowers and Paul Howard's Quality Serenaders; made his first records with those groups, "most notable of which was one called *Charlie's Idea,* a series of variations on the chords of *Tiger Rag."* With Louis, he recorded *Confessin', If I Could Be with You, I'm in the Market for You,* most of the sides Armstrong made on the Coast with the Hite gang. The experience with Louis left Lawrence with a never-ending admiration for the Satchelmouth.

He studied a little at Pasadena Junior College, medicine, criminology, but gave that up in favor of music. "It took all my time and spirit and energy. I got bogged down in my music. I just had to play." Joining Ellington was something of a blow to Brown's plans to see the world, to travel. But Duke told him of his plans to go to Europe in '33, and that was the clincher. He met Ellington on a Tuesday and was on his way back East with him on Saturday.

Lawrence was and still is a man of strong moral convictions. "Of course," he says, "you know I never smoke, drink, gamble or chew." But he doesn't preach, doesn't proselytize. Traveling back East with the band he allowed himself to be drawn out on these convictions just enough to state them and implement them, but not to the length of a sermon.

"See, fellows," he said, "I don't object to smoking, drinking, gambling or chewing in others, but I do think musicians are susceptible to extremes. It's inevitable in their world. I know that drinking has caused the downfall of hundreds of great talents; I won't let it get me. I think a musician should consider music as his first love, responsibility," he said, talking very quietly, almost whispering. "You have to be a businessman, almost, about your music. Be reliable. Mustn't get numb and not know what you're doing. There are tough enough obstacles in a musician's life without adding any more. All the vocational diseases, tooth and arm trouble, lung and muscle trouble. Add drink and you've got chaos. No, thanks."

One of the first dates the band made for Brunswick, when

E

it returned to New York, spotted *The Sheik of Araby,* on which Lawrence played what he says was one of the only two solos he ever planned through from beginning to end. The other was the famous *Rose of the Rio Grande,* which Ellington used to highlight the last set of dances. Both were killers, both jumped, both showed off Brown's great skill as a trombonist.

It was that very skill, however, which some of Ellington's most enthusiastic supporters, notably the critic John Hammond, found a very great fault, at least out of place in the Ellington band. Hammond, Hotchkiss-educated son of a wealthy family, was a vigorous supporter of hot jazz, friends of most of the men and women whom he admired as musicians and singers, a young man of violent likes and dislikes. His articulation of his feeling about jazz musicians was always provocative, generally musicianly, but sometimes based on personal feeling so strong that musical reasoning seemed to give way before emotional impression and political conviction. John's own musical background included years of study of the violin and viola; he had played often enough in string quartets and other chamber ensembles to be able to speak as a really informed amateur instrumentalist. And he'd been buying records ever since, as a boy in knee pants, he'd received his first sizable allowance and had been able to supplement this with borrowings from his sisters' allowances. All of this, the personal experience, the large record library, the close friendship with jazzmen, combined with a cogent writing style to make John Henry Hammond, Jr., America's first arbiter of serious jazz tastes. Whether or not he sought that position at the pinnacle of jazz criticism, his writing in the middle and late thirties for the popular music trade magazines, *Melody Maker* in England, *Down Beat* and, occasionally, *Metronome,* in this country, won him just that prestige. John was an influence.

About Lawrence Brown, John wrote:

> . . . He is a virtuoso of the first rank, one who is ever conscious of his technical ability Probably no other trombonist has his equipment.
>
> But I'm afraid that this brilliant musician is out of place in

Duke's band. He is a soloist who doesn't respect the rudiments of orchestral playing. Constantly he pushes himself to the fore-ground. In any other orchestra no objection could be raised; but Duke's group is very properly the voice of one man, and that gent is not Mr. Brown.

And Spike Hughes, "Mike" of the *Melody Maker,* an able musician himself and a critic of high standing in England, wrote from America on a trip to hear jazz at the source:

> The one person, to my mind, who is definitely out of place is Lawrence Brown. This artist is a grand player of the trom-bone, and would be a tremendous asset to any other band on account of his original style, but his solo work is altogether too "smart" or "sophisticated," if you will, to be anything but out of place in Duke's essentially direct and simple music. Brown is as much use to that band as Kreisler would be playing first fiddle in the New York Philharmonic. It is not that his individ-uality is too strong; just misplaced.
>
> This is, of course, only my personal opinion. I have nothing but admiration for Lawrence Brown's talent, as such, but by its very nature it seems to me to belong elsewhere.
>
> After all, can you imagine Hawkins or Armstrong in Duke's band?
>
> I can't.

The similarity of Hammond's and Hughes' opinions of Brown was more than coincidence: Spike's constant companion on his tour of New York jazz spots was John. Both men, too, make the same mistakes in analytical fact. Granting Lawrence his technical prowess, John says "he pushes himself to the fore-ground" constantly, which is wrong in an orchestra that is "the voice of one man," Duke. But, of course, whichever way you cut that, John is wrong: if the band is Duke's voice, then it is he who pushes Brown to the foreground; if the band is not Duke's voice, then each man is entitled to his own push. Actu-ally, the band was and is both a collective expression and an individual one. Lawrence stood out because Duke wanted him to, because Duke wanted the band to be a great deal more than his own voice: its greatness always had been in the freedom of musical exchange among the band's constituent musicians; there its greatness would remain.

Hughes' peculiar analogy is typical of the hysteria with which early supporters of Ellington greeted any change in his band. Kreisler would not be out of place as "first fiddle in the New York Philharmonic" any more than Benny Goodman is out of place in front of a band, or Tommy Dorsey or Louis Armstrong or any other virtuoso in or out of a band. And it is very easy to imagine Hawkins or Armstrong in Duke's band; one can do more than merely imagine, as a matter of fact. When Ben Webster joined Ellington in 1939, the band took on a tenor saxophonist with a style as close as possible to Coleman Hawkins', as individual as Hawk's and as brilliant technically. Ben fitted perfectly: he helped make some of Duke's best records. A few years later, Taft Jordan, an ardent Armstrong admirer and disciple, joined the Ellington trumpets and brought a voice remarkably like Louis's into the band. He has fitted beautifully.

John and Spike (using the pseudonym of "Mike") had other dissident commentaries to make about Duke and the band. Though in 1932 and '33 these eminent critics, and others soon to leave the Ellington camp, still supported Duke, still praised the band emphatically, still made generalizations of endorsement of his musical product, their suspicion and disparagement of much of the work was growing. They began to find records which weren't "the real Duke," though they never defined "the real Duke." Their taste, in general, was expressed by Hughes, who included the recording, *Jungle Nights in Harlem,* "among my favourite examples of Ellington music on account of its general 'low-downness.' "

These well-bred youngsters, very proper in look, manner and dress, wanted jazz to flagellate their sense of propriety. When Duke achieved any considerable mellifluousness in his music, when the sounds which issued forth from his band bore any resemblance to the conventional sounds of the symphony orchestra, they panned him. Their taste ran to blues, "low-down" blues, and when Duke escaped from the tyranny of that limited jazz form, being content to take from it what he could and add to it what he could, they beat a quick retreat from their earlier position of fawning adoration of Ellington. There were still a few years to go before John and Spike and their followers began their intense criticism of Ellington as "arty," "pretentious" and "not jazz," but the base was being laid with the criticism of Brown.

When the band returned to New York after the six weeks on the Coast, it got down to some serious recording activity, and not only did Lawrence Brown make his first appearance on records with Duke, but so did Ivie Anderson, Duke's first regular girl vocalist. There had been a few isolated vocals on Ellington records: those by Sonny, Dick Robertson's on *Sam and Delilah,* Adelaide Hall on *Creole Love Call* and *Blues I Love to Sing,* Baby Cox on the OKeh *Hot and-Bothered* and *Mooche.* Ivie was, however, the first girl Duke ever hired for the express purpose of singing with his band. She almost was the last: she stayed twelve years.

Ivie was born in Gilroy, California, and studied at a convent out there, St. Mary's, from the ages of nine to thirteen. Two years in Washington, some voice study in the capital city and singing in the glee club and chorus at school, and Ivie Anderson was ready for the Coast again and her first job. She worked at Tait's in Los Angeles and at the Tent, run by Abe Lyman's brother Mike. When a featured singer in the Fanchon and Marco revue starring the famous blues singer Mamie Smith became ill, Ivie stepped out of the chorus line to sing the soubrette's part on one hour's notice. Other jobs as a soubrette followed, leading to that role in *Shuffle Along,* a spot at Sebastian's Cotton Club, a five months' tour of Australia with a Fanchon and Marco unit, and finally her own group in a revue which toured West Coast theaters for twenty weeks. There was even one short engagement with Anson Weeks' white band at the Mark Hopkins Hotel in San Francisco.

In 1930, she was a featured singer in the show at the Grand Terrace Café in Chicago; she remained at the Terrace until

well into the winter of '31, until February 13. That was the day
she was asked to work with Duke at the Oriental Theatre in
Chicago.

"Go over and audition for Duke," Earl Hines, who led the
band and booked the talent at the Terrace, told her.

"Wouldn't think of it," Ivie replied. "I'm not good enough."

"Don't be foolish, baby, that's right for you, that's your
class," Earl assured her, biting harder on his big black cigar for
emphasis.

"All right, I'll work a week with him," Ivie promised, "if he
wants me." Duke did.

The week ran into four, the four Duke spent in Balaban and
Katz theaters in Chicago, and the four ran into a dozen years.
Ivie quickly satisfied Duke and was herself quickly satisfied with
the band.

The first record Ivie made with Ellington was the first record
the band made after returning from the Coast, *It Don't Mean
a Thing If It Ain't Got That Swing,* an Ellington tune which
Ivie had been singing since the middle of 1931. This, the first
song to use the term "swing" for jazz, made Ivie. It was one of
Duke's big record hits and one that, incidentally, used with
deadly accuracy the term which so many misused and abused
later on. Swing, in the jazz musician's lingo, was and is a way
of playing: it describes the lift which the propelling beat of this
music gives to solos and the jazz ensemble. With any kind of
feeling for jazz, you can tell whether a band or an individual
jazzman swings, gets a swing. Duke was confessing a cornerstone
of his musical credo when he said, "It don't mean a thing if it
ain't got that swing." His music was always in tempo, always
secure behind the drive of his rhythm section. At somewhat
greater length, in a somewhat more dignified diction, he reiterated this position in 1933:

> Our very lives are dependent on rhythm, for everything we
> do is governed by ordered rhythmic sequences: that modern
> dance music of the best type is completely rhythmic is only in
> accordance with natural law.
> Much has been said of the show part of the band—the melody

instruments—and I have grown a little tired of this perpetual eulogy, because everyone who really understands the dance band of today knows that it is the rhythm section which is by far the most important; without a solid basis of impeccable rhythm, no matter how brilliant the melody section, the band can never be successful.

Sonny Greer, sitting high atop his shining array of drums, was head man in the rhythm section. His sensitive understanding of Ellington as an individual musician and as a band leader made it possible for him to play without a score. Just give Sonny a brief rehearsal of a new thing, once, and he knows his part. Besides, Duke was always below him at the piano, "feeding the band with rhythm," as Duke himself put it. Duke's dictum that florid arpeggios and rapid chromatic runs are taboo until the pianist plays solo was closely followed. And Duke was a hard worker at the keyboard, feeding the audience with his flashy lifting of his hands, feeding the band with his rhythmic chording at the piano. He said in 1933 that the pianist must avoid the overwhelming urge to extemporize on the melody, "for once he begins to neglect his immobile rhythm, the whole section, which is dependent on him, immediately loses its snap and becomes ragged."

Nothing ragged or snapless about the Ellington band in 1932 and '33. There was *Rose Room,* with its very rhythmic, very mobile variations on the theme carried chiefly by Barney on clarinet—the other side of *It Don't Mean a Thing.* There were all the soft and sweet things, the relaxed music of *Lazy Rhapsody, Blue Tune, Blue Ramble,* and the steady jazz motion of *The Sheik of Araby* and *Ducky Wucky* and Freddy Jenkins' *Swing Low.*

Freddie Guy had not yet switched from banjo to guitar, and there is a faintly out-dated sound in the rhythm section of this band, but in everything else, this 1932 edition of Ellington has survived the years. Harmonically, melodically, in the tone colors, in the instrumental textures of the band, the sound of modern jazz is on those records. Sections and soloists were already being used in a free interplay which gave Duke's organiza-

tion greater musical latitude than any other jazz outfit ever
before him or contemporary with him.

The character of the organization seemed to have changed
once again in 1932, changed for the better musically, for the
worse from the point of view of the morale of the band. From
here on each musical advance was accompanied by a retrogres-
sion in the morale of the band. There was a clear advance, a
new musician added, more scoring possibilities, a fresh color
in the band. Somebody was sure to say, "Hell, this ain't no
band. But a couple of years ago, that was the band." Somebody
else would answer, "Time was playing was a kick. No more.
Yeah, we're going no place." And this routine obtained through
the ensuing decade and a quarter, right up to the present day.
The band is never as good as it was, even though the period
the musicians may be comparing it to was one they criticized
in the past.

It's hard for a musician in the middle of a band to hear the
music around him, of course. When the Washingtonians were
five and six pieces small, it was possible to lie back and hear
everybody else, then hear yourself as part of the ensemble. The
whole band wasn't bigger than the modern saxophone section
or as big as the present-day brass. Today, a musician in this or
any other jazz band is like the bass player in the orchestra at
the Metropolitan Opera House who finally got a day off after
several years of playing without a vacation. He took a musician's
holiday: went to the Opera. The opera that night was *Carmen*.
He sat excitedly through the performance, jumping up and
down in his seat, waving his hands, yelling and applauding
madly, as if he were one of the claque. After the opera was over
he hurried backstage. He greeted his fellow musicians, grabbed
them enthusiastically.

"You know, fellows," he said, "where I go mmmmmm-mp!
mmmmmm-mp!" And he imitated the sound of a full-drawn
bow against the bass strings, a loud sawing noise.

"Yes," the musicians acknowledged, "yes."

"Well," he went on, "while I do that, the rest of the orchestra goes mm-mm-m-m, hm-hm-hmmmm-hm-hm." And he went on to hum the *Habanera*.

To many of the Ellington musicians, it seemed that their work had become to a sad degree a journeyman's job, a stage super's, a small part in a large orchestra. They were all responsible to some extent for harmony notes, for filling out section voicings, ensemble chords; no longer was playing the exultant personal expression it had once been. But, strangely, in spite of a great feeling of being let down, their actual performance did not suffer, their technique became more polished, and their solos improved with their ensemble improvement. There was just as much original and effective improvisation as before; there was just as much sparkle and effervescence, as much rhythmic lift in their playing as in the days of Barron's and the Kentucky Club, and something else as well. There was, after all, a new variety of sounds. Instead of just one saxophone, a C melody or an alto, there were alto, baritone and tenor saxes, with doubles on soprano and clarinet. Instead of one growl trumpeter, there were three horns, one growl using plunger mute, and two open, with doubles on plain cup mute and work in derbies and with felt hats. Instead of one growl trombone, there were three of those instruments, Tricky still growling, Tizol pushing the valves down, and Lawrence responsible for anything and everything else which might strike Duke or any of the other writers for the band as trombone material. Instead of a two- or three-man rhythm section, there was a full quartet, with Sonny working from a battery of drums, right up to tuned timpani. The scorings could be as wide as anything of Stravinsky or Ravel, as lush as Tchaikovsky, as brash as Bartok and as full of the vigor and vitality and unorthodox sounds as all of jazz, from Buddy Bolden's New Orleans to Duke Ellington's Washington and New York.

Other bands and other musicians and singers were aware of the tremendous progress the Ellington band had made. Bing Crosby was delighted when the opportunity came in early 1932 to capitalize on his new success, and Duke's, by making a twelve-

E*

inch version of the *St. Louis Blues*, combining his crooning talents and the scoring and playing brilliance of the Ellington organization. Duke made *Swampy River* as a piano solo again, with another keyboard piece, *Fast and Furious*, on the back, and other pianists bought the record to determine whether or not the leader of this magnificent band was "any hell" as an instrumentalist. His playing had always been so much a part of the band they'd never been able to decide. The record didn't help: it was straight gymnastic stuff, piled with runs, filled with rather pleasant flash, but empty of much musical significance. The talk went on, as the records rolled forth. *Lightnin'*, which made musicians marvel again at Carney's command of his baritone. They complained when *Stars*, with a vocal by Sonny, was not issued in this country. They hummed and whistled *Drop Me Off in Harlem*, and used its bright figures in their own solos. *Merry-Go-Round* was another Ellington record issued overseas but not in this country. Musicians and dancers and Ellington fans knew it well: it was a band staple. But it wasn't until two years after it was recorded abroad that it was released over here, and then in a newer version. The score of Lew Leslie's epochal all-Negro revue, *Blackbirds of 1928*, first and most distinguished of a series, was still hit provender in 1933, and so Duke recorded the big tunes from that show. There was first a two-sided *Blackbirds Medley*, then, with Ethel Waters, *I Can't Give You Anything but Love, Baby* and *Porgy;* Adelaide Hall joined with the band to do *I Must Have That Man* and *Baby*, and the Mills Brothers, just emerging as stars, sang *Diga Diga Doo*, with Ellington support. One of the first jazz albums ever issued, this folio was printed in so small a number that its component discs soon became collectors' items, almost impossible to get. But here and abroad, individually and in the set, the '28 *Blackbirds* music as done by Ellington and Waters and Hall and the Mills boys was cause for excited talk. You couldn't see Ethel drape her large shape around the mike, fold and unfold her handkerchief, but you could sense her buxom personality in these records. Adelaide's nervous vibrato made *I Must Have That Man* effective all over again, and the bite of the band supplied what rhythmic feeling was missing from the Mills Brothers' rather straightforward, undramatic singing of a rhythm song.

The Cotton Club Parade of 1933 featured a score written by Ted Koehler (lyrics) and Harold Arlen (music). Duke recorded all of it; the music, so it was advertised, was played just as it was played at The Cotton Club. Ivie sang the four songs: three that did pretty well, *Raisin' the Rent, Happy as the Day is Long* and *Get Yourself a New Broom,* and one that swept a nation with its plaintive strains, *Stormy Weather.* The other side of *Stormy Weather* was occupied by an ambling tune based on a theme by Toby Hardwick, something called *Sophisticated Lady.* Before long the nation turned *Stormy Weather* on the other side and the lady of sophistication found herself the center of acclaim, much whistled at and danced with. This is one of the few sides still current on which Toby's creamy alto can be heard in solo. And then, just before the band left for Europe, four more sides: *I'm Satisfied,* in which Duke combined with Mitchell Parish, the writer of the lyric for Hoagy Carmichael's *Stardust,* in one of his first attempts to write an out-and-out commercial tune; *Jive Stomp,* bringing another new jazz word to record life, and showing off the drive of this jive; *Harlem Speaks,* jungle-istic in its growls, swingy in its rhythms, infectious music; and the beautiful remodeling of the American standard, *In the Shade of the Old Apple Tree,* in the tints of the new Ellington band.

The band left for Europe that June with a few misgivings, many complaints and a certain satisfaction. The money was coming in, the name was growing. For certain freedoms sacrificed, certain securities had been gained. And they could look forward to Europe, where they knew an eager audience awaited them, where there was no color line, it was said, and there was nothing but great love for the music and personality of the Negro musician. Perhaps in this new atmosphere, amid this broad tolerance, the band could really find itself. There was bound to be more understanding of its experimental kind of music in Europe than there was at home in America. And this was something the band wanted very much. As has always been true of the Ellington musicians, no matter how much they criticized Duke and each other, they defended the band as a unit to outsiders with all the temper and blood of which they were capable. Many of them were personally disgruntled as the band changed musical shape and individuals became somewhat less important than they had been, but all were convinced of the validity of this change. They wanted and expected substantiation of this conviction in the reception of European audiences.

Duke, too, looked forward to Europe for the same reasons. Only his musical life needed straightening out: his personal affairs were beautifully arranged in 1933.

CHAPTER NINE

HARLEM RIVER QUIVER

D UKE HAD SETTLED DOWN TO THE UNSETTLED LIFE OF THE late twenties and early thirties. It was time to take advantage of his new position, and he had. Not accepting favors from songpluggers, money or liquor or seats to the theater or prizefights. Not buying his way into the rackets, not participating in the business of bootlegging liquor, which he could have done at the lift of his little finger off the piano keyboard and at very great profit to that little finger. Just sitting back and enjoying some of the luxury his money could buy and more that his position afforded him. Extra-special attention all around, chefs bustling about to do his bidding in the restaurants he frequented (he frequented many), making him special dishes and giving him extra-large portions. Falling in love, and time to do something about it.

Edna had followed Duke to New York in 1923, and for a few years they had a wonderful time together. But somehow, after those first few years in New York, when Duke was at Barron's and the Kentucky, the old ties had broken and the old understanding had been replaced by a new misunderstanding. In Washington, Duke and Edna had had so much in common. In New York, after a while, the only thing they had deeply in common was young Mercer, and he was off at school in Washington, being looked after by Duke's folks.

In Washington, whenever Duke and Edna had a disagreement, or Duke was seriously disturbed by a personal problem, he could go into extra-plenary session with his mother. He would call to her and more than likely they would end up in the bathroom, where they could find real privacy and Duke could talk his heart out. In New York, there was nobody to talk it over with, and the misunderstandings grew far beyond patching. Duke and Edna reluctantly broke up their marriage.

There was a new girl in Duke's life. Mildred Dixon was her name. She danced in the Cotton Club show with Henri Wessons, the team of Mildred and Henri. Short, sleek, bright dark eyes on a soft coffee background. She spoke softly and earnestly, and Duke always felt a great conviction in what she said. And with that conviction went an intense interest on her part in what he said.

"Yes, yes," she would say, "go on." Duke would tell her of the latest band news, the latest news of music, what he had done and would do and could do. "Yes, yes," she would say, "go on."

Mildred and Henri opened at the Cotton Club in the same show that Duke did, opened on the same night, December 4, 1927. It was their first meeting. She'd seen him perform and appear at some of the late spots but had never met him. She was impressed at the Cotton Club. Duke, who always had an eye for beautiful young things, looked up from the piano and stared. Since he played with his feet well in front of him, and with his face turned to the audience, if he got interested in something other than the music, he could always fake the chords, just run his hands deftly over the keys and make it look right, even if he weren't playing a note. He faked the first time he saw Mildred. Soon after, when he felt secure in his position at the Club, he didn't play at all, didn't fake or anything else, just jumped off the stand and went to talk to her.

"Hello, baby," he said, as he bowed ceremoniously. "You certainly make that dress look beautiful."

Mildred became Mrs. Ellington. Duke moved in with her at her 141st Street apartment, shortly after. Things weren't perfect, but they were very good. It was so much fun together, they understood each other so well. Mildred knew Duke never knew where the hell he'd put anything and might at any moment yell for it. Oh, for shoes or socks or shirt, pants or jacket or tie, the comic papers or that book.

That book, those days, was generally one of the volumes in the big set of Historical Romances. They both got a big boot out of reading about the "great lovers of the past." Perhaps there was something analogous in their relationship, maybe not, but, though they didn't need the books to measure the depth of their attachment to each other, it was nice to bask in the reflected light of old loves as they dreamed their way through the new.

Something about the night light on Sugar Hill, the streets dancing away from the Harlem River, assuming animation underneath the Harlem moon. Something about the chicks, flouncing down the dancing streets in their tight skirts, bouncing along suspended on their French heels, clattering past the brownstone houses all lit up in the late night and early morning.

Brown was the color. Brownstone houses of a city's faded elegance, brownstone houses left over from the days of Harlem's first magnificence for these, its greatest times, moving along under the steady propulsion of a dozen rhythm sections, Duke's and Fletcher's and McKinney's and the Missourians' and others. Brown, mud-brown river and brown earth above it as the Hill rose over the Polo Grounds and the Bronx beyond. Duke wrote lots of river into his music. *Harlem River Quiver, The River and Me, Swampy River.* Sometimes he was writing about other waters, but the genesis was usually the river by the Hill. With only half an ear and less than a convolution cocked to their music, Duke was absorbing much of Ravel and Debussy. Their harmonic formulations came to him naturally, their symbols, the fluid sounds of the underwater naiads, were as much part of his life as of theirs. The brown water of the Harlem river. The brownskin girls and the brownstone houses. Something about the night light on Sugar Hill.

First it was Mexico's at 133rd and Lenox. That was the after-hours place, where the liquor was best and the noise most attractive and the faces most friendly.

Then it was to Jerry Preston's on 133rd that you went. That was because Mexico had gone West where the weather would protect his bones from the rheums which rain brought and the money would still be comfortable. Jerry Preston's to talk and drink and eat at, and meet your friends at, four and five and six in the morning. There was a remarkable clarity about those early-morning conversations when all the facts of life somehow lined up and identified themselves. The blue and red light of the little basement-café stimulated thought and brought clear articulation about the aims and the means of achieving the aims.

"Peace is what I want," Duke murmured as he speared a thick slice of sirloin.

"Peace is what you've got," Mildred reminded him.

"Peace and calm," Duke reiterated, as if he hadn't heard her.

"Peace and calm are what you've got," Mildred repeated.

"Peace," Duke sighed.

He was expressing a philosophy of life, a yearning. Peace was possible. Peace, maybe, at any price.

"Those arguments at the club. Don't like 'em," Duke said.

"Can't be helped," Mildred suggested.

"Don't like 'em."

Duke ate some more and waved hello to friends coming in from other parts of the city, arriving as fast as the subways and taxis could carry them, as this club and that speakeasy and the other private party let out.

"How about Mills putting his name on your music?" Mildred asked.

"We've talked about that before," Duke answered.

"How about it?"

"If it makes him happy. . . ."

"You'll have peace and calm at any price," Mildred assured him. "You have."

"Peace is what I want," Duke murmured, as he swallowed the last piece of steak.

The routine was the same wherever they went. New York or Chicago or Philadelphia or L.A. There was always some after-hours joint, some place to eat or drink or talk or do two of them or all three. In New York, it might be fried chicken at somebody's grill, and in Chicago it was pretty sure to be ribs, the pick of the country's hogs for a lover of the short ones, the spare ribs where they were least spare. Crackling with the heat of the spit, black embers where the fire had burned the edges, black embers against the mahogany brown of the close meat on the short ribs. Dip it into a tongue-splitting "hot sauce." Or cover the ribs first with the sauce and then reach down with your fingers into the thick goo for the rough morsel, feeling the sting of the red pepper on your fingers as you made for it. "Oh, Miss Jaxon," Duke later wrote in a lyric, "you've got some fine barbecue . . . Your ribs are Leviathonic, super-Herculeonic . . ."

In New York, they developed a pleasant routine at the Cotton Club. Into the early hours of the morning they would play cards, Duke and Mildred and Herman Stark, who managed and later owned the place, and Frenchy. Frenchy, who was associated with the syndicate which ran the Cotton Club. Frenchy, who loved Ellington's music and was devoted to Duke.

"Anything you want, Duke," Frenchy was wont to say, "anything you want, you just ask for it, and it's yours." And he could make good his offer, as few others could.

First they played whist, that ancient game, predecessor of bridge, honorable and ancient and a little wearing after a whole night. Then pinochle. Pinochle was the great road game in those days. Something about the smaller deck and the lush colors of the double number of face cards seemed right on the road, on trains, in hotel rooms and backstage dressing-rooms. Finally rummy, which was the easiest time-killer, the least arduous and the best to eat and drink and talk with. It was much easier to interrupt the matching of nines and the arranging of ten, Jack, Queen, King in sequence, with eating and talking and drinking, than to burst in upon the complicated melds of pinochle with a new joke or a great quaff of beer.

And you might have some good stories to tell, too. You might tell them about that guy who requested the *St. Louis Blues.*

"He danced up to me with this girl he was dancing with," Duke told them. "Tall, skinny guy, with a friendly manner.

" 'Please play the *St. Louis Blues*,' he asked me. 'I can't dance,' he explained, 'unless I can sing the words to my girl. And those are my favorite words.'

"Not once or twice, mind you, but fifteen times this cat comes up to me and asks me to play the *St. Louis Blues*. I play it for him. At the end of the evening he comes up to me again.

" 'How about once more, huh?' he asks. He's a friendly fellow. I play it for him again. He comes up to me after I finish.

" 'Thanks, fella,' he says. 'I really appreciate that. Here, boy,' he says, 'buy yourself a cigar.' I look at what he gives me and it's a thousand dollar note.

" 'I don't know where I can buy a cigar that expensive,' I say.

" 'That's okay,' he says, 'I like that. It's worth another.' And he gives me another G-note. 'Anytime anybody can make me laugh it's worth a grand to me,' he says." Duke laughs. "Yeah," he says, "a friendly guy."

"Anybody I know?" Frenchy asks.

"Yeah," Duke answers, "somebody you know. Legs Diamond."

"Oh, that Legs," Frenchy comments. "What a character! They say he's got diamonds and rubies and emeralds in the holes on his legs and stomach, wherever they shot him."

"Hmm," Mildred says, "hmm."

In 1930, J.E. and Aunt Daisy came up to New York to see their boy and they were impressed. A year later they came to stay, Ellingtons, senior, and daughter Ruth and Duke's son, Mercer. They all moved over to one of Harlem's best apartment houses, 381 Edgecombe Avenue, overlooking the river. Five rooms were spread among them, three bedrooms, living room and kitchen. Duke spent to get the place in shape. A full-stocked larder and easy furniture and, for his parents' special convenience, one of those long Pierce-Arrows, a sixteen-cylinder automobile, low to the ground. A boy was hired to drive the car and serve as personal aide to Duke's parents, particularly to look after them when Duke was out of town. This aide, Tommy Lavigne, gave Duke a new name. Duke was called

Edward by his parents, by his sister, by many of his friends. Tommy called him Governor. The next step was easy.

"Guvvy," Ruth called to her brother.

"Guvvy," Mildred called to Duke.

"Guvvy," even J.E. chimed in.

It stuck. So did the name of the Guys, Freddie and Minnie. Freddie and his wife lived in the same apartment house, 381, as the Ellington brood, and spent great quantities of time with Duke and Mildred and the family. They played cards at each other's apartment after work and ate in the early morning hours together. Duke, who put away horrendous amounts of food at that or any other time, was beginning to develop a profile below the chin.

"Hey, Dumpy," Freddie would call to Duke.

"Oh, Dumpling," Mildred amplified.

'Dumpy, dear," Ruth began conversations.

The "Dumpy" shortening for "Dumpling" satisfied the family and close friends as a description of the bourgeoning Ellington figure. It stuck, too.

The family was a close unit. Duke was overwhelmed with the pleasure of having family and Mildred and his work so closely juxtaposed. Ruth adored Mildred. Mildred was so sweet to Ruth. Whenever Mildred went on a shopping tour to buy anything, anything of size or of no consequence at all, she took Ruth along and bought something for her, too. And Ruth, just approaching college age when the family moved in with Duke, was more than ordinarily appreciative. Silks and satins had the usual allure for the adolescent girl, silks and satins and other stuffs of attractive color and texture.

"Come on, honey," Mildred would say to Ruth. "Let's go downtown."

"What for?"

"You need a new coat, baby."

Coats and hats and shoes and exquisitely sheer silk stockings for young Ruth, growing up to look so much like her brother Edward.

"One thing you can say about those Ellingtons," someone in the band said, "they sure look it."

Even little Mercer was beginning to show signs of the Ellington physiognomy. His eyes were dark and mournful like his father's, but not so often set in a poignant face. His face was long, like Duke's, but not so rounded. His figure was lithe, wiry, and gave signs of developing into athletic build. But athletics weren't Mercer's major interest. Airplanes were. He built hundreds of model planes and gave serious thought, as serious thought as a fourteen-year old might, to a career in aeronautics.

"Hey, Father Edward," he said to Duke, "I'm gonna be an aviator."

Another time, it was, "A mechanic, I'm gonna be."

"What about it, Eekie," Mildred asked. (Eekie, still another nickname, came from Duke's initials, E.K.E.)

"I dunno," Duke said, "dunno at all."

"Why don't you know? The boy's got a perfectly wonderful ambition, and it's a real one. You can see by the way he fools around with model airplanes that it's real. You don't know!"

"No, Sweet Bebe, it isn't as simple as that, you oughtta understand. Mercer's not just a little boy interested in airplanes. Mercer's a colored boy. And I'm not sure, not so sure."

"But, Eekie darling, why not? I know it won't be easy for him. Nothing's easy for any of us. Why not get his licks in the airplane business as much as any other?" Mildred was, if not adamant, at least devoted to Mercer's cause.

"Some businesses are harder for us than others, you realize that. The airplane business is a young one, new and uncertain. Anything this new isn't gonna have room for a colored boy. Don't forget that. I don't mean a little boy like Mercer, either, I'm thinking of a kid who's well-educated and older. But he's a Negro and they're not going to make opportunities for him. That's such a lot to overcome."

"I'm sorry you feel that way," Mildred said.

"Aw, Sweet Bebe," Duke comforted her, "don't act as if there's nothing Mercer can do. There's always the music business, you know."

Duke was concerned about the future of his music, and he thought a great deal about Mercer and that impressive and important bounty he would some day leave him.

"Don't you see, darling," Duke said, "who else am I gonna leave my music to? Somebody's gotta have it, and Mercer is the logical person. And, anyway, the music business is our business. He isn't gonna have such a struggle just to keep his head above water. I like that, see?"

Mercer had made some forays into the music business, just the simplest of entries. He'd studied some piano and absorbed more of the art and the business hanging around the band. In Salem, in summers, he'd been able to hear a lot of his father's music and musicians, and after coming to New York he didn't miss many appearances of the band. The airplane ambitions were not killed, however, with Duke's expressed doubts. Mercer was a brilliant mathematics student, the considerable envy of Ruth, who was fighting the hard fight with the ciphers at Wadleigh High School, where she finished secondary school education in New York. Mercer was a bright boy in the sciences generally and continued to show interest in aeronautics. A few years later, Mildred made serious inquiries about a good technical school in that field, and settled, reasonably enough, upon the Massachusetts Institute of Technology. Mildred was a Boston girl and had contacts. Since they fitted in well with airplanes, she made contact with her contacts, and in spite of a low colored quota, she was able to obtain entrance for Mercer. That is, he could get in if he could pass the entrance examinations. He passed them and everything looked set, until Duke's old doubts popped up again, and in such force and with such fervor that gainsaying them was difficult for everybody in the family from J.E. down to grandson Mercer, the one most concerned. Mercer, fortunately, wasn't too seriously disappointed. He liked music and respected the word and thought of his father. And it really looked liked a dubious field for his people, then. The future war boom in airplanes was hard to predict in the mid-thirties.

J.E. was an intense participant in family discussions, and his counsel was sought after. But J.E. sought after far more than family discussions. Harlem was a holiday to Duke's father. Like son, like father. Though devoted to his wife, he had an eye for the chicks. His line was, if anything, better than his son's, based upon longer experience. He was more of a verbal philanderer than anything else, but the words were true to the mark and the charm of his personality so great that it was pretty hard, if you were a girl in the show at the 125th Street Apollo Theatre, say, or a hostess at the Savoy Ballroom, perhaps, or in the Cotton Club line, to escape entirely from his spell.

He was known all over Harlem. People would see him coming.

"Here comes old Uncle Ed," a girl would say, smiling to her friend, who kicked across the same row of footlights she did.

"Hello, my darling," Uncle Ed would greet them. "My," he continued, "you look tuckered out today. I don't know what it is about the younger generation, something about these boys that always leaves the girls looking tired. Now my influence is more restful. What you need to do is to hang out with Uncle Ed more often." He usually concluded his speeches with, "Won't you join me?"

Duke's father was adored wherever he went. The young girls would trade banter with him. The older ones would enjoy talking more seriously with him, exchanging stories about Washington and New York and what J.E. could remember of the South directly and indirectly through his father's tales. As a blueprint-maker for the Navy, he had led a semi-privileged existence, with more of the comforts than most of his people experienced in the Nation's Capital in those days. He had spent his leisure time well, reading and talking with stimulating people, and when he came to New York, having retired, at Duke's insistence, he could spend all his time in those pleasant pursuits. He looked extremely well, a great deal younger than his fifty-two years when the family moved to New York: he looked in his forties. Close-cropped hair and a head shaped more like his grandson Mercer's than Duke's gave his face a sturdy look. A square jaw, added to a natural stubbornness, sometimes made him seem the least conciliatory of men. But his eyes often softened beneath his rimless eye-glasses, and the line of his upper lip, just like Duke's, rose to a middle peak from either side, edged by a mustache which added sparkle to his face.

Daisy Kennedy Ellington was sweet: that is the dominant impression people carry of her. She was considerate of their feelings, anxious to make visitors at the apartment feel at home, and deeply aware of family responsibilities, an awareness she passed on to her son. She would often pat Mercer on the back and send him off to see Edna, who lived near by. But Mercer needed little prodding: he was then, as he is now, deeply devoted to his mother.

Everybody who knew Duke knew his mother and father, and their life at 381 was full. From the Mills office to the acts which shared billing with Duke in the cafés and stage shows, close friends and professional acquaintances, people uptown and downtown and midtown knew them. As the long, low Pierce-Arrow made slow progress through Harlem's streets, there would almost always be someone at a street corner, somebody crossing the car's path between corners, to hail Duke's parents, to say hello to Mercer or Ruth, maybe to ask how Duke was.

No doubt about it, Duke would say to himself, things are going pretty well. In 1931, things went so well, so damn well. Something had to be done about it, Duke decided. At Christmas, something was done.

They were playing a theater, Christmas week, 1931. First thing to do, Mildred decided, was fix up the place. She chose one of the more commodious dressing rooms—none was especially large, but this one would do. She decorated the room, hung it with holly wreaths and fir branches. She got a fair-sized tree and suspended a galaxy of lights from it, so that it fairly shouted the season's greetings. Over one corner of the room she even hung a dab of mistletoe. This would be a Christmas. Then the bandboy was sent around to ask the boys in, everybody, the acts on the bill, everybody in any way associated with the band.

"Duke says come to the dressing room on the second floor," the bandboy announced.

"What dressing room?" Barney asked.

"Second floor. Empty one."

"What the hell for?" somebody else asked.

"Isn't that a damn shame?" somebody asked of everybody. "Christmas and we gotta go to a dressing room. Run over a new arrangement, huh? Or just talk about something. Ain't that a damn shame?"

"I'm not going," somebody said flatly.

"Better go," the bandboy warned. "Duke says come."

"I'll be damned," somebody said.

"Let's go, fellas," the bandboy said.

Grumbling as they went, wondering or just annoyed or bored, the Ellington musicians went to the dressing room on the second floor to see Duke Ellington.

"Everybody in?" Duke asked.

"Not yet, Dumpy," Freddie Guy informed him.

Finally, everybody was in. Duke turned to them.

"Look, fellas," he said.

"Here it comes," somebody whispered to somebody else.

"Look, fellas, this has been a good year, a very good year all around. This is a very Merry Christmas for me, and I sincerely hope it will be for you, a very Merry Christmas. I got something for you, don't know whether it suits everybody's taste, after all, some people like different colors, different models. You know how it is. But maybe you'll like this stuff. Mildred's taste is impeccable, you know. Anyway, here they are. Let's pass 'em out," he concluded to Mildred and the bandboy.

They shouted the names, as the packages came up. "Cootie." "Barney." "Rabbit." "Posey." "Tricky." "Carney." "Tizol." "Freddie Guy." "Sonny." "Braud." "Arthur." Then, "The Steps," and the Four Step Brothers, who danced on the bill with the band, stepped up. "Sam," and Sam Fliashnick, road manager of the band, took his. The bandboy (the youngster responsible for setting up music stands, packing and unpacking instruments, doing errands) and even a couple of theater employees, were given packages.

The packages were of a dozen different sizes, large and small

and medium. Wrapped in almost as many colors, they were
gaily festooned with shining ribbons. The Christmas spirit
shone in them as it did on the tree, on the branches and holly
and mistletoe around the dressing room. They were opened
with the happy noise that always attends the opening of Christmas packages, a crackling and groaning of paper, a tense
ripping-loose of the reluctant string. Cootie and Barney and
Rabbit, Posey and Tricky, Carney, Tizol and Freddie Guy,
Sonny and Braud and Arthur Whetsol, the bandboy and Sam
Fliashnick and the Step Brothers opened their packages, looking
for ties and socks and suspenders, maybe a shirt or two or a
sports jacket.

Sonny was the first.

"I *like* this color, Duke," he said. "I like it fine."

"Yeah, Duke," Tricky said in his high, soft voice. "Fine
color."

"Green, green," Posey Jenkins murmured, "green like
mother earth. Green is my color."

"That's very good of you," Harry Carney said with some
formality.

"Gee, Duke," the Steps acknowledged.

They were all pretty happy, and quick in one way or another
to acknowledge their happiness, to make their Christmas obliga-
tion known. They had all received money, in varying amounts.
The boys in the band got $250 apiece; the Steps, $50, and the
bandboy and some of the theater people the same; Sam Fliashnick, $100. Wrapped in all the different-sized packages, an-
nounced so inauspiciously, the recipients of ducal pleasure that
Christmas hadn't looked forward to quite so much and were
that much more surprised, of course, when they opened their
packages.

Christmas was the time, too, to exchange enormous tokens of
family affection, wrist-watches and other jewelry of consequence,
the best Duke could obtain, and even an auto, once, for Ruth,
but that was a few years later. Duke would lose track of the
presents to him shortly after getting them and might even forget he'd ever received them, but on Christmas itself he was all

arms, receiving with as much pleasure as he'd given, and giving all the more pleasure to his family as a result.

The money was flowing gaily away. Mildred and Duke talked about it occasionally, usually around the subject of Irving Mills.

"Where does it all go?" Mildred asked.

"All over, all over," Duke explained noncommittally.

"That makes it all clear," Mildred said.

"God, Bebe, look, there are the expenses at home, right?" Mildred nodded. "And the expenses on the road?" She nodded again. "And the expenses of the family. That all adds up."

"Do you bother to add it up yourself?" Mildred asked.

"No, not really," Duke answered.

"Have you ever figured Mills' take, and all the other business expenses?" Mildred asked.

"No, not really," Duke answered. "But look, Sweet Bebe, if, after home and the road and the family, there's anything left, Mills and anybody else is welcome to it. Anything they can find, let 'em take."

Duke meant that, at the time; he was damned if he'd worry about an extra dollar or hundred or thousand. He'd lived just long enough in that era of thousand-dollar tips and frenzied spending to lose concern for money as such. Just as long as he was free from worry, as long as he could buy the Pierce-Arrow and pay the salaries and have the little and large comforts he wanted, everything was all right.

Yes, Duke was damned if he'd worry about an extra dollar, but, on the other hand, he seemed to be damned. It was damnation by force or forces unseen. Some of the symptoms were clear, some of the damning powers were obvious, but they didn't explain everything.

The early thirties were a strange and difficult time for a musician like Ellington. That was one source of worry. For the early thirties, unlike the early twenties, were years of the locust in jazz. The field was overrun with "Mickey Mouse" music, "cheese" or "toy" bands, as the jazzman calls orchestras which rely upon synthetic sounds rather than music for popular appeal. Jazz had taken shape under the direction of the New Orleans originators, Joe Oliver and Louis Armstrong and the Original Dixieland Jazz Band. It had gathered tyros and made them into professionals in Chicago and Kansas City and New York, as jazz sped up the Mississippi River to points North and West and East. There were an impressive few years in Chicago, with Oliver and Armstrong and Earl Hines and Jimmie Noone leading the way, more or less in the New Orleans tradition. Then, in the early twenties, the big bands started going, Fletcher Henderson and Duke, and, less significantly, Bennie Moten and McKinney's Cotton Pickers and the Missourians and a host of lesser outfits which could boast a star soloist or two. Even Paul Whiteman and Ted Lewis, the leading white show bands of the time, were infected by the virus. Whiteman, at various times, featured such jazz stars as Joe Venuti and Bix Beiderbecke and the Dorsey Brothers, Mildred Bailey and Red Norvo. Muggsy Spanier and, later, Benny Goodman and Fats Waller recorded with Ted Lewis.

By the late twenties, the taste for jazz was beginning to wear off in American audiences, though great music was still being played. Chick Webb started his band and Ben Pollack his, with Jack Teagarden and Benny Goodman and Gene Krupa and Glenn Miller and other such stars. Red Nichols made lots of fine records, some of the first to employ modern dance band arrangements, using most of the white stars mentioned above. Andy Kirk had a good band going in Kansas City. But Chick and Pollack and Kirk worked in comparative obscurity, and though Henderson and Ellington had audiences of some size, and Jean Goldkette and McKinney, in their Detroit headquarters, won some support for jazz, the big trend seemed to be to another kind of music.

By the early thirties, the other kind of music had taken over. Nichols was finished as a recording artist. The colored bands, Smack and Duke and Cab excepted, played only for colored audiences in colored quarters. Guy Lombardo was the hottest thing in the country—paradoxically: music couldn't be colder. His simpering saxophone voicings, pinned to an alto, usually overbearingly sharp, were universally accepted as the "Sweetest Music This Side of Heaven," which, as an identifying tag, should have been enough to confound it. Ben Bernie and Isham Jones and Abe Lyman and Wayne King and Jan Garber and Horace Heidt were the big names. They had radio commercials, and their music, which in the case of Jones, at least, had occasional merit, was hardly in the jazz groove. Hal Kemp, who had started out as a leader of a jazz band, switched to the twitch-rhythm school and made a reputation and a fortune. And what jazz there was seemed to be entirely of the flag-waver school, screaming, badly played, with incredibly fast stomps; that was Henderson at his worst and the popular Casa Loma band at its average. Cab Calloway, whom Duke had discovered singing at the Plantation Club in 1929, was now fronting the Missourians. But Cab's success was not due to music of any high quality: it was strictly Cab's wild singing and dancing, his sleek, exaggerated Harlem dress. It was all pretty discouraging. Such good jazz as there was sneaked in by back doors. The future for Duke's type of music didn't look too good.

There was another worry. The men in the band were sort of prima donnas. Never had there been such a distinguished collection of jazzmen in one band, and never was a collection of jazzmen so well aware of how distinguished they were. There were great shows of temperament, salary disputes, lots of bewildering unpleasantness. It was bewildering because these were Duke's old friends, his associates all the way back, most of them. It was bewildering because the band had jumped from what was really a collective organization to one led by a leader, a genuine leader, by musical and social and psychological personality a leader. The band had made that jump with little to soften the blow, to assuage the feelings of those left behind, still in the band but no longer equal to the leader. They were closer to Duke than other musicians to their bosses, but they had been still closer and there were some hard feelings.

Duke's feelings of self-satisfaction and of social achievement, his delight in the establishment of a new family circle in New York and a balanced relationship with a girl he loved, these things were severely modified by the worries. He worried about where his band stood in relation to the times, to those times and the years still to come. He worried about the delicate web of personalities and temperaments which tied his band together. He just plain worried.

Th nk God, Duke said to himself, for Europe. Europe is ahead. He looked forward to it in early 1933 as a dental patient with a raw nerve looks forward to novocain. Europe, Duke said to himself, thank God for Europe.

"What about me?" Mildred asked.

"What about you?" Duke countered.

"Do I get to go along?"

Duke answered slowly, "No, baby, I'm afraid not. No, I guess we'd better not do that."

"What do you mean 'better not do that'?" Mildred asked.

"I mean God would punish me if I took you along, sure as can be," Duke answered. "It would be too much. Just having Europe now is so wonderful. Having you along too would be too much. I'm not meant to be that happy. Maybe nobody is. But I certainly know I'm not meant to be that happy."

CHAPTER TEN

HIGH LIFE

Louis Armstrong had been to England in 1932, but he hadn't made a great impression. Just a good "nigger" band, the English said, using the word with some degree of patronization, but without any serious edge. They awaited Duke with somewhat greater interest. He was preceded in the spring of 1933 by a terrific advertising and publicity campaign organized by Jack Hylton, the bandleader-promoter who was bringing the Ellington band to Europe. In the London papers and magazines, for weeks before Duke arrived, there was talk about the ensuing events. The *Evening Standard,* day before the band reached London, said:

> Duke Ellington, "hot gospeller" of crazy jazz music and Haarlem rhythm, arrives from America on his first visit to this country to-morrow. London will be invaded by 5000 dance bandsmen from all parts of the country for the purpose of hearing a demonstration by his band of 13 players of the latest dance music.

Certainly interest among musicians was high enough to bring 5000 of them to London to hear Duke, but there is no record of any such concerted invasion of the short-haired folk. The "hot gospeller" appellation was undoubtedly the work of a Hylton press-agent, and the description of the genre as "crazy jazz music" was probably occasioned by the fact that Ellington was booked for an appearance at the Palladium, most famous for its so-called "crazy shows." The British temperament conceived of anything as far from the suitable decorum of everyday life as a slapstick comedian as "crazy."

There was some griping in the press about Hylton's not being allowed to play in America (because of conflicting labor union laws) and Ellington's being free to play in England. Hylton was in fact turning the other cheek, or it was frightfully cheeky of the Americans, or something. The other cheek was quickly withdrawn, however: when Duke returned to Europe, six years later, England had engraved in her statute books a law forbidding foreign performers who were not members of the English performing unions to appear in Great Britain. In any case, on this, his first trip, a warm welcome awaited him.

Cedric Belfrage in the *Sunday Express* said, "This band, consisting of America's eighteen hottest rhythm boys, all of whom are negroes [always with a small n in England, to the considerable annoyance of the N.], is considered by experts to be the finest hot-cha turnout west of Land's End." In discussing Ellington and jazz, the British writers achieved a gaucherie of phrase unmatched in the field of music criticism until two and a half years later when the "swing" fad hit America.

An articulate, aggressive group of jazz writers, critics, editors, and Hylton and his associates obtained for Ellington one forty-five minute broadcast over the British Broadcasting Company National network at a fee. B.B.C. never brought in a band from a remote location, hotel, night club or ballroom and had never before paid for dance-band performances except those played by its house orchestra, a pallid organization directed, at that time, by Henry Hall. Some newspapers made bitter comment about the payment to the band. The Manchester *Dispatch* bristled:

> This month [Jack Hylton] is bringing the American jazz king to England—Duke Ellington—for whom he has booked an engagement at Broadcasting House at an unusually high fee, which touches three figures. Trust an American to make money records!

And it was with a touch of more than ordinary snobbery that Cedric Belfrage reported:

> Ellington, you know, is no ordinary negro jazzist. His advance press agent describes him as "well-educated and gentlemanly in his bearing."

Spike Hughes writes to me from New York declaring that "Ellington and Walt Disney seem to be the only great men that America has produced without the help of the Jews."

"Be that as it may," Belfrage concluded cryptically, not letting his readers know whether he wanted Hughes' Nazi-like statements or the claims of Duke's advance man to be as they may.

There was some resentment that the Palladium bookers couldn't find sufficient talent in Britain "and that America is the only remaining source of material." Resentment, amazement, and disbelief. "They have lost the art of creating British stars," was the bitter comment of *The People*. "The material is there. But no one can develop it."

Along with the snide cracks and the patriotic pique, however, there was enormous interest in Ellington, a genuine interest. Much was made in the British press of Australian-American composer Percy Grainger's comparison of Ellington to Johann Sebastian Bach and to Frederick Delius. Delius was England's own and a serious comparison of "America's coloured king of jazz," as many referred to him, and a contemporary English composer, by a musician like Grainger, was to be taken very seriously. The top London papers, the *Daily Express* and *Daily Herald*, not only covered the appearances of the band but gave Ellington great space before he arrived. His picture appeared in the *Herald*, *Sketch*, *News-Chronicle*, *Evening Standard* and *Sunday Referee*. All over the country, newspapers, large and small, hailed his forthcoming appearances. The *News-Chronicle*, in a story announcing his arrival at London's Waterloo Station, hailed Ellington as "the most celebrated negro bandmaster in the world." Perhaps they were thinking of Duke as another Jim Europe, the famous Negro regimental band leader in the last war, whose big brass crew was the first to introduce American jazz to Europe.

The trip over was not especially noteworthy. The band was feted on board the S.S *Olympic* from the day it left New York, June 2, until it arrived in Southampton a little after noon one week later. Freddie Guy, who had been teaching himself the differences in fingering and chording a guitar, six strings after the four of the banjo, had switched instruments. Everybody had drunk a lot, balled a little, Toby swaggering a little as he explained the incidentals and fundamentals of travel on a transatlantic liner. The two girls with the troupe, Ivie and Bessie Dudley, a dancer, were lionized. There were some rehearsals.

At Southampton Jack Hylton met them, shook hands around and got everybody set for a series of pictures for the newspapers and the trade weekly, the *Melody Maker.* All the traditional shots on the deck of the *Olympic.* Smiling standing. Smiling seated. Duke on the top deck, at the head of the stairs, waving hello to England. They boarded the train for London and Duke met a crisis. He was introduced to gin and tonic.

"It was a terrible thing. I could never acquire a taste for *that!*"

At Waterloo everybody was impressed. The boat train was full of diplomats of international renown going to the London Conference, one of the dozens of between-wars naval parity conclaves which claimed headlines and photo space in the world's newspapers in those years. But the photographers shot Ellington and his bandsmen. Instead of the Ambassador from the United States, they took the country's jazz minister plenipotentiary. The cameramen got set for poses.

"We posed back!"

In London there were headlines. They weren't simply headlines announcing the band's arrival. They were something different from what the musicians had expected.

NO HOTEL FOR
A NEGRO BAND

JAZZ "KING"
WILL
LEAD THEM

18 PLAYERS ALL
MUSICIANS WANT
TO HEAR

PROBLEM FOR JACK
HYLTON

The story was unpleasant. "No hotel wishes to board eighteen negroes." "I cannot very well send the jazz-monarch to a hostel," said Jack Hylton, "though at the moment that seems to be the only solution. My staff have ransacked the town and suburbs for rooms, and failed."

The *Express* asked the question, "Is it possible for a negro to find accommodation in a first-class hotel in London?" A representative of the newspaper toured well-known London hotels and tried to book a room for a West African negro, as a test case.

"We are extremely sorry, sir, but we have not a single room vacant," was one reply.

"Hopelessly full up. . . . World Conference and Ascot, you know?" was another.

"We can put him up for one night if he is well-behaved," was another.

"Is he very black?"

Another clerk explained the hierarchy. "There are blacks and blacks. The type with flat noses and crinkly hair have less chance of securing rooms than any other type."

It was possible for *a* Negro to find accommodation in a first-class London hotel. Duke was booked at the Dorchester, one of the city's finest and best-known hotels. But then, as one of the newspaper columnists summed him up, "He is not very black. He is a master of harmony. He wears a brown suit and a yellow tie that harmonise with his skin." The British were perhaps more curious about these American Negroes than prejudiced against them.

It was not possible for eighteen colored musicians, even of the stature of Ellington's men, to find similar accommodation. They were quartered in various Bloomsbury hotels and rooming-houses, set away in the district of London which corresponds to New York's Greenwich Village, where there is no color line and there is much freedom, of all kinds.

Duke made a quick change when he got to the Dorchester and hurried past Hyde Park in confoundedly tangled traffic to Jack Hylton's for a cocktail party. Everybody was there, columnists, conductors, musicians, "heavy conductors, heavy musicians," as he called the big men in classical music who were there to do him preliminary homage. Tommy Driberg, who wrote a much-read column for the *Daily Express* under the signature of William Hickey, cornered Duke.

"Duke?" Tommy said, with a questioning tone.

"Mmm," Duke answered, with typical faraway tone to match the guileless look on his face that indicated tolerance, interest perhaps, but certainly not conviction, conviction about anything.

"Duke," Driberg continued, "what is hot?"

"Oh, hot," Duke repeated, "hot. Why hot is, er, hot is. Yes, hot is like a tree. Hot is a part of music, like the root is part of the tree, and the twigs and the leaves and the trunk; hot is to music as a root, a trunk, a twig, a leaf is to a tree." Duke really felt "hot" was like the fruit or blossom of a tree, its efflorescence. But he felt the distinction was too difficult to make. "Why, in England," he mused, *"Mood Indigo* is hot . . ."

Driberg didn't "dig" Duke, perhaps, but he was impressed. He did understand that there was something different about his music and the way it was written. He gleaned something of Duke's working routine and the atmosphere that surrounded him from their conversation together and in a column written a few days later he explained that "Ellington drinks sparkling Burgundy while he is composing," that "he composes best at five or six in the morning," that he didn't get up at that early hour to write but hadn't retired yet, that he would often play cards after work until the next noon, that going to bed before lunch-time is "regarded in Harlem as going to bed early."

Hylton's guests, most of England that was interested in the arts and many of its people who were not, were fascinated with this man and his bizarre world, where the hours were topsy-turvy and the very atmosphere turgid with intoxicated creativity. They were amazed that from America, from "Haarlem," as they insisted on spelling New York's Negro quarter, where everybody was so fabulously dissipated and the life was so perilously close to a numbing degeneration, such courtly manners could come. "He is quiet, friendly and deferential. When introduced to anyone he bows from the waist. He has a charming smile and plaintive eyes." "A pleasant cultured voice." An editorial in the *Express* nominated Duke as a representative of the colonies in the House of Commons. A good sample, a dignified representative. England wondered.

Hylton's house was a Mayfair showplace, a converted old building, long, low-roofed and patterned in black and white bricks. Very heavily luxurious appointments and at this cocktail party for Duke a great show of West End people. The door stood open from six that evening until nine as people flowed in to meet Ellington. The *Melody Maker* man covering the party was impressed by Duke's "wonderful and rare ability of making every single person to whom he spoke feel that that person was the most important in the room."

At nine Duke was rushed over to Broadcasting House with Jack Hylton and ten minutes after the hour the orderly reading of news bulletins was interrupted to put the two men on the air. A new kind of Duke spoke to England. All ad libbed, the conversation was as relaxed as some of the chats at Hylton's reception. They discussed Duke's music and his musical aims. Duke ended the program with solemn and honest affirmation of a fact.

"I am of little value," he said, "without my band."

The Dorchester was "overserviced," Duke says. He moved from one room to another. "It took them from four o'clock in the morning until seven that evening to find out I had moved." They didn't notify Duke of a change in program at the Palladium, where he was to open his first Monday in London, so he was late for the first show. He came on in time to make a bow. The audience had been made sufficiently impatient by the late placing of the band on the variety bill, thirteenth, but the smooth pacing of the band's show appeased them and they didn't seriously miss the absent leader.

Duke's Palladium program provoked serious criticism from his most earnest English fans, who wanted to hear *Blue Tune* and *Blue Ramble* and *Rose Room* and *Creole Rhapsody*, music that was less showy than what he did play but more important,

they felt, more fully representative of the band. They felt let
down by the presence in the band's portion of the bill of Bessie
Dudley, a hip-shaking dancer, and the tap team of Bailey and
Derby. But they did acknowledge that "the band was perfec-
tion in every note it played." And the audiences at the Palladium were wildly enthusiastic, pounded ·their applause at such
length that Ivie stumbled through *Stormy Weather* in tears at
the intensity of their feeling and the warmth of their appreciation.

Ring Dem Bells and *Three Little Words* opened the program. The Amos 'n' Andy film had reached England, and Duke,
mindful at this point of commercial tie-ups (Irving Mills was
with him on the trip), wasn't missing an obvious opportunity.
Ivie sang *Stormy Weather* and one of the bright pieces of
double-entendre patter which soon became standard stage stuff
for her, *Give Me a Man Like That*. The audience roared at the
wryness of Sonny's interpolated comments on Ivie's ideal man.
Bessie Dudley danced but the Ellington fans shielded their eyes
to pay better attention to what the band was playing, the
bumptious *Rockin' in Rhythm,* which they knew so well from
records. *The Whispering Tiger* was next, a pianissimo version of *Tiger Rag.* Duke had learned the value of understated
dynamics since his recording of *The Mystery Song* in 1931, in
which the number's theme was made mysterious by the way it
was first stated—so soft, way down. *Black and Tan Fantasy* kept
the mood quiet and restrained, with an added touch of the
lugubrious. Then Freddy Jenkins stomped on to stage center,
posed, and sang, danced and trumpeted his way through the
torchy song which Sophie Tucker had made an international
success, *Some of These Days.* Posey scored. Neither he nor the
audience wanted him to return to his seat to beat some cymbals
and clown in the background and carry his responsible trumpet
section load. Then the familiar strains of *Mood Indigo* elicited
enough attention to quiet the thrilled spectators and bring the
program to a properly triumphant conclusion.

Duke remained at the Palladium for two weeks, selling out at
each performance and getting all the response he and Mills

could have wished for from the press. Even the *Times* allowed some of the excitement to creep into its review of the show. From the heights of its austerity it granted that "Mr. Duke Ellington . . . is exceptionally and remarkably efficient in his own line. He does at once and with an apparently easy show of ingenuity what a jazz band commonly does with difficulty or fails to do. And the excitement and exacerbation of the nerves which are caused by the performances of his orchestra are the more disquieting by reason of his complete control and precision. It is not an orgy but a scientific application of measured and dangerous stimuli. . . . The expert, who could disregard their emotional effect," the *Times* conceded, "might conceivably derive an artistic enjoyment from his rhythms. But the ordinary listener probably does not and is probably not intended to do so. It is enough that the effect should be immediate and violent."

The broadcast from the B.B.C. studio caused considerable controversy. There was no audience to display its frenzy, and no room, therefore, for dyspeptic comment such as the *Daily Mail's* summing up of the effect of Ellington on England, a greater success "even than the Russian Ballet at its best . . . The primitive raw quality of his playing seems to have found an answering chord in the mentality of youth." There were other protests, however, letters to papers all over the country, such as one in the Sunderland *Echo* in which the writer thought "that in view of the present state of unemployment in this country the BBC could do much better by employing British artists, as it is with British money that the BBC is made possible." Some outlying papers were displeased. The Manchester *Guardian*, traditional Liberal voice of the British press, was stanchly conservative, if not reactionary, in its review of the Duke's broadcast: "When all arguments are finished it is surely true to say that something that is thoroughly ugly from start to finish is fairly to be opposed. Even the 'music' would be more bearable if the words were not so stupid and if the ideas which exist vaguely behind it were not so pathetically crude." The wonder is that the *Guardian* reviewer granted the existence of a realm of ideas in Ellington's world. Under the heading of "Enough Said," a reviewer in the Yorkshire *Observer* summed up his bad feeling: "Duke Ellington I suffered for 15 min. and then switched off. Give me Henry Hall every time."

It is hard to understand just what offended these reviewers. The broadcast on June 14 was an impressive review of the tunes by which the Ellington band had made its dual reputation among hot fans and with the larger unhep public. *East St. Louis Toodle-Oo, Lightnin', Creole Love Call, Old Man Blues, Rose Room, Limehouse Blues, Best Wishes* (specially composed for and dedicated to Great Britain), a *Blackbirds* medley, *Sophisticated Lady, It Don't Mean a Thing* and a few pop tunes not of Ellington authorship, headed by *I've Got the World on a String. Mood Indigo,* establishing the routine of all the programs on the European tour, was the finale. An engineer's fade-out on this Ellington staple brought the program to a close on diminishing sound. There was an abundance of good music on the forty-five-minute broadcast, very little talk, and, judging from the favorable comments of radio reviewers in general, it was a well-balanced airing carefully monitored by the B.B.C. engineer in charge to capture the strange sounds of this exotic organization.

Most of the response to the broadcast was favorable. The B.B.C.'s weekly newspaper, *Radio Times,* stuffed a full column with listeners' comment, almost all of it enthusiastic, some of it frantic with zeal. Interest in the band's first *Melody Maker* concert, on Sunday evening, June 25, was pitched to skyscraper height by the broadcast. There was wide debate on the merits of the orchestra and upon the particular value of the so-called commercial numbers.

After the concert, given at the Trocadero Cinema, dissension was not merely sharp: it led to talk of such bitterness that out of it grew the new anti-Ellington school with Patrick "Spike" Hughes at its head. The concert had started out in Ellington's mind as "the real, the true Ellington—no commercial endings at all." But half-way through the program Duke decided against that purist procedure. The audience, he could see, was fine on the hot numbers, "but on the slow numbers they sat back and said when do we get started." For the second half of the concert, "I went back and gave a vaudeville show with the B & K endings thrown in." (B & K are the initials of Balaban and Katz, owners of the leading chain of theaters in the Chicago area and famous for the elaborateness of their stage shows; each of their orchestral numbers ends with a coda thick with fanfare and flourish.) At a table afterward, Hughes and the other critics, amateur and professional, gave Ellington hell.

"That isn't you," they said, as if they really knew.

"Those people wanted something and I gave it to them," Duke said.

"You must show independence," the critics asserted.

"If they don't go for my high-powered jive," Duke answered, "then I'm going to lay down a little street for them."

"You have no Spirit of Independence," the critics returned, in an appeal to Ellington's American patriotism.

Jack Hylton and his wife sided with Duke, but they were "commercial," of course, and they, the Hyltons and Duke, lost the argument. At the next *Melody Maker* concert, three weeks later, the audience was presented with instructions by Spike, whom Ellington called the "Hot Dictator." When Tricky Sam plays you mustn't laugh, was the gist of Hughes' directions; it's art; and no applause in the middle of numbers. The audience didn't laugh, but Duke did, thinking about the wraps which Spike had thrown about Tricky's playing and the reaction to it. This was Duke's farewell appearance in England and the crowd that turned out listened with reverence to the program, carefully supervised by Spike and very satisfactory to that painstaking gentleman. Under the "Mike" alias he reported in the following week's *Melody Maker* that he enjoyed himself "so much last Sunday that there is very little for me to say in the way of criticism. . . . If a couple of thousand people have learned within three weeks that Cootie and Tricky are really expressing something extremely personal and moving, then there is indeed some hope that these same people will realise, by the time Duke gives another concert, that applause during the performance of a piece of music is not done in the best circles." He rather wished that the attack of gastritis which Freddy Jenkins suffered during the program had dampened his spirits, because "some of his antics were most distracting. . . . There is a time and a place for everything, but the muted brass passages of this piece are not an occasion for the waving of hands and such. On Sunday afternoons, in England, the stage is not a stage, but a concert platform, when it isn't a pulpit." After a remarkably personalized review in which Spike cited what "suits me" and indicted what did not, he ended with another reminder of audience etiquette. "P.S." he said. "Remember about the applause next time, won't you?"

Between concerts, the band toured England: Birmingham, Bolton, Liverpool, Blackpool, a number of theater dates and one or two dances, arranged by Hylton. In Liverpool, the band and the audience were surprised by a visit from the Prince of Wales, who was in town on his way to the international golf competition for the Ryder Cup at Southport. The Prince and his party took their places in the two-shilling seats, front row of the stalls (orchestra), in the middle of one of the early turns on the bill and remained through to the end of the show. He requested one or two numbers which the band played with pleasure: "We played like mad." The musicians were all so set up by the presence of the Prince that "we didn't know when to stop." Finally, they played *The King (God Save)* "very majestically."

"I am very sincere about *The King*," Duke says.

When Duke got to Scotland to play a week at the Empire Theatre in Glasgow, just after his first concert in London, he found eager reporters, anxious to know all about him and his music, men who had read every word printed in the London papers and thought he would be good copy.

"Some people say that my music is uncouth," he told Glaswegians, "and without form—a weird conglomeration of blatant discords which never has and never will mean anything at all. But what, may I ask you as Scotsmen, do the same people think about bagpipe music?" He twinkled.

F*

"My contention about the music we play," he continued, "is that it is also folk music, the result of our transplantation to American soil, and the expression of a people's soul just as much as the wild skirling of bagpipes denotes a heroic race that has never known the yoke of foreign dictatorship."

Duke warmed to the subject. "There is an inherent feeling for wild music in Scottish nature and there is a definite relationship between the rhythms of reels and the Highland fling and the music I play."

He spoke of "the fury with which people have attacked me through the press and personal letters," noted several examples of choice invective and rude metaphor which had been leveled at him, and then answered "one gentleman" who wanted to know why his music was called "hot music." But then, Duke said, "So do I. My music isn't 'hot music.' It is essentially Negro music, and the elaborations of self-expression." After his trip to England, for many years Duke called his work "Negro music," declining to have it classified as "hot" or "jazz" or "swing" or any other categorical name which might be given it.

As were the English, the Scots were impressed with his dress and his manners, "of the public school quality—or better." The space devoted to him in the Glasgow papers was large, and universally receptive articles filled it.

Meanwhile, in the London papers, the controversy over the Ellington band spread from the gossip columns and the theater reviewers to the dignified pages of the music critics. Such eminents as the old Ernest Newman and the young Constant Lambert stated their positions. Newman was not pleased. In a memorable phrase, he termed Duke "a Harlem Dionysus drunk on bad bootleg liquor." Lambert, a vigorous and talented composer himself *(Rio Grande)*, did not answer Newman directly. But several of his pieces in the *Radio Times* and the *Sunday Referee* came right to the point. Their directness and their freedom from moral or pigmentary prejudice gave them distinction. The logic of Lambert's musical analysis added critical conviction. He summed up for the defense:

The orchestration of nearly all the numbers shows an intensely musical instinct, and after hearing what Ellington can do with fourteen players in pieces like *Jive Stomp* and *Mood Indigo,* the average modern composer who splashes about with eighty players in the Respighi manner must feel a little chastened. All this is clearly apparent to anyone who visits the Palladium, but what may not be so apparent is that Ellington is no mere bandleader and arranger, but a composer of uncommon merit, probably the first composer of real character to come out of America.

Until Duke left England, the controversy was continued in the dailies and weeklies. Stanley Nelson kept up a peppery discussion of the aphrodisiac qualities of Ellington's music in *The Era.*

ELLINGTON—AND AFTER

ART OR DEBAUCHERY?

MUSIC OF REVOLT

And then another: "SEXOPHONE" AND SIN. Nelson said that he refused to go along with Freud on the ubiquity of sexual desire and stimulation and made a serious distinction between the reaction of listeners and the intent of composers. He contended that Ellington's music "possesses as much of variety of appeal as even the Masters." Not denying that "music has well-defined links with sex," he added that he had little doubt that many musicians had been successful because of "their attractive qualities in the physical sense." He told the story of James Huneker, famous American music critic early in this century, "who, after a recital by Paderewski in New York, went round counting the number of seats in the hall affected by the emotion of the occupants."

In an article in *New Britain,* critic John Cheatle gave Duke credit for creating a mob hysteria much like that attributed in later years to Benny Goodman and then to Frank Sinatra. The members of the audience "sit and clutch hands, gasp, goggle their eyes and jig their knees to the rhythm . . . [they] need to be psycho-analysed." Reviewing a quotation from Ellington, he was vitriolic.

Ellington:

> . . . The characteristic melancholy music of my race has been
> forged from the whiteheat of our sorrows, and from our grop-
> ings after something tangible in the primitiveness of our lives
> in the early days of our American occupation.

Cheatle:

> Now I agree that the "melancholy" of the Negro Spiritual in
> its primitive form, before it was ruined by concert arrange-
> ments, was a significant and moving thing. . . . But it is infuriat-
> ing to be told that a bunch of highly-paid, over-sophisticated
> jazz players, whose music is almost entirely European in char-
> acter, are entertaining us with racial tears in their hearts.
> Down, Pagliacci! Out, Sonny Boy! I submit that Duke Elling-
> ton's delicious Blues have no more to do with the Sorrows of
> Captivity than De Falla's Ballets with the Defeat of the Spanish
> Armada.

Cheatle hoped, he said, that the quotation was "the work of
a too-enthusiastic press agent; to whom we may also owe the
statement that in America Duke Ellington has been seriously
compared with Bach and Delius." Wrong on both hopes, of
course. Duke actually did say that he believed his music came
from the Negro's sorrowful past; Percy Grainger really had
compared him to Bach and Delius in a lecture at New York
University. Cheatle was willing to accept the Delius comparison
because of the patent similarity of chords and progressions of
the two composers. He rejected Bach: "The only thing the two
composers have in common is a certain rhythmic persistence. It
were as sensible to compare a geranium with the Botanical Gardens."

Whether or not Ellington's stature is in any way comparable
to that of Bach or Delius, lesser than the former's, greater than
the latter's, perhaps, or incomparably different, as different as
jazz trumpets from Spanish tambourines, is all beyond this
story. But Cheatle's disavowal of racial antecedents in Duke's
music is highly questionable. Ellington did not and could not
claim that his music expressed something in his blood, something he was born with that took musical shape almost auto-

matically. He was talking of the culture of his people, a culture
shaped by years of servitude and of inevitable sorrow, of a melancholy of a people that is beyond contention if you know the
people. Surely the pay and the sophistication of the performers
are not guarantees against a sadness they see all about them
and inherit along with the color of their skins. It isn't a congenital melancholy: it is in the world about them and it is almost impossible for a Negro to live without it. These are not
Pagliaccis: when they laugh, it is not through tears, but rather
in alternation with their lachrymose laments. And if at times
this interchanging of tears and laughter presents the bloody
aspect of a Pagliacci it is because the world has made such
clowns of its dark-skinned entertainers. To their glory they
have made high art of this sometimes piteous buffoonery, something more than can be said for Leoncavallo's drum-beater.

From every point of view, Duke made exciting copy during
his trip in England. Writers moralized, praised and censured;
they admired and reviled his music. The staid British were left
with a deep concern for jazz and for the man they accepted as its
high priest. Some mounted pulpits, real or imaginary, to con-
demn the music of Ellington; others gave it a place beside that
of the titans of traditional music. His imprint upon the national
consciousness was deep and indelible; it is still with them.

As the press gave itself over to lengthy discussion of the virtues and defects of his music and to starry-eyed wonder at the
courtliness of the American Duke, so did British society lionize
him. There was the first cocktail party thrown by Jack Hylton,
and a reciprocal fete:

Mr. Irving Mills and Mr. Duke Ellington
request the pleasure of the company of

———————————————

at a
Cocktail Party
at 5 p.m., Friday, July 14th
in the
Park Suite, Dorchester Hotel, W. 1
on the occasion of a
Presentation to Mr. Jack Hylton

R.S.V.P.   Dorchester Hotel, Park Lane, W. 1

Handsomely printed cards set in script announced the party. An impressive crowd greeted their American hosts and wit-nessed the exchange of felicitations between Ellington and Hylton.

There was the party thrown by the ornamental members of Punch's Club, at the Mayfair Hotel in London's West End. Duke and the band played at the party, and the rotogravure pages of the Sunday supplements and the social pages of the monthlies noted the elegants of British society, the characters out of Evelyn Waugh, Lords and Ladies and the Maharajah of Rajpipla attentive to *Mood Indigo,* film stars dancing to *Sophisticated Lady.* "A Syncopated Brew," the *Bystander* called it. "Punch's Club parties are more exclusive than the Royal Enclosure," the *Daily Express* explained to its readers from the lower world and added that six hundred people got invitations to a room that usually holds three hundred—and they all came. A Duke was a greater draw than a Maharajah that night. The King's oculist, an important gossip writer and Irving Mills were almost refused admittance, and the gossip columns were open-mouthed. The spaces between the lines were bigger than usual: "I saw many coloured dresses—and many coloured faces," one wrote. "There was the brown-faced Maharajah of Rajpipla. And, of course, Duke Ellington and his band."

But the big party was Lord Beaverbrook's, a party given for the Prince of Wales. "We were way up," Duke says, "feeling mellow. They were serving nothing but wine all night long—good nectar, too." For every drink served the guests, there was one for the band. "I had a rich feeling," Duke remembers, "playing piano and posing."

A slight-looking man came up to Duke, bent over the piano and asked a question.

"Hm?" Duke replied.

"Would you play *Swampy River?*" he repeated.

"You know how it is," Duke answered, "I never play piano solos. You know how it is."

The man left, but soon returned to ask for *Swampy River* again. He was persistent. So was Duke.

"I never do solos," Duke explained patiently. "The solos are for the boys in the band."

The slight man departed and Irving Mills caught Duke's ear. "Know who that was?"

"No."

"That was Prince George."

Duke took an extra-long gulp of his drink, "a deep breath of wine." Then he heard his name mentioned, and there in the middle of the floor was the Prince of Wales speaking about him. A long eulogy, an extravagant speech. He was impressed with Duke. Needless to say, the Duke was impressed with the Prince. After the speech the Prince approached him.

"Won't you have a drink with me?" Windsor asked Ellington.

"Delighted." They found their way to the bar together.

"What are you drinking, Duke?" Edward asked Edward.

"Why, gin."

"I'll have the same." (Up to that time Duke had always thought gin was a sort of low drink. "Since that time," he says, "I've always felt rather grand when I drank gin.")

Before many drinks had passed, Duke knew both Princes at the party and Prince George came over to play some piano with Duke. Then the Prince of Wales turned to Sonny.

"Sonny," he said, "how'd you like me to show you how to play drums?"

"It's all yours. Take over," he said, and bowed. The Prince returned the bow.

"Lord Fauntleroy stuff, I'll bet," Sonny whispered to Braud, the bass-player. He decided differently, though, when the Prince had played a set with the band. "Good hot drums," Duke said, and he meant it.

Just before leaving England, the band hurried to Decca's studios to do one record date. Ellington's contract with Brunswick had expired with his last recording session before leaving New York and his new one with Victor was not yet in force, so the Decca tie-up was feasible. But there wasn't much time, and when something went wrong with the machines, turning out several masters off-center, they had to be content with only one master for the last record, *Chicago*, which was not just unorthodox but dangerous in case something happened to it. The only set piece at the session was *Harlem Speaks*, which the band had done at its last American date. The others, *Chicago, Ain't Misbehavin'* and *Hyde Park*, were all head arrangements, sequences of solos with roughed backgrounds. *Hyde Park* was based on the chords of several songs and first was named *Park Lane*, after the street bordering Hyde Park on which the Dorchester Hotel was located; it was advertised under its first title in Paris, when the band got there, but its tony name was relinquished in favor of the less chic but better known home of England's soap-box orators. The record sounded more like rabble gabble than like the dulcet sonorities of Duke's social friends.

Prince George wanted to be in on the record date, but at the last minute Scotland Yard vetoed his plans: too many people knew about his coming, they said, and they would not be responsible. The band had a ball, anyway, loading up at the next-door pub, Six Bells (after which Spike Hughes named his best known jazz composition, *Six Bells Stampede*), before going into the studio. "By the time we got to *Chicago*, the last of the sides, we didn't know whether we were in Chicago or Egypt."

The band stayed high in Paris. There were three concerts, two at the famous Salle Pleyel in Paris, on successive Saturdays, July 22 and 29, and *"enfin avant de s'embarquer pour l'Amérique, Duke Ellington et son fameux Orchestre donneront leur dernier concert en Europe, Dimanche soir 30 Juillet, au Casino de Deauville."* The rest of the time, the boys partied. Toby refurbished old friendships, and Bricktop, overjoyed to see all her Washington and New York friends again, threw a terrific ball for the band. Most impressive moment of the evening was the carrying-in of the huge champagne bottle, taller than any of the bandsmen, so big it had to be held by four waiters. The sparkle that was seen that night!

Paris was ready for Duke. A few years earlier the distinguished critic, Henri Prunières, the French opposite number of the London *Times'* Ernest Newman, had written his impressions of the band in *La Revue musicale:*

> *Duke Ellington ne fait qu'un avec ses musiciens. Assis au centre, tournant le dos aux trompettes et au trombone, il dirige au moyen des mouvements du corps. Il est placé face à la batterie qui le sépare des saxophones et de la clarinette. Derrière les saxos, le banjo, la contrebasse (utilisée comme percussion) et les tambours. Ainsi l'orchestre forme trois sections. Parfois une section se lève en jouant. L'emploi de ces sections qui opèrent à l'intérieur de l'orchestre offre de grandes ressources, surtout si l'on se sert des solistes. On peut ajouter à tout ceci les effets de la "perspective," par exemple, lorsqu'on renverse la position respective de la melodie et de l'accompagnement. Les combinaisons semblent illimitées.*

The French musicians who worked in the music of tradition were fascinated by the instrumentation of the Ellington band, by the inner voicings of Duke's writing, by the texture of his sound. Like Prunieres, they concentrated on the seating of the band, and noted their amazement at the great resources the four saxes, six brass and four rhythm provided. "The combinations seem unlimited."

Prunières and others were interested, too, in Duke's much-repeated assertion that he would not read Rimsky-Korsakov's Treatise on Harmony, which had been sent him, or any other basic musical text. *"Il croit que la musique a perdu de sa force depuis qu'on l'a enfermée en des formules,"* Prunières explained, *"et vraiment il a poussé au plus haut point le système de l'improvisation collective."* The French, engaged in the production and appreciation of the most lusty classical music of our day, that of Ravel and Honegger, Milhaud and Ibert, were more than merely tolerant of Ellington's jazz. They were delighted to hear the original music which had been imitated so often by "Les Six," Milhaud, Honegger, Poulenc, Germaine Tailleferre, Auric and Louis Durey. They were delighted to hear original music.

The large numbers of hot jazz enthusiasts in Paris were, of

course, overwhelmed by the presence in their city of their idol. Hugues Panassié and Charles Delaunay, whose writings formed the base of the European jazz movement, were in constant attendance upon the band and showed Duke such of Paris as Bricktop and her associates did not know or care to show. From all over the near-by continent, Ellington enthusiasts came to hear the band, from Holland, Belgium and Switzerland, from Germany. There were the foreign jazz magazines to hail the coming and get the audiences out—*De Jazzwereld* in Holland, *Music* in Belgium, *Jazz* in Switzerland, *Jazz Tango Dancing* in France (Panassié had not yet started his magazine, *Hot Jazz*), *Musik Echo* in Germany. These jazz journals had antedated by some years the serious appreciation of the art in this country in magazines of its own. Their followers turned up in ardent numbers in Paris during Ellington's week there.

The band sailed from France on the *Majestic*, everybody still loaded. Duke was carried along on champagne and brandy ("That is the most glorious glow—and good for seasickness").

Somebody commented on how drunk Duke was.

"Not drunk," Duke explained, "just unworried. That's the way to travel the ocean. You must go on board right, with no worries, no weight on your mind. Then take it slow and it goes easy, it goes on in pastels."

Just as he had hoped, the European trip had proved a heady, happy tonic for Duke. For him it was one long ball. With the traditional attitude of the publicity-seeking gentleman, "I don't care what you say about me as long as you spell the name right," he had provoked as much controversy and won as much newspaper magazine space as English channel swimmers, winners of the Loterie Nationale and murderers, and over a much longer period than those three-day wonders. And since most of the controversy was honest and Duke's participation in the tortuous musical discussions entirely sincere, the space had been well won. He genuinely didn't care what people said about him, though he did want more than his name spelled right: he wanted his views presented properly. He could not have gained more co-operation toward this end if he had bought the space.

There was some disappointment among the boys in the band, a reinforced bitterness about the bigotry of whites the world over. However, they couldn't help being flattered by the meticulous attention that had been paid their every recorded note and by the way their footsteps were dogged by fervent admirers all over England, and again in Paris and Deauville. And for all the contagion of America's prejudices, which had carried in some degree overseas, the general attitude of the English and French had been one of warm friendship toward the musicians. No matter what the disappointments, Europe left the Ellington musicians with almost as much self-confidence as Duke himself felt. Duke put it succinctly, if somewhat melodramatically. "The main thing I got in Europe was *spirit;* it lifted me out of a bad groove. That kind of thing gives you courage to go on. If they think I'm *that* important," Duke mused, "then maybe I have kinda said something, maybe our music does mean something."

CHAPTER ELEVEN

DALLAS DOINGS

I WON'T GO SOUTH," DUKE HAD SAID, MANY TIMES.
"I don't care what they offer me," he told Irving Mills. They offered a lot of money. Mills turned down one-nighter fees of $1500, which was very big money in the thirties and isn't too small even today. But Duke didn't want to go South. He didn't like the thought of going down where his people had been so miserably treated, where the treatment was still so bad, where Negroes were lynched and, like "Untouchables," sat in the back of busses and trolley cars and trains in special Jim Crow sections. He didn't want to play in ballrooms and theaters where the colored patron would be forcibly separated from the white.

When Duke returned from Europe, however, some of his objections to the South had been dissipated. He was no longer a stranger to strangeness; he was willing to experiment at almost anything. His spirits were sufficiently buoyed by that European trip, by the magnificent reception abroad, so that even the South seemed a real possibility; Mills got to work and turned up with a lucrative trip through Texas for the autumn of 1933. It was epochal journey: it was the first complete tour of Interstate s in the Texas territory by a Negro band. And with the ater tour, dances were booked, some white, some colored, some mixed (though separated by balcony or boxes from a direct contact).

Dallas, Texas, went wild. Long before Duke arrived in the big city, its newspapers were filled with stories about Ellington and his musicians. It was like England all over again. There were the routine stories, announcing the booking of the band for the Majestic Theatre for a week's engagement with subsidiary billing for Ivie Anderson, "well-known blues singer," and Snake-hips Tucker, "gelatinous dancer," Bailey and Darby, the dancers who accompanied Duke on the European tour, Jess Cryor, a singer, and Sonny Greer. There were great streamer headlines in the white as well as the Negro newspapers.

DUKE ELLINGTON, ONCE SODA-JERKER, SLIPPED INTO MUSIC RACKET

AMERICA'S "HOT AMBASSADOR" TO VISIT DALLAS THIS WEEK-END

DUKE ELLINGTON TO INVADE DALLAS

DUKE ELLINGTON—HERE NEXT SATURDAY

MAJESTIC MAKES SPECIAL PREPARATION FOR ELLINGTON

Great black banners across the top of amusement pages of Dallas newspapers, headlines accompanied, as often as not, by pictures of Duke, pictures of a size and dignity with the headlines. Negroes were very rarely seen in Dallas or any other Texas newspapers. The *Dispatch* reproduced from the movie short, *Black and Tan Fantasy,* a shot of piano and hands in the foreground and Duke's shadow large in the background; it seemed to fit the caption, "Dusky Player of Weird Melodies"; it obviated the necessity of printing his picture in that paper.

The *Dispatch* also used cartoons to avoid using Duke's photograph: one of Duke alone, one of Ivie and Duke and a clarinetist who, in this strange caricature, bore no relation to anyone in the band. The *Dispatch* ran the sketch of Ellington right underneath a photo of Carole Lombard, whose movie, *Brief Moment,* was being shown with Duke's stage show at the Majestic. The juxaposition of white and colored, even if the latter were caricatured, was an innovation in Texas.

The *News* printed a close-up of Duke's hands at the piano,

with the head, "Another Pair of Hands in History," and the caption, "The square palms and spatulate fingers of Duke Ellington are gaining a certain immortality in the field of jazz, a field that draws nearer and nearer to classical music."

There were stories on "Duke's Jazz Glossary," a rather fancified sketch of the verbal idiom of jazz gleaned from Wilder Hobson's article in *Fortune* of that year 1933, *Introducing Duke Ellington*. There were others outlining the history of the band and its triumphs at the Kentucky and Cotton Clubs and before European royalty. As in England, Percy Grainger's comparison of Duke with Bach and Delius was given wide airing. Delius, though not a native son as he was in England, had lived in Florida, and he was better known in the South than other contemporary British composers. The comparison was well made for Texas appreciation.

References to Duke were not always as leader of a Negro band, but Texas readers were not to forget the color of his skin or his musicians. "Dusky" was the adjective and it was used over and over again. "Dusky entertainers." "The dusky Duke Ellington." "Duke Ellington and Cab Calloway own the two most famous negro [sic] bands in the world are both dusky instead of dark skinned."

When the band finally made its appearance, the newspapers went far out of their way to give its stage show great space and thorough review. Their enthusiasm was unbounded. Under heads about the "Greatest Band of Today," "Harlem's Aristocrats of Rhythm," "Greatest Jazz Band Today Sends Crowds Into Cheers," they hailed the Ellington organization. "Ellington is by far the greatest player of jazz sitting at the piano today." "It was a great show. . . ." "Duke Ellington does not possess the sensational showmanship of Cab Calloway, who brought the first big negro band to the Majestic theatre last spring . . . [but] his stage show . . . is a much better show than that presented by Calloway. His band is far superior to Calloway's." Comparisons between Duke and Cab were inevitable. Close friends, the one discovered by the other, they were each other's closest rivals in the decade between 1930 and 1940.

Again there was the intense audience reaction. "At moments when the band got really 'hot' the audience was worked into a frenzy. A symphony of tapping feet, humming voices and clapping hands permeated the Majestic."

Dallas turned out to hear the man so highly praised by its newspaper writers. All records for the theater were broken. Two dances, one white and one colored, had been scheduled for the Ice Palace. An additional one was set at the Baker Hotel Peacock Terrace, Dallas' premier dance spot, the night of his last show at the Majestic. Into the early hours of Saturday morning, Dallas whites danced to the music of "the greatest of jazz bands," a Negro orchestra. ". . . Our grandfathers would have given any odds as to the improbability of his appearance," one Dallas writer said. Another, interviewing Duke just before he left Dallas, reported on the arrangements made for quartering him and his musicians: Duke lived in an apartment on Caddo Street, "where with a rented piano he works on new compositions. . . . Ellington's musicians, several of whom are accompanied by their wives, live in private negro homes or in apartments during the engagement at the Majestic and also in other Southern cities." This same writer reported on Duke's projected "negro suite . . . five parts. . . . [which] will trace negro music from its source in the African jungle." He quoted Duke directly and fairly, though Duke's concluding words were strong for a white newspaper in the South: "I shall look into the future for the fifth and last movement, probably a hundred years from now, and give a recapitulation, an apotheosis aiming to put the negro in a more comfortable place among the people of the world and a return to something he lost when he became a slave."

Dallas had been interested in everything Duke did or said, where and how he and his musicians lived. It was the same all over again in Fort Worth, near-by Texas metropolis, which had been infected with the Ellington disease while Duke was playing Dallas. The same articles, many of them, or rough paraphrases of the Dallas originals, appeared in the Fort Worth papers. And the people responded all over again. Wherever the band played in the Southwest, on the Interstate circuit, the Dallas pattern was repeated. Duke's fears for his people in the South, though hardly groundless, were palliated for himself.

In spite of the good treatment he'd had, Duke was fearful as he approached an interview over a Missouri radio station. The announcer called him *Mister* Ellington. Duke thought he detected an ironic edge in the salutation.

"*Mister* Ellington," the announcer asked him, after they were on the air, "how do you compose your music, what procedure do you follow, *Mister* Ellington?"

And later, "*Mister* Ellington, what is your own favorite of all the music you have written?"

Routine questions were mixed with a few that seemed as pointed as the *Mister*. These were questions about the luxury of his Harlem home, his eminence as a bandleader, his large number of records. Was the announcer, with his *Misters* and his detailed picture of the financial and social and musical success of the "Nigra" Duke Ellington, suggesting that Duke had no right to his success, that no Negro had a right to any such success?

By the time the interview was over and he and the announcer had exchanged a few informal words, Duke decided he had been wrong. The announcer was genuinely respectful; he was genuinely interested in Duke's music and personality and habits of living. Duke made a·few more adjustments in his thinking about the South. There were still more to come.

A trip to New Orleans a year later brought Duke South again. This time the band traveled in two railroad cars of its own, because no matter how much better the South seemed now than it had in Duke's mind before his first-hand experience down there, he had seen little dissolution of traditional color bars and he did not want to have to hunt for accommodations in some back-of-the-tracks slum. A baggage car held their instruments and the band's music; a sleeping car bedded the organization. The cars were rolled into the New Orleans station, pushed onto a siding and the band had a home for the duration of its stay.

The first thrill in the city below the bayous was the reception for Barney. Barney Bigard was a native son, New Orleans' own, and New Orleans remembered. A huge crowd down to meet the band broke up into smaller contingents which huddled around their favorite musicians. Then the great mass of the people surged forward as they saw Barney.

"How yah, man?" they asked the clarinetist.

"That's our Barney," they yelled.

"Hooray for Barney," they cheered.

Barney was escorted through the streets of New Orleans. He was followed whever he went in the jazz quarter, close to old Storeyville, where he and most of the other famous New Orleans jazz stars had played. The home town boy had made good.

In New Orleans, too, a children's club, an all-white organization of youngsters, demonstrated fervent support of Duke and his music without a moment's attention to differences in color or background, without prejudice. Duke was deeply touched.

Duke ate in New Orleans, ate as he had eaten in New York, Chicago, and points West, in London and Glasgow and Paris. He discovered a few dishes that ranked with the best he'd had in Europe or New York or Chicago. He discovered that the reputation New Orleans enjoyed as a great eating city was well deserved. He discovered gumbo, gallon-large portions of it, New Orleans fashion, crabmeat on the soft-shell, chicken or lamb, chunks of some other meat, shrimp and rice, covered with a very thin but very hot sauce. Duke ordered it by the pail. When he left New Orleans, he took a pail with him. He had to have some on the train. He walked down to the train swinging a bucket of gumbo, good Creole gumbo, in front of him. About a block from the station he noticed that there was a huge crowd gathered. He wondered what was up. A few steps farther and he saw. Spotting a few of his bandsmen's faces, he realized that the crowd was down to see the Ellington crew off, the crowd was down in force. He looked at himself. Dressed in sloppy sports attire, hat slouched back on his head, brim up, swinging a pail of gumbo, he looked like a happy worker on a day off. He couldn't face the crowd that way. He decided to walk all the way around the train and come in by the last car.

Arrived at the last car, Duke tried to open the door. Locked. He walked around the other side, tried that door. Locked. He rapped on the door. No answer. He banged. No answer. He kicked at the door with his feet. Finally a steward screamed from within.

"Go away, man, git."

"What you mean, git?" Duke screamed back. "It's me!"

"Me who?" the steward yelled.

"Duke, Duke," Duke identified frantically, as he heard some young fans come dashing down to his end of the train.

The steward opened the door just in time. Duke made an unceremonious exit from New Orleans, but he didn't spoil the glamorous impression he and his music had made upon the people of the city, white and colored.

Along with the happier impression of the South which Duke's first two long-delayed trips to that region left with him, there was a sad and bitter one. Noting the extraordinary courtesy of gas station attendants, of hotel workers and little people everywhere in the South, Duke made a conclusion. With this courtesy, he paired the excessive poverty he saw throughout the Southern states he visited.

"Hungry people are nice," Duke summed up his impression. "It's not pleasant to see that and know it, but it's true. Hungry people are nice. And the South is full of hungry people."

Duke did find more than the hungry people nice. He has felt ever since those first trips South that the future of that region, associated with such sorrow and pain and ugliness for his people, might very well be a good future. The South, Duke felt, was a source of both misery and happiness for the Negro, and after close personal contact with it, and with its people, he felt the misery might be overcome and the happiness elevated and widely disseminated.

CHAPTER TWELVE

STEPPING INTO
SWING SOCIETY

T HEY WEREN'T CALLING IT "SWING" IN 1934, BUT THE GERMS
of something new were taking hold. Duke was doing all
right, his reputation big, his one-nighter money holding
up, and movies beckoning. The Mickey Mouse bands were
doing all right, too. But something else, not Mickey Mouse
certainly, fairly close to Duke, but closer, really, to Fletcher
Henderson, was coming up. Benny Goodman made a stab at the
bandleading business at Billy Rose's New York cabaret-restau-
rant, the Music Hall, and as one of the three bands on the
National Biscuit three-hour airing over NBC Saturday nights
(the other two were Xavier Cugat's, and a studio outfit under
Kel Murray). They were only stabs that Benny and a few other
men made in 1934. Duke wasn't bothered, and the music world
didn't pay much attention.

Duke went out to Hollywood, to play Sebastian's Cotton Club
and to make a couple of movies for Paramount. He was set
first for *Murder at the Vanities,* a mystery film built around
Earl Carroll's Hollywood theater-restaurant. The band came on
in eighteenth century costumes, bewigged and befrocked and
bejabo-ed, because some anachronistic studio designer thought
the eighteenth-century costumes proper for the performance of
Liszt's *Second Hungarian Rhapsody,* an *echt* nineteenth-century work. After just enough measures to recognize the Liszt
warhorse, a quick dissolve brought the boys back in dinner
jackets and a change of tempo. The *Hungarian* became the
Ebony Rhapsody, and was submitted to a vigorous Ellington

revitalization. Rewriting Liszt wasn't Duke's idea; it was Sam Coslow's and Arthur Johnston's. They did it and Duke improved upon their "improvement."

Coslow and Johnston were *the* writers that year: they wrote twenty-eight songs, almost all hits. Duke recorded two big hits from *Murder at the Vanities*—*Cocktails for Two* and *Live and Love Tonight*. They were recorded in Hollywood, with Toby and Tizol out of the band. Toby just missed the recording date; Tizol had been out for a year, reducing the trombones to a duo.

That pairing and *Ebony Rhapsody* were successful records, but there was more distinction in seven earlier sides he made for Victor in Chicago, in 1933 and 1934, and more money in at least one of them. The distinction may be found in abundance in *Daybreak Express* and *Dear Old Southland*. The one was an imitation, chug for chug, toot for toot and choo for choo, of a railroad engine, just as brash as Arthur Honegger's famed *Pacific 231*, and much less monotonous, as a result of being confined to the length of a three-minute ten-inch record. The other was the popular tune fashioned from the spiritual, *Deep River*, given new color and added poignancy by Tricky Sam's growl trombone. Louis Bacon, Ivie's husband, was added to the trumpet section very briefly, and sang *Southland* and *Rude Interlude*, which was more complete than an interlude, and much more reflective than rude. *Delta Serenade* was in this same mood; *Dallas Doings* and *Stompy Jones* were jump tunes, the last as infectious as its name. *Blue Feeling* expressed just that. These were seven distinguished sides, all as impressive today as when they were made, but none the moneymaker that the eighth turned out to be.

Solitude was recorded in Chicago on January 10, 1934. A little over a year later it became an enormous hit, Duke's biggest to that date. Fitted with lyrics by Eddie De Lange, it sold thousands of records and hundreds of thousands of sheet-music copies. When Duke moved back to Brunswick in 1935, he had to record it all over again. Will Hudson used the chords of an earlier Ellington tune, *Lazy Rhapsody*, and fashioned another tune from them, *Moonglow*, which went on to the same great success; in mood and manner it was much like *Solitude*. Duke recorded *Moonglow* and backed the second version of *Solitude* with it.

After *Murder at the Vanities*, Paramount found a few spots for the band in the Mae West film, *Belle of the Nineties*, just getting under way. The band did two more Coslow and Johnston tunes, *Troubled Waters* and *My Old Flame*, and its record performances of these songs, coupled together, sold very well. Ivie's sensitive singing of imaginative tunes and lyrics was probably responsible for the record's success, but, as usual, she got backing from the band consonant with the songs and her singing of them.

Two full-length movies completed, Paramount made use of the band for a short, *Symphony in Black*. Ten minutes long, the short employed most of the clichés usually associated with the dramatic presentation of Negroes. Right out of Oscar Hammerstein's lyric for *Ol' Man River*, big, black colored men sweated and strained, loading heavy bales into storehouses on river wharves; they stoked blast furnaces. And then, for surefire audience appeal, there was a brief little story, the eternal triangle, the theme of jealousy underlined heavily and the figurative blues accompanied by blues figurations. But the music was good, and when the short was issued in 1936, it won some acclaim, though no award as *Black and Tan* had. Perhaps the prizemakers had begun to spot the disquieting overtones in the hoked-up stock Negro characters.

The movies were good, and they paid off, but the Coast wasn't as interested in 1934 as it had been in '32. Audiences were sparse at the Cotton Club: only Ellington diehards, the true fans and musicians, came around to pay their respects and Mr. Sebastian's tabs. Wingy Mannone, the trumpeter, singer and character, who made California his headquarters, summed up this apathy: "Swing," said Wingy, a few years later, "hadn't come over the mountain yet."

The rest of the country was more interested. There were the Southern jaunts, filled with expectations, with fears and hopes

and genuine thrills as Duke and the boys discovered some signs
of health and tolerance below the line. There were one-nighters
through every state in the union, and theater tours, with ups
and downs, but just enough of the former, as the band broke
records, to keep salaries comfortable and squawks down to a
minimum. There was talk of an engagement at the leading
Chicago night club, the Chez Paree, or the College Inn of the
Hotel Sherman, where most of the leading dance bands of that
era played. But neither materialized. James Caesar Petrillo,
President of Local 10, the white Chicago local of the American
Federation of Musicians, was very anxious to keep all out-of-
town orchestras, white or colored, from his city. He didn't rule
against them; he just discouraged their booking.

The band stumbled from one one-night stand to another.
There were hardships on the road, difficulties of securing living
space in some of the towns, Jim Crow hell in others, and the
eternal grind, from ballroom to ballroom to ballroom with
little time or space between to breathe, to sit down and rest
a little and live like other people. There was a good quota
of grumbling in the band, and ugly rumors began to spread in
the music business. George Frazier, who ran a jazz column in
the *Boston Traveller* under the head of *Swingin' Lightly*,
swung heavily:

> The greatest jazz band of all time may break up! Word is
> making the rounds that seven of Duke Ellington's boys are soon
> to leave him—the entire sax section, Wellman Braud, and two
> others. . . . It's not the easiest thing imaginable to think of
> Duke's working without that sax section. . . . There are innu-
> merable arrangements that he never bothered to transcribe to
> manuscript paper, a fact that makes one just a bit worried
> about his losing men whose playing is permeated with the dy-
> namic Ellington personality. It'll be a bad bringdown if that
> band of his splits.

Actually, two men did leave. Braud, the least effective rhythm
man Duke ever had, left, and Duke hired two bass players to
take his place—not because two were needed to equal Wellman,
but simply because Duke wanted to hear lots of bass, and really

score for the instrument as a harmonic adjunct to the band. Billy Taylor, who had played a big-toned tuba and then a string bass for McKinney's Cotton Pickers, came in first. And then Hayes Alvis, who sold ladies' hats in a business association with his wife, took over the other bow. Whetsol left, too, but only briefly and because he was ill with the beginnings of a disease which was to wrack his body and torture his mind and finally kill him. For the few months he was gone, Charlie Allen took his place and played a competent section trumpet in his place.

The grumbling was growing; there were these rumors. There were genuine hardships, and then a serious blow. Mildred had wanted to speak to Duke about his mother, but she was hesitant. Since 1933, Dr. Thomas Amos, Mildred's doctor and consequently Duke's, had been warning Mildred.

"Mrs. Ellington is a sick woman," Dr. Amos said in 1933.

"She ought to go to the Medical Center," he said in 1934.

"She must go," he insisted later that year. But Aunt Day was afraid of surgeons and distrustful of hospitals. She refused to go.

By September, 1934, Duke's mother was aware of her illness. She knew she had cancer and she decided to go home to Washington. She would feel right in Washington; she would take massaging treatments. They would help, surely. She left New York.

Aunt Daisy refused to worry about herself. She was much more concerned about others. When Duke asked her about herself and about the treatments she was taking, she turned him aside.

"Never mind, Edward," she said. "How are you? How is your opera progressing?" She asked about individual members of the band and business associates, and refused to talk about herself. But talk about herself or not, the tissue-eating disease was slowly eroding her flesh. She allowed herself to be moved to Providence Hospital, a distinguished sanatorium and research center in Detroit. Duke arranged his bookings so he could be near her.

The move came too late. On May 27, 1935, with her children and husband beside her, Daisy Ellington died. Duke had spent the last three days of her life with his head on his mother's pillow. His customary love of food was gone and his sense of time departed with it. Such time as his mother had left he was determined to spend with her. He missed few of her sleeping and none of her waking moments, on May 25 and 26 and 27.

His mother's death was a terrifying shock. Duke repaired to the Bible, always a great solace, and to the inner confines of his own mind. He brooded, hours at a time.

"I have no ambition left," he told friends. "When Mother was alive, I had something to fight for, I could say, 'I'll fight with anybody, against any kinda odds. You wanna fight? O.K., because I'm fighting for my mother and the money I get will go to her.' Now what? I can see nothing. The bottom's out of everything."

The bottom did seem to be out of everything. It was hard to understand what was happening on records. Just signed with Brunswick, the first date had been a complete bust, apparently. None of the four sides made was released. Duke remade two of them: one, *Admiration,* in the remake, was released coupled with the new *Merry-Go-Round.* Another three sides, made later, were not issued. And of the eight sides which were issued, only four were Ellington originals. And of the four Ellington originals, the tune which became the biggest hit, *In a Sentimental Mood,* sold many more records for Ozzie Nelson and Benny Goodman than it did for Duke. This was another Hardwick song: you can hear Otto in one of his rare latter-day appearances on this record, better by far than the Goodman and Nelson performances which outsold it.

Discouraged and bewildered, Duke turned to his music and turned out a masterpiece, one of his few large-scale works, the first one since *Creole Rhapsody* and the first of a new series of compositions. This was *Reminiscing in Tempo,* four record sides inspired by the mood of his moment, the brooding over his mother's death. "It was written," Duke says, "in a soliloquizing mood. It begins with pleasant thoughts. Then something gets you down. Then you snap out of it, and it ends affirmatively." The four record sides follow a pattern roughly like

Duke's soliloquies, with alternate sadness and gladness expressed by his piano, the saxophones, muted trumpet and trombone. There is particularly moving plaintiveness in Cootie's muted trumpet solo on the second side, the third theme introduced in the work and the most enduring. This side ends with a brilliantly chorded piano solo, from which jazz pianists have been borrowing ever since. The plaintive trumpet tune comes back in statements by full orchestra and clarinet bringing the third side to its end. The last side, the most cohesive, is a recapitulation of the previous three, with solo trumpet and ensemble—carrying the thematic weight and the solemnity and the melancholy of the earlier portions of the work—giving way to something which, if not joyful, is at least not tearful. ". . . You snap out of it, and it ends affirmatively."

The reaction to *Reminiscing in Tempo* was angrily mixed. John Hammond, by this time Duke's severest critic, gave it scathing mention in *Down Beat*. "Arty" and "pretentious" were his words. Others praised or damned it, but without any attempt to analyze it, to identify the themes or call the solos or assay the mood. Even in England, there was such blank criticism as Edgar Jackson's in *The Gramophone:* Jackson admitted he did not understand it, though there was nothing, surely, so knotty about the music. In another English magazine, Leonard Hibbs gave *Reminiscing in Tempo* its only critical break: he submitted the composition to extended analysis. Hibbs admitted he thought at first, "it was dull and meaningless. . . . It wasn't jazz and it wasn't music. . . . At the same time, I had too high an opinion of Duke to think he would willingly perpetrate anything like the pointless joke that this appeared to be. . . ." After many listenings Hibbs saw the relation of the themes, a pattern of statement and restatement, and some organization of solos. The conclusion was easy: "Very briefly, I believe that Duke has allowed us to 'tune-in' on his mind at work."

The greatest controversy caused by the work was among college students. Caught up in the swing movement which Benny Goodman had brought to full flower, these youngsters through-

G

out America followed the time-honored procedure of their predecessors among hot jazz fans, the English Rhythm Club members and the French enthusiasts. They met over hot records, instead of hot stoves, and discussed with a fervor they did not bring to their more conventional studies the fine points of Bix and Fats and Jelly Roll and Benny. To their credit may it be said that in those first years of "swing," there was more interest in the live jazzmen than in their dead or putrefying progenitors. *Reminiscing in Tempo* satisfied this interest admirably. The debates rocked the country's campuses. The trend was to Goodman and Bob Crosby, to loud flag-wavers or "killer-dillers," with screeching trumpets and pounding rhythm and one improvised solo after another. That was swing, the kids decided. But was *Reminiscing in Tempo?* That was the question. This work of Duke's was twelve minutes long, four times as long as the other band pieces on records. It was carefully organized, not actually "more arranged" than the three-minute pieces of Goodman, but its solos were more a part of the conception of the whole than in Benny's jump numbers, and there was less rhythmic regularity here, abrupt changes of tempo, wandering in and out of tempo. This was a work more easily comparable to a short tone poem than to a swing number. And swing was the thing in 1935 and '36.

Duke had described "swing" in 1932. "It don't mean a thing if it ain't got that swing," he had said, and defined it. Swing was and is the way a jazz number is played, the syncopated lift a performer or ensemble gets into jazz performances. In the middle and late thirties, swing lost its standing as a verb and was elevated to the stature of a noun and a category. Jazz was dead, long live swing. There was no difference between the two kinds of music: they were and are one and the same, but distinctions were being made. Out with the old jazz, in with the new swing. Swing meant arranged big-band jazz to the majority of fans and musicians, who used it to denote and connote the new music. That was the explanation of the categorical difference. Now what about its musical meaning?

Benny Goodman's band had perpetrated this thing called swing; it was logical to ask Benny and his boys what "swing" meant. They had some interesting, conflicting and rather ambiguous answers.

Gene Krupa said it was "complete and inspired freedom on rhythmic interpretation." That was a drummer's answer, *the* drummer.

Jess Stacy, Benny's pianist, said it was "syncopated syncopation."

Benny himself said, "See John." John Hammond was Benny's aide, confidant and critical adviser. He spoke for Benny. With Marshall Stearns, president of the United Hot Clubs of America, English teacher at Yale, John produced a definition: "A band swings when its collective improvisation is rhythmically integrated." The best thing about this definition is that it uses the word properly, as the majority of musicians had been using it for years, as a verb.

Wingy Mannone explained swing: "Feeling an increase in tempo though you're still playing at the same tempo." He and Stacy were referring really to the setting of two rhythms against each other, triplets against steady quarter notes, three against two, polyrhythms, the thing Duke had been doing for years.

Glenn Miller, who in those years was identified simply as "swing trombonist," said it was "something that you have to feel; a sensation that can be conveyed to others."

Chick Webb, who didn't need to be identified, drew a picture. "It's like lovin' a gal, and havin' a fight, and then seein' her again."

And Louis Armstrong summed it all up: "Swing is my idea of how a tune should go." Nothing very clear, and yet something all the musicians knew and felt and understood, "how a tune should go." Swing was and is susceptible of definition: it is the rhythmic integration, but not in waltz or march tempo, of soloists or groups thereof or whole bands or just a section of a band. In the thirties, the more articulate musicians could have told anyone what swing was. But the commercial value of the commodity was in its mysterious elements and so swing was something indefinable, hazy and wonderful.

With the interest in the new jazz, swing, there was a concomitant interest in the language spoken by the swing musicians, not their musical language, unfortunately, but their "Swinglish." Musicians obliged. They spoke about their "licorice sticks" (clarinets), "dog houses" (basses), "slush pumps" (trombones). They talked the language of "jive," seriously misusing the word itself, which meant then as now to kid somebody, to lead them on, to joke with them. That was as a verb. As a noun, jive was one of a hundred synonyms for marijuana. The musicians themselves used some specialized words, of course. "Schmaltz," from the German, denoted lush music, accordions and tenor bands and legato fiddles. "In the groove" described music that was "in there," that swung, that hit a steady tempo and held it and moved its players and listeners alike. If you were "sent," your senses were caught by the music, you were entranced by music in the groove. The genuine words mixed unhappily with the fake. Musicians rarely if ever called their instruments by the revolting terms thought up by the writers of magazine articles about jazzmen. They weren't inarticulate goons reduced to a vocabulary of crude metaphor and questionable simile. They were professionals with a specialized professional vocabulary, the best of it colorful and precisely descriptive, the worst of it clearly identifiable as such and quickly relegated to the limbo of forgotten phrases, to be forever afterward dubbed as "corny," from "cornfed," meaning from the sticks, the country. If you used these patently absurd words, you were corny, and no musician or fan wanted to be called that most horrible of names.

At first, Duke was left out of the growing swing ranks. Benny Goodman, Bob Crosby, Tommy Dorsey, Jimmy Dorsey, Fats Waller, Red Norvo, Jimmie Lunceford, Chick Webb, and, briefly, Willie Bryant and Teddy Hill, were the big swing names. That didn't mean that Duke was a box-office failure, that his music was to be shunned; it was the great music, the music in the background, the music that inspired all the other music, but it wasn't exactly swing, according to the swing lights. Actually, the bands which qualified as swing bands were simply those which were formed or came up during the so-called swing years, after 1935. The Dorsey Brothers didn't qualify with their jointly-led band: it was before '35. But their separate bands, formed in '35, did. Duke was an ancient in 1935, a twelve-year-old jazz antiquity; his music was reverenced but simply not regarded as swing. And though the money was still good, and the records selling fairly well, the first years of swing were not encouraging for Edward Ellington. He was laid aside for about a year and a half.

Then Ned Williams really went to work. He laid down a barrage of publicity for Duke and it helped. Ned was an important figure in Duke's life in the thirties. He was Irving Mills' publicity chief, a short, balding man who looked as if he sold something, something quite good, maybe. He always wore a flower in his lapel and waxed the ends of his mustache till they shone. He wore spats and, in short, dressed in the manner of spats, flower, cane and waxed mustache, double-breasted waistcoats, dark suits, gray ties. He talked easily, if a little nervously, and really loved Duke and his music and selling both.

"It took me three years, maybe," he said, "to get close to Duke, but, brother, it was worth the struggle. You see," he explained, "Duke looks you over, takes a time to make up his mind; but once it's made up, he's all out for you." He sold Duke to magazine and newspaper editors by telling them about his remarkable personality, the scope of his interests, the magnetism of his personality, always as if he were letting them in on a secret. There was something about his own personality that generally got across, and thus got Mr. Ellington across.

"How about that scrim in front of his band, the scrim with which he opens all his stage shows? That ain't jazz," Ned said, "but, brother, it sure is good."

When Duke opened at the Urban Room of the Chicago Congress Hotel on the eighth of May, 1936, things were better and were getting better all the time. He was following Benny

Goodman and Ben Pollack in a room that was apparently going to be dedicated to the bands that played jazz, that swung. Chicago was pretty enthusiastic about Duke. The enthusiasm grew as the Chicago Rhythm Club took over. E. M. Ashcraft, known as "Squirrel" to his familiars, was one of the moving lights of the club. An amateur musician himself, "Squirrel" was the scion of a wealthy suburban Chicago family; he could indulge his jazz fancies. Helen Oakley was the other Rhythm Club Force. Helen was the daughter of a Canadian wool manufacturer. But Helen was more securely attached to jazz than to Toronto society, and she left Ontario precincts early in the thirties to work in the music business she adored, for Irving Mills, Chick Webb and Duke at various times in the following years. In 1936, it was the Rhythm Club, with Squirrel Ashcraft.

The Rhythm Club was holding Sunday concerts at the Congress. The epochal afternoon earlier that year, when Teddy Wilson had flown out to Chicago from New York to play one with Benny Goodman, and remained to form the nucleus of the small Goodman unit with Benny and Gene Krupa, was already jazz history. Those concerts with Duke were memorable affairs, too.

There were also Concert Nights at the Urban Room. Full advantage was taken of Duke's eminence in the field. The Rhythm Club climaxed the afternoon and evening concerts with the presentation of a gold baton to Duke. Because Chicago musicians of white skin were not entirely free of prejudice, the presentation was not altogether as it should have been. But the desired effect was finally produced.

The Rhythm Club at first approached three well-known Chicago white jazzmen to make the presentation. They all refused, singly and collectively. The Club asked Eugene Stinson, who reviewed traditional music for the Chicago *Daily News,* to present Duke with his glittering stick. Stinson was delighted. He did it, at the first Concert Night. "I am aware of no race lines where genius is concerned," Stinson said, and with bows as gracious as Duke's, he handed Ellington his baton.

The Urban Room was the scene of a curious encounter between Duke and one of his severest critics. Said severe critic was
sitting with Helen Oakley one night in May, at a ringside table,
listening intently to the band he had once loved, but which no
longer stirred his passions. The band played *Clarinet Lament,*
featuring Barney Bigard, a moody work characterized by sweep-
ing glissandos on the solo instrument, by a feeling of searing
melancholy elicited from its minor tonality.

"Self-conscious," the critic said, "self-conscious and pretentious, like so much of Duke's recent work. There is an artiness
which pervades all of his writing today . . ."

"Oh, be quiet," Helen said, and laughed to cover the strength
of her feelings.

The band stopped playing. Duke sat down at the piano with
the look of faint, long-suffering pain with which he approaches
a long piano solo. His eyes wrinkled at the edges, his hands
suspended briefly above the keyboard, he approached a large
work. He played. The band played. He played some more. It
was something the critic didn't know.

"That's it!" the critic cried. "That's it!" He popped up from
his chair in his enthusiasm. He sat down again, his face in the
contortions of anguish that indicated for him great emotional
stirring within. He lowered his head in reverent appreciation
of the music. Helen smiled. When it was over, he spoke again.

"How wonderful, how perfectly wonderful," he said. "And
besides"—he added the Croix de Guerre—"the band swung on
it. How wonderful!"

Duke came up to the table. The set was over. He bowed to
the critic and smiled broadly. "How are you?" he asked.

"Very well, very well," the critic replied. "Duke," he said,
springing up to take Duke by the hand, "that was it!"

"It?" Duke asked, looking around to see what he was talking
about. The decoration, maybe? his manner assumed. Or that
lovely girl in the corner? You couldn't be talking about me or
my music, Duke's manner suggested. No, no, not that.

But he was, he was. "That last thing you played. Exquisite.
The real Duke," he told Duke, as if the man standing before

him with that name were a pretender to the throne. He was hot and bothered. "What was it, Duke, what was it?"

"Something new," Duke said.

"What do you call it?"

"No special name for it. It's just one of my new works."

"Well, that's it," the critic concluded, "that's it."

The music had been *Reminiscing in Tempo,* which this leading jazz critic had pulverized in his column in one of the leading jazz magazines. Duke never told him what it was. Neither did Helen. It remained a private joke between the two of them.

The Congress engagement was a happy one in many ways. Duke said hello again to Jack Hylton, who was in Chicago with his band, American musicians under an English leader. Hylton finished up at the Drake Hotel the night after Duke opened at the Congress. Jack had come to this country on the understanding that he could front a band, but that the personnel would have to be American. He got some lucrative locations and a radio commercial, and introduced some British variety acts to America on that half-hour weekly airing, such as the dialectician, Pat O'Malley. In Chicago, he and Duke talked over the kicks and breaks, the extraordinary success of the Ellington tour of England and France, and Duke once more renewed his promise to come over soon and repeat.

"There's a hitch, now, Duke," Jack said.

"I know, ole man," Duke acknowledged.

"Ministry of Labor," Hylton identified.

"So it goes. I sure wanna go around the world, though," Duke said. "I'd love to."

In spite of many news stories, column and trade paper reports that Duke would repeat his European tour, it didn't materialize in 1936 as it hadn't the year before, and wouldn't for a few more years: 1936 was destined to be another year of one-nighters, with occasional weeks at theaters. But at least the Congress engagement proved that Duke was still big-time, his name important at a hotel and in the newspapers, and the sense of achievement was large when organizations like the Rhythm

Club made such presentations and college kids began to worry about whether or not *Reminiscing in Tempo* was "swing."

Reminiscing was the last record of Duke's to be made in 1935. He made a half-dozen more sides for Brunswick, but they languished in the master vaults of the company, unpressed, as they still do in Columbia's shelves, the change in ownership and label having apparently made no difference. And so we shall never have the early versions of *Clarinet Lament* and *Echoes of Harlem,* first titled *Barney's Concerto* and *Cootie's Concerto,* or *Jumpy, Dinah Lou, I Don't Know Why I Love You,* or Duke's version of the traditional *Farewell Blues,* one of the classics of jazz.

The next year was not a big record one for Duke. No great song hits, no remarkable instrumentals, as stock arrangements for other bands to pick up. But 1936 saw the development of a new idea. Duke began to feature some of his star soloists in so-called concertos. They weren't bona fide concertos, in the sense that the Beethoven or Mozart or Tchaikovsky violin concertos are; they weren't cast in the classical concerto form because Duke's music never followed the episodic development of the sonata. But they were concertos in the sense that they presented soloists before the band, in the sense that the backgrounds Duke scored for the soloists were designed to show off the ideas and tone and color of these soloists.

The first two Ellington concertos were the most successful, the aforementioned *Clarinet Lament,* which was an utter triumph for Barney, and Cootie Williams' first concerto (there was another in 1940), *Echoes of Harlem.* The *Echoes* were made by Duke's two bass players, Duke's left hand, emphasizing the alternation of weak and strong beat, taking the place of hand-clappers in underlining the off-beat. Cootie's heart-blasting growling was set against the bass beat and low sound, building into full band statement, with the bass incessant beneath soloist and orchestra. The coupling of the *Lament* and the *Echoes* was a brilliant one.

Then came Lawrence Brown's pretty exposition of an Ellington theme, *Yearning for Love.* But this wasn't the perfect

G*

vehicle for Lawrence's beautiful trombone tone and remarkable facility on his horn. For one thing, the full piece didn't fit on a ten-inch record: it wasn't conceived in such brief disc confines. For another, its lush progressions weren't as suitable a display for Lawrence as the earlier *Sheik of Araby* or the later *Rose of the Rio Grande* or his numerous shorter solos, such as the wonderful measures he plays on *All Too Soon*.

Trumpet in Spades was an allusion to Rex's formidable technique and it was a demonstration of it. Rex, too, had to wait for a truly satisfactory show-piece. He had joined the band in 1934, Christmas week, to the misgivings of many, not his or Duke's or any of the guys' in the band, but those of critics and some fans. Rex was a hard blower, a wit on his horn and a jazz veteran who had been playing since his fifteenth year as a professional of distinction. He had been playing with a whole lot of bands, most notably with McKinney's Cotton Pickers and Fletcher Henderson. When he brought his bulbous dark figure into the Ellington organization there were crossed fingers and shaking heads. The fingers shortly were uncrossed and the heads quieted. Rex proved himself on one record and in one performance after another. But the full force of his bright little personality was not felt until 1937, while the biggest commercial hit he ever had sprang full-blown from record grooves in '38 when *Boy Meets Horn* was made. *Trumpet in Spades* was pleasant and impressive but not the imperious command to attention that any side presenting Rex should have been.

There were some pop tunes, four in a row, *Isn't Love the Strangest Thing, No Greater Love, Love Is Like a Cigarette* and *Kissin' My Baby Goodnight*. These were heavily criticized: criticizing Duke had become a favorite indoor sport in the trade by then. "Not the real thing; dull arrangements of dull tunes." But they have weathered the years remarkably well. The arrangements are anything but dull and convert ordinary tunes into extraordinary music by a kind of full scoring that didn't become really popular until three years later, when Glenn Miller made his reputation. Then there was Louis Armstrong's big hit from the downtown Connie's Inn show, *Shoe Shine Boy*, which Ivie sang with plaintive conviction; *It Was a Sad Night in Harlem,* Duke's number in the same sad key, and *Oh, Babe! Maybe Someday,* a bumptious promise of love to come, which Ivie sang with the same understanding and kicks she brought to the sad songs. Ivie was really singing in those days; five years with Ellington had brought her voice and personality to maturity. On these sides and the four first named, she showed that sympathy for a lyric-writer's lines and that feeling for a musical phrase which made all her appearances, in the flesh or the radio tube or phonograph disc, such a delight.

Duke's *Uptown Downbeat* and *In a Jam* brought the year to a conclusion. They were precisely what their titles indicated, records that got a Harlem beat, that presented Ellington soloists in a jam session. They swung as no other swing bands swung, with greater looseness and more drive than their competitors. They presented greater soloists than other bands could, Johnny Hodges and Tricky Sam, Cootie and Lawrence.

For a little while, the swing craze had left Duke behind, not musically, simply in fan attention and general band publicity. But it wasn't long before he caught up. At the end of 1936, though Benny Goodman and Tommy Dorsey were the biggest names in the business, and Duke wasn't winning any band polls, his musicianship and box-office appeal had both proved themselves again. When he could get good bookings, he was doing fine business, and his records, when they were issued, sold well and, more important, were on a high musical level. *It don't mean a thing if it ain't got that swing*—Duke said it first, and he proved it first and he continued to prove it while some other boys were being discovered for doing less effectively what he had done years earlier.

The Columbia Broadcasting System made a concession to the swing movement in the Saturday Night Swing Session, which made its first appearance early in 1937. Before that series of Saturday evening half-hours left the network air, Duke made three appearances. It was the obvious recognition of his stature as a swing or jazz musician or any other name that might be given to his function by the press agents and fans of popular

music. Duke was now an accepted apostle of the new dispensa-
tion, swing, if not its savior. In Chicago, the *Examiner* said,
"ELLINGTON MASTER OF SWING MUSIC." In Cleve-
land, they were more simple, withholding the praise for the
article itself; perhaps conferring the verbal description was
honor itself. "ELLINGTON BAND SWINGS IT AT PAL-
ACE" was the Cleveland paper's streamer head. When *Life* did
a story on "Swing" in August of the following year, its writer
classified "Swing's Black Royalty: King—Joe "King" Oliver;
Duke—Edward Kennedy "Duke" Ellington; Count—Bill
"Count" Basie."

Duke was involved in a series of discussions about swing from
coast to coast, in newspaper after newspaper, small and large
and in-between. The controversy over the merits of swing was
still on in 1937; it lasted until 1940. Comments, anodyne, anile
and, very rarely, accurate and to the point, were quoted from
everybody connected in any way with music.

Arthur Cremin of the New York Schools of Music (the same
organization which had in 1932 given Duke its annual award
to an American composer) spoke up. Arthur Cremin attributed
the 1937 wave of sex crimes to swing. As later on Artur Rodzinski called "boogie woogie" the source of juvenile delinquency,
this authority with the same Christian name thought he had
found one of the basic causes of depravity in our time, swing.
Duke had an answer.

"Music is known to be a stimulant," Duke said, "and while it
unquestionably invigorates emotions to a certain degree, so do
checkers and ping-pong.

"If, as Mr. Cremin says, music can be proved to be a neurotic
influence then I'm certain you'll find Stravinsky's *Le Sacre du
Printemps* a great deal more exciting emotionally than a slow
ride arrangement of *Body and Soul* or even a fast rendition of
Tiger Rag."

Duke called attention to the ancient hue and cry against any
popular music. "This excitement harks back to the turn of the
century, when doting mothers taught their daughters that the
Indian squaw in the forest was safer than the American girl in a

ballroom." He quoted from a document of the Free Tract Society of Los Angeles: "The younger generation of those pioneer days was warned that 'women, agitated by voluptuous music, will speak and listen to words that would have been deemed unpardonable in calmer moments.'" Duke suggested that Mr. Cremin debate the virtues and vices of *They're Hanging Danny Deever in the Morning*, and similar songs.

Duke not only defended it, he insisted on making clear just what the term "swing" meant. He defined it carefully.

"Swing," Duke explained, "is not a kind of music; it is that part of rhythm that causes a bouncing, buoyant, terpsichorean urge." He settled down with his interviewer, from a magazine, a newspaper or a radio station. He was prepared for long sieges. He was anxious to make himself and the subject clear.

"Look," Duke said, "swing is something that affects the emotions, not a melody. Musicians have been using the word for years, long before it replaced 'jazz' in people's vocabularies."

He fought a losing battle. In Toronto, for example, the *Globe-Mail* headed an interview in which Duke expressed those sentiments: "SWING IS NOT MUSIC, KING OF SWING ADMITS."

From experiences like those, Duke developed his intense fear of being misquoted in interviews and a sharp distaste for statements which commit him to a position on anything, be it musical, moral or political. Worn out by both misquotation and the failure of a dozen causes he has fought for, some minor, some very important, Duke was for a long time given to the tangential and oblique statement.

Another word which was being kicked around in 1936 and 1937 and 1938, as it continues to be, is "jive." Duke tried to straighten out an interviewer.

"Jive is just fooling around, in any way, on your instrument maybe. Just as when you meet a friend on the street you say, 'How are you, pal? You're looking very well!'—and the man might have just come out of the hospital."

"Jive" continued to be used as a synonym for jazz or swing. It is still so used, with remarkably consistent incorrectness.

While he was at the Cotton Club, while he was involved in these endless discussions of the meaning and significance of swing, Duke took part in swing demonstrations, demonstrations which were far more inclusive than that designation would suggest. But that was the term, and Duke's fight to change it was useless. The United Hot Clubs of America held a meeting at the Master studios and leading musicians played to exemplify "hot" at its best. "Hot" or "hot jazz" was the term these connoisseurs used. Duke played as part of a trio, with Chick Webb on drums and Artie Shaw on clarinet. In spite of the sedate organization, the insistence by its governors upon the use of their term, the assemblage of fans and musicians and learned aficionados, 300 strong, was dubbed a "swing session" by trade papers.

When Duke played at Randall's Island, with twenty-four other bands, in a five hour and forty-five minute "Swing Festival," on May 29, 1938, his music was called swing and there was nothing he could do about it. The affair was organized by WNEW "disc jockey" Martin Block at New York's East River Island Stadium, for the benefit of the Hospital Fund of Local 802 of the American Federation of Musicians. It was characterized, as the staid New York *Times* put it, by "frenzy." The *Times* writer, like almost all others at the time, caught up by the swing fever, tossed off the current phrases with dignified aplomb. He talked of "jitterbugs" and "alligators—more conservatively known as swing music enthusiasts. . . . A blond vocalist" with Vincent Lopez, he said, one "Betty Hutton, tossed off her saucer hat to demand: *Who Stole the Jam?* and the crowd went wild.

"Then Duke Ellington began sending his *Diminuendo and Crescendo in Blue*," the *Times* man continued, demonstrating his intimate knowledge of the terms of the profession, "and a pair of little Brooklyn girls, wearing beer jackets with swing jargon written all over them, ran screaming onto the cinder track to Lindy Hop. . . . Ivy Anderson tore off the *St. Louis Blues,* leaping high into the air and smacking Duke on the back. The bull-fiddler 'smacked his doghouse' till it groaned, the boys were all jiving and the crowd was like jelly." If swing was here to stay, then the New York *Times* thought that it was news fit to print and that it was proper to use its language.

Swing or something very much like it certainly was here to stay. Music with a pronounced beat, played by big bands, was to become more and not less popular, in firm contradiction of the predictions of doom which its ill-wishers made every week with boring regularity, in magazine articles, Sunday supplement pieces, in the gossip and opinion columns and editorial pages of the nation's newspapers. Swing was to grow and its audiences to mature at least to the point where it didn't matter whether or not it was called "swing" or "jazz" as long as it did have "that swing" and the solos were good and the arrangements were musicianly. With that growth, Duke grew in public stature, the bookings got better and he could find some solace in the present and hope in the future. He had proved himself once more, as he apparently was required to do periodically. He had found his place in swing society.

CHAPTER THIRTEEN

MAIN STEM

ONCE MORE THE COTTON CLUB WAS ASSOCIATED WITH DUKE in 1937 and 1938. The Palais Royal, famous as the New York home of the Paul Whiteman band in earlier years, was converted into an all-Negro club in '36, when Connie Immerman moved his uptown house, Connie's Inn, to that site. Next year the Cotton Club interests, Herman Stark presiding, took over, and the big room on the top floor of one of Broadway's most successful "tax-payers" achieved great musical distinction again. For two years Duke headed its top shows, opening in the late winter and staying through early spring.

Before coming into the Cotton Club, in 1937, the Ellington organization stomped around the country, playing one-nighters again and theaters and brief locations. In November of '36, after a successful three-day stand at the Texas Centennial Exposition in Dallas, the band played a week at the Chez Maurice in the same city. Dallas papers made much of the fact that this was "the first extended appearance of a Negro band at a downtown spot" in that city.

The band moved out to the Coast, for another stay at Sebastian's Cotton Club out there, mixing again with the cowboys and Indians who people Culver City. Just before the Cotton Club there, the band played the Los Angeles Paramount Theatre, and with "swing" still making newspaper headlines, garnered a good share of space with that appearance. At Sebastian's, Duke served notice of his new conception of the band. He played a swing concert. But, as one of the reviews of the evening by a discriminating critic in the Beverly Hills *Script* put it, it wasn't "a swing concert. It was, rather, a recital—a recital of the Ellington compositions and technique and soloists, executed with a maximum of sincere feeling and a minimum of yeah-mans . . . for in the absence of insincere and artificial gestures and shouts, the Duke's music becomes not the product of 'the weed' or gin or hysterical shouting, but a sincere product of the Negro, built basically on some obscure rhythm of Africa and the Deep South, decorated by the sophistication that civilization has lent to the Duke himself. As such it is individual and distinctive. . . ."

The amount of sincerity or insincerity present in other jazz musicians' "artificial gestures and shouts" is certainly not susceptible of exact appraisal, and Duke's rhythms were not then nor are they now "obscure." But this critic's appreciation of the essential dignity of his presentation, and the high degree of musicianship inevitable in a recital of Ellington compositions, was a kind of introductory chord to a new treatment of Duke. Wherever he went now, there was a respect accorded his work which other dance band leaders and composers didn't get. Duke was a veteran, not an old man in the business, but an originator with unusually practiced executants of his originations.

The band played a concert at the University of California in Los Angeles, first of several on college campuses. This was an extension of the concert or recital idea. There had been the Rhythm Club concerts and the Concert Nights at the Congress in Chicago, the Sebastian's Concert and now this. Duke was moving along.

On the Coast, too, Duke made a movie, nothing terribly important, but one which added money and perhaps a vestige of prestige to his name. For Republic, one of the smaller companies which specialized in class B thrillers and sprawling musicals, Duke cued the trend to name bands in motion pictures. He did *The Hit Parade*, in which the orchestras of Eddie Duchin and Carl Hoff were also featured. Duke played *I've Got to Be a Rug Cutter*, a song in tune with the times, its title reviving one of the traditional words of jazz. "Rug Cutter" was one of Harlem's terms for a jitterbug, a technically skillful dancer, fast on his feet and "hip" (in the jazz or swing know).

Fletcher Henderson had used the term many years earlier in his *Rug Cutters' Swing*. The movie set the band in a background of palm trees and low lighting, with the moving bodies of the musicians reflected in gyrating shadow on the backdrop of their bandstand. Harry Carney, Rex Stewart and Hayes Alvis, a hastily improvised vocal trio, sang Duke's amusing words.

Ivie took time off on the Coast to make a movie at M-G-M. She appeared in the much talked-of colored sequence of the Marx Brothers' *A Day at the Races,* in which Harpo led a group of Negro children and adults in a modern version of the Pied Piper of Hamelin story through the pleasant phrases of *All God's Chillun Got Rhythm*. The song was a pseudo-spiritual, but Harpo's infectious personality and the warmth and grace of the colored dancers and Ivie's superb singing gave it credence. The presence of Ellington musicians in the recording orchestra which played the sound-track background for the dancing and singing helped, too.

Before leaving the West Coast, the band had some dates to play in the Pacific Northwest. One was memorable. It placed Duke in a bracket with Katharine Cornell. The Seattle papers made much of that.

The band was due at the Palomar Theatre in Seattle on a Tuesday afternoon. The previous Friday, it had left San Jose, just below San Francisco. Rain and snow impeded the progress of the train through the Coast's traditionally icy February road-banks, but everybody believed they would make the Seattle engagement on time. At Dunsmuir, the train was halted, but not so long that it couldn't make Tacoma on time for a Sunday night stand. Then Bellingham on Monday. It looked all right. But in Bellingham the weather grew more savagely wintry. The steam engines froze, the train cars became unendurably cold. The band was moved, with some of its baggage, into a hotel, the musicians stamping their feet and clapping their hands and burrowing their heads into their coat collars to keep warm.

"Oh, my hands," the saxists mumbled, "oh, my hands!"

"I am so cold," Duke complained softly, "so damn cold."

The quick transition from Southern California sun to Washington ice and snow was expected of dance band musicians, particularly of Negro jazzmen, who always played one-nighters, whose schedules never permitted them to sit down for very long in any one spot. But this was tougher than usual. It was so cold.

Next day, the train pulled laboriously toward Seattle and managed to arrive there at 1:45 in the afternoon, just about in time to make an appearance at the Palomar. But another crisis interfered. The baggage car locks were jammed, the cold had left its mark on the inanimate iron; it, too, was frozen stiff, and the musicians couldn't get clothes or instruments. Fortunately, there were enough instruments in the sleeping car to play a show, and so, after several vain attempts to break into the baggage car, the musicians piled into cabs and were rushed to the theater. But it was very late.

At the Palomar the manager was worried. He remembered the Katharine Cornell incident of a few months earlier, when the actress and her company had been stalled on their way into Seattle by driving rains and icy blasts of wind. They had arrived hours late, with little hope of performing that night. But in the early hours of the morning, with Seattle citizens still waiting patiently to see and hear the Cornell troupe, they had arrived, and, after the proper speeches, put on *The Barretts of Wimpole Street* in modern street dress. There was hope, then, for Ellington. The manager screened a Lowell Thomas short subject for the second time. He was greeted by whistles and shouts and derisive applause from the impatient audience.

"Wait," the manager said, as he mounted the Palomar stage. "The Duke never disappoints." As he spoke, somebody connected with the theater mounted the stage and whispered in his ear. The manager turned to the audience and smiled. "They're coming," he said. "I've just got word that Duke has just left the station."

The Lowell Thomas short was run through again, and then, after a short stage wait, the curtains parted and revealed the Ellington group clad in a motley assortment of street clothes, sport shirts, business shirts, some with, some without ties. Duke

himself was in street clothes. The audience pounded away its
gratitude for the quick transformation from cold musicians to
hot, for the abandonment of face, clean, and body, neat. The
newspapers picked up the story and made banner headline feature material of it.

DUKE'S BAND CONQUERS TROUBLE;
PANICS PALOMAR
Patient
Fans Are
Rewarded

One writer summed up the effect of the band upon shivering
Seattle: "Fifteen bandsmen, including the Duke, run wild in a
fiery blast of red hot rhythm, then cool off to deep, rich tones
of velvety smoothness. A treat to the eye as well as to the
ear. . . ."

Duke continued to make newspaper headlines in 1937.
Deems Taylor credited him and Guy Lombardo with being the
first orchestra leaders to determine the scientific possibilities
and limitations of the microphone in radio broaacasting, in an
article in the magazine, *The New York Woman.* Taylor pointed
out the unusual sensitivity of the microphone and the delicacy
required to handle it properly. Ellington and Lombardo, he
concluded, were most successful in their use of radio as a musical medium. Hundreds of newspapers from coast to coast used
the story, some merely as filler material, some as a full-length
feature, with Duke's name prominent in the headline.

Fred Waring, in San Francisco with his Pennsylvanians playing a theater engagement, was interviewed in the *Chronicle.*
Queried about his musical tastes he cited several bandleaders
he admired, Benny Goodman, Cab Calloway and Duke, whom
he mentioned first, and with the greatest superlatives. "I think
that Duke Ellington is the genius of the commercial musical
world," he said. "He has paved the way for modern music as
we know it today and is a really great creator." It is news when
one leader in a profession goes out of his way to praise another

and not merely as a capable colleague, but as "the genius" of his world. Newspapers again picked up a story on Ellington.

Only the colored press drew attention to a signal honor paid Duke. A firm of British contractors, Alexander Wells, Ltd., having completed a group of apartments in one of London's better districts, at 29 Sloane Square, S.W. 1, Southgate, decided to name them Ellington Court after Duke. The apartments, in the international style, were in the tradition of Le Corbusier and Erich Mendelssohn, great architectural originators of our time. It seemed logical to name them after an innovator in another field, an art to which architecture has long been compared ("Architecture is frozen music," said the nineteenth-century German philosopher, Friedrich von Schelling, in his *Philosophy of Art,* and Madame de Staël echoed the sentiment and gave it long life). The Wells firm explained its decision in a letter to Duke:

> It is the practice in this country to give names to blocks of apartment houses and, like the buildings to which they are applied, these often appear somewhat dull or dead. Convinced that our improvement was neither dull nor dead, we took the liberty of naming it after your good self. The considerable interest aroused is a valuable indication of the popularity you enjoy in this country.

There was some interested comment in the columns, a flurry of excitement, as Duke joined with eight other bandleaders in the Mills stable in the creation of a popular song, each to write two measures. The idea was Milton Berle's, and like some ideas of any comedian, big or little, it fell flat.

The biggest talk around New York was occasioned by the opening of the second show at the downtown Cotton Club. Cab had opened the transformed Connie's Inn. Duke followed with a fabulously long revue, with ten featured names, from his band and Ethel Waters, down to the Three Giants of Rhythm. In between, there were the tap-dancers, the Nicholas Brothers; singer George Dewey Washington; Renee and Estela, crack Cuban rhumba team; shake-dancer Kaloah; Anise and Aland,

Bessie Dudley and Bill Bailey, all dancers. Kaloah wiggled her belly to Duke's *Black and Tan Fantasy;* Bessie Dudley shook her hips to *Rockin' in Rhythm,* as she had on the band's European tour. There was very little else representative of Ellington in the show, except a medley of his hit tunes, an inevitable part of any Ellington show from then on. The chorus danced to *Peckin',* credited, at first, to Harry James and the Three Chocolateers, who made the tune famous. But *Peckin'* came straight out of Cootie's solo in *Rockin' in Rhythm,* and Duke's name was eventually added to the long list of composer credits. With *Peckin',* then, Duke was indirectly represented in the Cotton Club show, and directly with the medley and some background music for dancers, but that's all. Ivie sang a rhumba, *Chile.* For Ellington fans, the breaks came during the dance sets, of which there were precious few. But these and the plentiful air time and the generous space in the city's night-club columns reminded readers and listeners that Duke was a polished night-club entertainer, one of the first bandleaders to shine in the field, and that his band was well-nigh incomparable.

Irving Mills took advantage of Duke's presence in New York for an extended period to make a flock of Ellington recordings for his own new firm, Master Records. The company was short-lived, but during its existence it pressed a large number of first-rate performances by most of the ranking colored names of the late thirties, all that Mills himself managed, and some that he didn't. Duke and Cab and Don Redman, Lucky Millinder's Mills Blue Rhythm Band and a large number of small bands specially assembled for the purpose made records for Master, Mills' 75¢ label, or Varsity, his 35¢ disc. In addition to these records, Mills brought out a series introducing for the first time small Ellington units, seven or eight men recruited from the Ellington band, under the leadership of Barney Bigard, Johnny Hodges, Cootie Williams or Rex Stewart.

Barney and Johnny had dignified label names: Barney Bigard and His Jazzopaters; Johnny Hodges and His Orchestra. Cootie and Rex, as trumpeters, were traditionally entitled to more jivey names: Cootie Williams and His Rug Cutters, Rex

Stewart and His 52nd Street Stompers. Explanation of the 52nd Street alliance in Rex's case is his use of a few musicians outside the Ellington band, guitarists Ceelle Burke and Brick Fleagle and drummer Jack Maisel. Ceelle played a Hawaiian guitar; Brick scored then, as he does now, for Rex's small band dates; Jack Maisel drummed often for Duke in studio rehearsals of the big band.

The first records made by those small Ellington units were memorable. Barney made the first date late in 1936, an Ellington standard, *Stompy Jones,* two in which he had a composing hand, *Clouds in My Heart* and *Frolic Sam,* and the first recording of Juan Tizol's classic contribution to the Ellington library, *Caravan.* Johnny made a lot of pops which sold very well to the growing audiences that hovered around the country's juke boxes and across the record store counters. The sinuous alto and soprano style of the Rabbit was a commercial natural. It carried a musical innuendo that never missed fire, at slow or middle or up tempo, in an ordinary popular tune or one of his own imaginative creations.

Cootie produced records which reflected his own personality and that of his horn. The growl of good cheer, the grunt of ironic jeer, the musical sneer and leer and sorrowful inner stirrings mixed through *Downtown Uproar, Blue Reverie, Diga Diga Doo* and *I Can't Believe That You're in Love with Me,* first four tunes recorded by the Williams group. Rex gave Ceelle Burke wide berth through *Lazy Man's Shuffle;* he carried the other tune made at his first date himself, named after himself, *Rexatious.*

When Mills' firm was transferred, lock (the door to his Broadway studios), stock (names like Duke and Cab and Hudson–De Lange) and barrel (a number of fine records still unreleased), to the American Record Company, these small Ellington units continued to make dates. They appeared on the ARC's 35¢ label, Vocalion. And one impressive coupling after another was issued during '37, '38, and '39. When the band moved to Victor in 1940, the small units transferred to the Bluebird label, to make fewer but not less effective records.

Outstanding on these records is the balance of scored backgrounds and improvised solos. The personnels were interchangeable, with Cootie playing for Barney and Johnny as well as for himself, Carney in all four units, and the rhythm section, usually the big band's regulars, down to Duke himself. Seven or eight men with the same horns and personalities played at one time or another for each of the four leaders, yet the records managed to preserve the character and musical temperament of the four different men. Naturally, they themselves took great chunks of solo wax, and this gave individual stamp to their records. In addition, however, they determined tunes and times and helped to put the background scorings together. The result was a most distinguished series of small band recordings—with those made by Benny Goodman's Trio, Quartet, Quintet and Sextet, perhaps the finest music ever committed to disc grooves by small jazz groups.

For Master, Duke departed from time-honored Ellington procedure himself. He made piano medleys, his four biggest hits on the two sides of one record, *Mood Indigo, Solitude, Sophisticated Lady* and *In a Sentimental Mood*. The band made four negligible pops, the movie tunes, Duke's *Rug Cutter,* and the mock-spiritual Ivie had sung for the Marx Brothers. It did *The New East St. Louis Toodle-Oo* and *The New Birmingham Breakdown,* recreating theme and piano flash of ten years earlier, when the band had made its first important records. *Caravan,* building into a big hit, *Azure,* in the *Indigo* mood, *Scattin' at the Kit Kat,* a brash riff tune, and the poignant *Alabama Home* completed the Master file.

At the Cotton Club, it was slow going at first, playing more background music than anything else. But there were compensations. Leopold Stokowski came in one night. He sat alone in a box under the cupid-strewn heavens of the Cotton Club ceiling. Duke noticed him and joined the white-haired conductor. Stokowski rose to meet him.

"I have always wanted to meet you and hear you conduct your compositions," Stokowski said.

"This is one of the proudest moments of my life. I've always had the greatest admiration for you," Ellington said.

"Tell me," Stokowski continued, after a further exchange of proprieties, "what are you striving for in your music?"

"I am endeavoring to establish unadulterated Negro melody portraying the American Negro," Duke explained.

"I would like to sit here and listen to your interpretations. It would be enlightening," Stokowski decided.

Duke played his concertos, *Clarinet Lament, Echoes of Harlem, Trumpet in Spades, Yearning for Love.* Stokowski sat as if stunned by the extraordinary virtuosity of the soloists, Barney, Cootie, Rex, Lawrence Brown, wishing, perhaps, that his brass section in the Philadelphia yielded such color and vigor. Duke played *In a Sentimental Mood* and *Rockin' in Rhythm,* a good sampling of the moods and their manners of expression by his orchestra. Stokowski applauded loudly.

When Duke returned to his box, the classical conductor expressed his thanks and his reaction.

"Mr. Ellington," he said, "now I truly understand the Negro soul. Perhaps you would honor me by attending my concert at Carnegie tomorrow evening."

Next night, Duke sat alone in a box at Carnegie and listened, as one of the New York columnists, Louis Sobol, put it, "while the Caucasian conductor led his vast orchestra [the Philadelphia] in an interpretation of the vague white-folks' soul."

Stokowski remained a champion of Ellington and of jazz. He stanchly supported the music of America's great dance bands as this country's most original and most vigorous expression in the art and answered Rodzinski firmly and intelligently when the New York Philharmonic-Symphony conductor attacked "boogie-woogie" (meaning all of popular music) as an incitement to juvenile delinquency.

Duke continued to speak for "Negro music." Fed up with the loose use of the term "swing," he insisted that his music be called after his people, "Negro music." At one point, he made a savage distinction between his work and that of the so-called swing bands.

"Swing is stagnant and without a future," Duke said, explaining that he meant music which emphasized "the type of musical rhythm that causes a bouncing, buoyant, terpsichorean urge" to an exaggerated degree, forgetting all other planes of popular musical expression. Most swing, he said, is "like the monotonous rhythmical bouncing of a ball. After you hear just so much, you get sick of it because it hasn't enough harmony and there isn't enough to it.

"There is something lasting, however, to be obtained from the Negro idiom," he said. "I predict that Negro music will be alive years after swing is dead. Negro music has color, harmony, melody and rhythm. It's what I am interested in, and I am going to stick to it. Let the others whirl and jerk, like ickies and jitterbugs, on swing, and let me sit back and drink in the music."

Writing a guest column for the Pittsburgh *Courier*, the country's top-ranking Negro newspaper, he expressed the conviction that "a new cycle of interest in colored entertainment is just starting." He implemented his generalization. "More and more colored bands are taking their place on the screen, and this last season saw the first successful all-Negro radio program, headed by the inimitable Louis Armstrong [for Fleischman's Yeast], whose work in Paramount Pictures is also something to talk about.

"All of these things are good for the race," he continued. "The man of color has a wealthy heritage. His capacity for music and entertainment is an infinite one."

He concluded with a hopeful Amen. "We long have passed the era when twanging a banjo, singing a spiritual and doing a shuffling dance were popularly supposed to be the extent of a Negro's talent. We don't have to list all of the outstanding musicians, performers and artists of the race to convince you of this point.

"We must be proud of our race and of our heritage, we must develop the special talents which have been handed down to us through generations, we must try to make our work express the rich background of the Negro, something that our orchestra always has tried to do and constantly will strive to attain."

Agreement that Duke had succeeded in doing just that came from an unexpected source. The Greensboro (S. C.) *News* editorialized:

"If we were asked to name the ten best American composers, living or dead, we would put Duke Ellington on the list, not because of the intricacies of his compositions, but because he has expressed the soul of his people better than any other man."

The white South concurred.

With editorial recognition came more lucrative acceptance of his music in the South. He had already broken down restraints and bars in Texas and Louisiana and a few other Southern states. In December, 1937, Duke broke another. He played in a theater on the Main Street of Memphis, Tennessee. The newspapers trotted out their wooden block letters again.

DUKE'S BAND BREAKS PRECEDENT AT ORPHEUM.

The precedent broken was an important one in Memphis. The big papers were impressed. "The Duke and his aggregation did something that has not been duplicated in the Bluff City since the days of Bert Williams and the blues king, Handy," the *Commercial Appeal* explained under the banner headline quoted above. "He played an engagement at the Orpheum —a colored attraction was billed in a Main Street theatre." Exclamation points were implied.

The shattering nature of this booking can be further explained. The Orpheum was the same theater which had paid the salaries of a group of colored actors who were booked to play there but didn't perform, despite the fact that they were contracted for a week's work. They didn't perform because there were loud complaints from whites at the appearance of colored actors on the stage of a playhouse in downtown Memphis.

With Duke's booking, the second balcony was opened to colored patrons for the first time in many years. And with a nice touch of irony, this first colored booking for downtown Memphis in many years took the Orpheum out of the red. The advertising for the event was not free of patronizing lines. Ivie Anderson was billed as "The Slick Saffron-Skinned Singer"; the whole program was dubbed "A Sepian Revue." But the caricatures of Duke which accompanied these lines were not laboriously dotted with half-tone dots to make his pigmentation clear, and the band was given top billing over the Mickey Rooney picture which accompanied it. In show-world parlance, Duke got 100 per cent billing to Mickey's 25 per cent.

One of the local colored papers commented humorously on the booking, parodying the Uncle Tom diction in which most writing about and for the Negro by whites is done:

"Well, Sir, for the first time since Grant camped on Beale St. a cullud attraction will play the Orpheum. . . . Cullud folk, I understand, will be given not only the gallery but the balcony in which to sit. In short, the Orpheum management apparently takes the position that now is a good time to see whether or not Memfus cullud folk will show any real appreciation for high class entertainment and better accommodations. . . . Here's hoping that Ellington will crack the ice so wide that even the white folk of these parts will stand in line for more cullud attractions. It'll go far toward making Memphis the theatrical capital of the Mid-South, as it should be, for God's chillun with their world of talent."

The head on this piece was a suitable show of irony. "Black and Tan Fantasy," was the short slug.

There was further recognition for Ellington's "Negro music." In broadcasts to England, carried by the British Broadcasting Company in that country, and by the Columbia Broadcasting System here, Duke was heavily toasted. Some of the immense esteem in which the British held his music was reflected on two half-hour programs, the last on his thirty-ninth birthday in 1938. It was pleasant that the British listeners should hear the superlatives; it helped for Americans the land over to be serenaded with the music and a generous appraisal of it.

Before opening at the Cotton Club in 1938, Duke and some

of his musicians played in a "High-Low" concert held in late February at the Viennese Roof of the Hotel St. Regis, one of New York's sleekest inns. The concert was held for the benefit of the League of Composers, America's leading organization for the propagation of the faith in modern classical music, and the crowd attracted was social. The same class which supports the League turned out in dazzling numbers to patronize "high" and "low" music. As it happened, the "low" was the "high" of the concert. So distinguished an authority as Cholly Knicker-bocker, famed society columnist of the New York *Journal-American,* said so: ". . . And Duke Ellington," Cholly chortled, "was the undeniable 'hit' of the evening." Cholly stooped to use the colloquialism, "hit," so carried away was he. So, too, were others, Cholly reported.

"One of his [Duke's] most enthusiastic listeners—and ap-plauders—was the stunning Mrs. Samuel Barlow, who rushed up to him after the concert was over to express her great delight at his program. No one looked lovelier that evening than Er-nestina Barlow. . . ."

Back to the "low" atmosphere of the Cotton Club Duke trudged in March, a polite success on New York's East Side, but a sensation on the other side of town. This new show, with even more supporting acts than the first downtown bill, was, nonetheless, a greater triumph for Duke than the Ethel Waters–Nicholas Brothers collaboration had been. There he was play-ing background music and broadcasts. Here, the band played Ellington all night long. The score for the show was Duke's, and one of his most effective.

There was a lot of specialty stuff for the show's featured per-formers. The Peters Sisters, Peg Leg Bates, Mae Johnson, the Chocolateers, Aida Ward, Anise and Aland, and the chorus line. *Swingtime in Honolulu* was written for the Peters'. *I'm Slappin' Seventh Avenue with the Sole of My Shoe* was for Peg Leg Bates. *Carnival in Caroline* was a chorus number. *The Scrounch,* which was spelled "Skrontch" until it was recorded, was for the "grand finale," The Cotton Club Parade of 1938's bid for dance honors as a possible successor to the Lindy Hop, the Susie-Q, Truckin', Peckin' and other successful jazz dance steps which the Club had originated in its revues. There were some pallid ballad numbers which got nowhere in or out of the show and then the three masterpieces of the score.

Braggin' in Brass was just that: first the trumpets, then the trombones, then Rex solo. It moves. The other two songs in this bracket move, too, but in a different way. *I Let a Song Go Out of My Heart* and *If You Were in My Place* are touching torch-bearers; both burn as a result of Johnny Hodges' gracious scoops of alto pitch. The first was a revamping of Johnny's tag solo on *Sunny Side of the Street*, the second strictly a pop. Both carried lyrics by one of Broadway's prime characters, Henry Nemo. Nemo, a solid citizen (about 250 pounds), was a singer, dancer, comedian and songwriter, who entertained anywhere, anytime, at club dinners, stag parties, or right on the street in front of the Brill Building, site of a working majority of the country's song-publishing firms. His rotund person was always good for a few laughs; from the heart buried deep below all that flesh came some sensitive songwriting, too. For Duke he turned out several excellent lyrics. For himself, he tooled two of the loveliest popular songs ever written, *Don't Take Your Love from Me* and *'Tis Autumn*. It was hard in 1938, and it still is, to associate the Neem, whose brand of fast talk is famous (for example, his self-description, "The Neem is on the Beam"), whose speech, even when the entendre is unmistakably single, drives at nerve-wracking pace, with delicate images and soft verbalizations. But the man who claimed he put the hoi in hoi polloi was capable of just such thinking and feeling and execution, and his collaboration with Duke was most successful.

At the Cotton Club, Duke renewed acquaintance with Will Vodery, the colored arranger who had been one of the big boys on Florenz Ziegfeld's staff. Vodery directed a choir in the '38 Cotton Club Parade, and he and Duke spent much time at rehearsals reminiscing. They thought back and talked back to *Show Girl*. They talked over a lot of Follies. Vodery had been the musical supervisor of just about every Ziegfeld show from 1911 to 1932, a dignified, quiet man who worked behind the

scenes. After Ziegfeld died he went to work for Rudolf Friml,
Jerome Kern and Fox Films. This was the man Duke had always claimed had taught him almost all he knew about orchestration.

"Lookit this man," Duke said, pointing to Will Vodery,
speaking to Cootie.

"Looking," Cootie said.

"I can remember when he had a rehearsal in the old Ziegfeld
days, all the great arrangers on Broadway were in the audience
listening to the new Vodery arrangement. Why?"

"I'll bite," Cootie said, "why?"

"Because at each of the rehearsals something new came out."

"You used to be there a lot," Will said.

"Yes, I was," Duke said, "but I wasn't one of the regular
audience boys."

"Why not?" Cootie asked.

"Because I was not accepted as an arranger in that time. I
was wearing out many pairs of shoes peddling songs. But regular audience boy or not, Will was a strong influence on me.
His chromatic tendencies penetrated my ear and are largely responsible for the way I think music, even today."

The Vodery influence is not to be underestimated in any
analysis of Duke's music. Duke had little direct contact with
the main stream of traditional music. Will had had, and his
supple, vital orchestration of one Ziegfeld score after another
reflected Debussy and Ravel and one or two more strident
voices in contemporary music, reflected them and their antecedents. He was a schooled musician, with a variety of influences
extending back to arranging for John Philip Sousa and leading
a military band during the First World War. From Vodery,
Duke derived a feeling for the pentatonic constructions of
Claude Debussy and his followers. From Vodery, as he says
himself, he drew his chromatic convictions, his use of the tones
ordinarily extraneous to the diatonic scale, with the consequent
alteration of the harmonic character of his music, its broaden-
ing, the deepening of his resources. It has become customary
to ascribe the major classical influences upon Duke—Delius and

Debussy and Ravel—to direct contact with their music. Actually, his serious appreciation of those and other modern composers came after his meeting with Will Vodery, after his years as, first an irregular, then a steady "audience boy." Vodery had already assimilated the classical experience and translated it into the terms of the musical comedy pit band. It was more easily assimilable for Duke in those terms and made far more of an impression upon him than it would have in its original form. No, the Vodery influence is not to be underestimated.

When Duke met up with Will again in 1938, he was himself a well-rounded musician, a major influence, not only upon the jazzmen of our time, but upon classical musicians as well. Duke was, according to *Life* magazine, one of the "Twenty Most Prominent Negroes in the United States," placing only two other musicians in that select list, William Christopher Handy, the "Father of the Blues," and William Grant Still, outstanding composer in traditional forms, whose *Lenox Avenue Suite* and *Afro-American Symphony* had become part of many symphony orchestras' permanent repertories.

As a "prominent" composer, Duke was invited to write some large-scale works for other orchestras. Paul Whiteman asked five young American composers, in 1938, to contribute pieces to a suite of bell tunes, tunes which suggested or employed the tones of bells, the organum of the clanging metal, tunes which were in some way inspired by bells. He asked Ferdie Grofé, his old standby; Raymond Scott, whose six-man Quintet had made its debut on Master Records' first list, sharing billing honors with the Ellington band; Bert Shefter, a duo-pianist and radio arranger of good standing; Walter Gross, a single pianist and radio conductor of similar reputation; and Duke.

Duke, in character, wrote of very different bells, of *The Blue Belles of Harlem*, a title which to a degree reflected the sound of bells; it rang with multiple meaning. It was a paraphrase of *The Bluebells of Scotland*, of course. It employed the requisite word in its title, bell(e)s. It spoke of Harlem's brown belles as blue, blue with melancholy, and, in effect, compared them with the flower, the bluebell. The music was written like the title, off the tongue just removed from cheek. It was scored for piano and orchestra, with heavy duties assigned to the keyboard artist. Light in touch, it was permeated with genuine blues feeling and a touch of ragtime, with a kind of plaintive nostalgia. Successful at its Carnegie Hall debut under Whiteman, *The Blue Belles of Harlem* made its deepest impression on an audience five years later, when Duke played it at his first Carnegie concert.

Duke glided into 1939, a recognized "major influence." The dates the band played were still beneath the dignity and stature of the man at the head of it and those who followed the beat of his foot and the stroke of his pen. In New York, they did no better than Loew's State, least of the Broadway theaters which accompanied films with stage shows. There were interminable rounds of one-nighters, it seemed, with no end in sight, New England, to New York, to New Orleans. There was no longer a run at the Cotton Club to interrupt this merry-go-round: the downtown spot had folded—there just weren't enough attractions of the caliber of Ellington and Calloway and Waters and Robinson, apparently, to keep the place going between engagements of those titans.

There had been twenty-seven records in the preceding two-year period (with one coupling unissued), and only one very large success, *I Let a Song Go Out of My Heart*. The musical level of the other fifty-three sides was very high, but the market for the discs actually was smaller than that for the records of the little units, Johnny's especially. Duke composed one of his more ambitious works, *Crescendo and Diminuendo in Blue*, a bright exploration of the expressed dynamics within the blues frame. Most of the critics were puzzled by it, reflecting their inadequacy and the low state of jazz criticism rather than any deficiency in the music. Today, some of the brass writing sounds rhythmically old-fashioned, but the basic lines of the *Crescendo and Diminuendo* are if anything more effective, our ears having become accustomed to more vigorous experimenta-

H

tion on the part of jazz bands. Even after many years, some of the scoring still presents great difficulties for the saxophonists and trumpeters.

Duke rescored *Black and Tan Fantasy* as a two-part work. The whimsical executives of the American Record Company issued the two parts on separate records and the second part first. He did some very slight things, such as *La De Doody Do*, in collaboration with Edward J. Lambert and Stephen Richards; its words followed the continuity of Billy De Beck's syndicated comic strip, *Barney Google*, which in July, 1938, was muddling briefly through swing. Damon Runyon explained this preoccupation with nonsense syllables in his syndicated column. "*La De Doody Doo* is the name of a new song. Kindly do not blame us. It is the trend of the times. When you hear a fellow chanting something that may strike you as strictly Zulu, he may be conveying a message in swing language quite intelligible to millions of listeners—like *La De Doody Doo*. They tell us it is a hit." It wasn't a hit, millions of listeners did not find it intelligible—millions of listeners did not find it. But it might very well strike you as strictly Zulu.

Records like *The Lambeth Walk, Love in Swingtime* and *Watermelon Man* might very well strike one as strictly wasteful of Duke's talents and his band's. But there were tie-ups, such tie-ups! *The Lambeth Walk* was, of course, the Cockney dance step which was imported to this country by a wide range of entrepreneurs, dance teachers, song publishers, record company executives. To the Lambeth walkers' "Oy!" American audiences replied, "Oy, yoy!" and the dance died on its feet. *Love in Swingtime* was the title of a serial romance ghosted under Tommy Dorsey's by-line in the Hearst papers and whichever other journals wanted to purchase the gory tale from the King Features Syndicate. As a song for Ellington, it was a sad experiment: it neither was romantic nor did it swing.

But these were mutations. The general product of the years 1937 and 1938 was first-rate. The first-mentioned works, *Crescendo and Diminuendo* and the Cotton Club score and *The New Black and Tan*, were followed by such handsome explorations of section and solo sound as *Riding on a Blue Note, Lost in Meditation, The Gal from Joe's, Prelude to a Kiss, Blue Light, Subtle Lament, Please Forgive Me* and *Pussy Willow.* The mood was, as Duke himself put it, in one of his song titles, *Way Low.* Volume low, horns low, manner low-down. From soft plaint to bitter complaint, the music expressed unhappiness. Duke was *In a Mizz;* he said *You Can't Count on Me.* The band recorded *Something to Live for,* but the sentiment was Billy Strayhorn's, not Ellington's. It introduced Strayhorn to the Ellington organization.

Something to Live For also introduced Jean Eldridge. Jean was, like Strayhorn, from Pittsburgh. But she came by way of Buffalo; he came directly from the Smoky City. Jean was one of two "vocal discoveries" made by Duke in 1938. One was Dolores Brown of Brooklyn; the other, Jean. Both played several theater tours with the band, not replacing Ivie, just supplementing her. Dolores didn't last very long: she was prettier than she was able, and she soon departed the Ellington organization to make her way among some lesser bands and as a single attraction in small night clubs. Jean lasted a little longer: she was, and is, an excellent singer, with an intriguing vibrato and a very good sense of song meaning and style. There is more of her on Teddy Wilson's records than on Duke's: she joined Teddy's brilliant big band after leaving Duke in 1939. Though Duke wasn't ready, in 1939, to carry several vocalists with his band, he had really made a discovery in Jean Eldridge.

There were experiments, like the "discovery" of singing talent and the temporary assimilation of this talent in his organization, to beguile Duke. The coming of Strayhorn was an important event, the full significance of which Duke didn't perhaps entirely appreciate, but he did give Billy the widest possible encouragement. And he was taken into the Ellington family household, moving in with Mercer and Ruth. There was Ruth's trip to Europe. And there were the solid musical achievements of his own. But Duke was down. His personal life wasn't right.

Things had happened. For every good break Duke got

there was one equally bad. The things that happened seemed to happen at the frivolous invitation of a flippant fate. When people die and close family ties dissolve, when every attempt to meet the frivolities of destiny half-way is turned to disaster, things aren't right. Duke had felt that some dire punishment was in store for him if he were to take Mildred with him on the first trip to Europe; that would have been too much pleasure, so much more than he was entitled to. But even though he had practiced a large degree of self-denial, his life seemed to remain at the whim and fancy of thrusts into a grab-bag.

CHAPTER FOURTEEN

SADDEST TALE

SADDEST TALE told on land or sea
Is the tale they told
When they told the truth on me

THAT WAS THE "VOCAL CHORUS" DUKE TALKED, HIMSELF, IN croaking, halting, feverish voice on a record made in 1935. The record was called *Saddest Tale*. It was made shortly before the death of Duke's mother, at a hard time for Duke. Life was very, very hard for him in the years between November, 1937, when J. E. died, and March, 1939, when the band sailed for Europe again.

The death of Duke's father was not without forecast. J. E. had lived intensely; he had lived almost as fast a life as his son. He'd been warned about that cough, but hadn't taken it too seriously. The summer of 1937 he went away to the Catskills, for the cleanness and freshness and restfulness of mountain air. But even up there, with the sedative atmosphere of a summer resort, friends around him and a routine of pleasant ease, he was restless. Ever since his wife's death, he and Edward had been very close. Any time the band came back to New York, he rushed down to the city to spend a few days with Duke. Like an eager son, he dipped into Duke's luggage to see what gifts he had brought back from his cross-country travels, to see what new acquisitions he had made for himself or the home or Ruth or Mercer. The family was a tight unit, and J. E. didn't want to miss a moment of its gay unity.

When he returned from the Catskills in the fall, Uncle Ed, at fifty-eight, was not in good shape. His lips were drawn and his

look was haggard. He was suffering. The cough turned to a
clearly diagnosed case of pleurisy. The pleurisy turned to gal-
loping consumption, to a ravaging tuberculosis, the onslaughts
of which could not be stopped. Uncle Ed went up to Presby-
terian Hospital at the Columbia University Medical Center,
168th Street and Broadway, not far from his home on Edgecombe Avenue. Duke and Ruth spent a lot of time with him.
There wasn't much time left. On a Thursday night in early
November, at 11:18, he died, his children beside him.

Ruth, a year from the completion of her studies at New College of Columbia University, bore up pretty well under the
strain of her father's death. She managed funeral arrangements, the service at the New York funeral parlor and that in
Washington, at the John Wesley A. M. E. church to which J. E.
had belonged all of his life.

Duke didn't take it nearly so well. For a long time, he did
no composing. He went through the routine appearances, theaters, one-nighters, talked about doing the score for a ballet for
the Ballet Russe, looked with pleasure at the results of the band
poll in the English magazine, *The Melody Maker,* in which
his orchestra topped all others—Benny Goodman, Tommy Dorsey, following behind him. In his own country the poll results
weren't so good, but that didn't bother Duke too much.

He was able to joke with politicians, with Southern white
politicians. His sense of humor did not desert him. Meeting the
City Manager of Knoxville, a week after J. E.'s death, Duke
compared notes with him. He discovered that the Manager was
running for Mayor.

The Manager discovered that it was Duke who had written
Mood Indigo.

"Yes," said Duke, "we wrote it," using not the royal but the
band "we."

"A very fine piece of music," the City Manager commented.

"I hope I won't have to play *Mood Indigo* for you after the
election," Duke said.

"You won't," the City Manager assured him, laughing.

There was added satisfaction in the fact that the leading

white newspaper of Knoxville, the *Journal,* printed a picture of Duke and the candidate for Mayor together. Satisfaction? Maybe not. After all, a picture with Duke was good campaign material for the man. It would go a long way toward getting the votes of such Negroes as were allowed to go to the polls.

There was little satisfaction in what was happening to Arthur Whetsol. The oldest of Duke's trumpeters in years of service, his friend and associate all the way back to Washington beginnings, was in very poor health; he had been for a few years. Shortly before Duke left the Coast in 1937, after making *The Hit Parade* at Republic, he phoned Mildred.

"It's bad news, baby," Duke told Mildred.

"What do you mean, what do you mean?" she asked seriously.

"About Arthur, Sweet Bebe."

"What about Arthur?" But Mildred knew.

"He's pretty far gone," Duke said.

"My God," she said.

"You'll have to prepare Marguerite," Duke said.

"I know," Mildred said, "I will."

Arthur's wife would have to know, of course. Mildred went to see her.

"Arthur's such a proud man," Marguerite said. "He wouldn't go to a doctor when he might have saved himself all this pain. He wouldn't ever admit he could be that sick."

'He's very sick," Mildred said, "very sick. His insides have just been eaten up; he's lived so hard and worked so hard. And Duke says it's gone to his brain. You must bear up, darling—but sometimes, Duke says, he doesn't make any sense at all, just mumbles."

"Oh, my God," Arthur Whetsol's wife said, "my God."

Arthur returned to New York. That's when Danny Baker and Wallace Jones came into the band, first Danny, then Wallace. And the position of lead trumpet diminished in importance: Arthur's sweet tone and exacting musicianship were not duplicated in that chair until years later, when Harold Baker joined the band. And Duke was further saddened, further weakened, made to feel his life was further without hope.

Arthur lingered for three years, lingered through 1939 and into 1940, when the last convolution in his brain snapped and he went. Another tie with the Washington past was broken. Another bulwark against the problems and perils of the future was broken. Duke was almost broken. Saddest tale. . . .

There was another loss: Freddy Jenkins, out since 1935 with tuberculosis, came back briefly in 1937. He didn't last very long.

"Doc says I'm all right. Means I'm all right to blow horn," Freddy said.

"Crazy as ever," Duke commented.

"Don't hurt yourself, Posey," the boys said, "please."

"Never fear," Freddy said, and bowed his acknowledgment of his colleagues' concern.

But Freddy did hurt himself. His lungs weren't up to the severe strain of day and night blowing, the intense activity of the big Ellington band of 1937. He succumbed once more to the dread disease of wind-instrumentalists, particularly the high-flying, chest-confounding jazz hornmen. For months and months he lay flat on his back, dead, for a man of his ebullience, to the world, but preciously alive to Duke, who secured specialists, made sure he had every attention, as he had with Arthur Whetsol. Freddy had to live. He had to live. He had to. Years later, Freddy recovered. His illness had been tiring, fraught with dramatic crises and frightening uncertainties. But Freddy wanted to live and he did.

Duke was almost without resources for family life. His mother dead, his father dead, his close friends in the band, Arthur and Freddy, terribly sick. Then, in 1938, the May following J. E.'s death, Ruth left for a summer in Europe, to study in Paris. She was taking her Master's degree at Columbia University Teachers College and wanted to supplement her work in biology with study abroad; Duke felt that Europe was the thing for her, as it had been and would be again for him. With Mrs. Minnie Singleton, an old family friend, as companion, Ruth sailed on the S.S. *Washington*. Duke was left with Willie

Manning, his chauffeur, "man," assistant bawler-out and friend, as his family that summer.

"Now is the time to get that operation done," Arthur Logan, Duke's new doctor, advised.

"You're on," Duke conceded. In the past he had been reluctant to attend to his own medical needs, though very solicitous about the pains and ills of others. "Must have a specialist," Duke always said, as soon as the symptoms of anybody's illness became fairly specifically apparent. For himself, a mild dosage of anything that might narcotize his pain and calm his disposition was sufficient. But after the death of his parents, he was much more concerned about himself. He knew that, as Arthur Logan had said, this was the time to have the herniotomy performed. And so it was.

As with most of the events, small and large, in Duke's life, great ceremony attended the preliminary arrangements and the subsequent convalescence in hospital and home. He was much photographed at the Wickersham Hospital in midtown New York, abed clutching music manuscript paper to his bosom. His son stood proudly by the side of his bed, looking even younger than he was because of a bright bow tie. The photographers cocked their shutters and snapped the picture, Duke looking happily paternal, right index finger pointing in the air as he admonished Mercer.

"Now grow up," he told Mercer, "and be a great composer." Duke laughed.

"As you say, Father Duke." Mercer smiled back.

When he left the hospital, it was with full entourage, Arthur Logan, his doctor, Jerry Rhea, his aide, Jonesy, his valet, and Mercer. They posed leaving the hospital and arriving at the house. Once home, there was the same round of visitors there had been at the hospital. Interviewers came to seek information of future plans.

"What next, Duke?" they asked.

He answered as he always had for three or four years. "My *African Suite:* five parts, Africa to the present; the his-

H*

tory of the American Negro." He joyfully detailed the work which eventually became *Black, Brown and Beige*. For years it was "just short of completion," "just a few pages to go," "almost done." While it was in this state, Duke formulated the program of the work. He'd done a lot of solid thinking about it at the hospital. Soon, now, he said to himself, soon.

There wasn't much time to work on Duke's three B's. There were so many unpleasant little details. And some not so little. The personal affairs. The business affairs. Sad tales.

For some years, the Negro press had been taking shots at Duke's business arrangement with Irving Mills—first with a fowling-piece, then, along with the rest of the world, writers for the colored papers adopted a program of heavy armaments. Porter Roberts in his column of "Praise and Criticism" in the Pittsburgh *Courier* had something to say.

"Rudy Vallee (a very fair white man to all regardless of color) made big time in 1928. He is now worth over $2,000,000," Roberts began. "Duke Ellington made it about the same time and has EARNED something like $2,000,000—for somebody else . . ." Roberts was also concerned about another thing. "No Negro writer has written the lyrics for any of Duke Ellington's melodies since he has been under the Mills banner. What's the matter, Duke? House rules?"

Duke always turned aside criticism of Mills. He was grateful to him for early financial support, for wise business counsel, for an association which, he really believed, had been directly responsible for his international success. Irving had early seen the wisdom of enlarging the band, had secured its best bookings, arranged first-rate recording tie-ups. He was a sagacious booker of talent; he had spied Lawrence Brown in a floor show at Sebastian's, put together some of Duke's best stage shows. He had profited, himself, yes, but so had Duke. After all, as he told Mildred, many times, with all the dough he spent, at home, on the road, for the family, there wasn't much left, there couldn't be. Nevertheless, in 1939, he left Mills.

The immediate cause of the separation of Ellington and Mills was "lack of attention." That was Duke's complaint and that of his associates. The band wasn't getting enough of Irving's time, they said, now that he had become such a big publisher and booker of close to a dozen outfits, large and small. And then there was the afternoon Duke walked into Mills' office.

"May I see my books?" he asked one of the secretaries. He smiled at her and she brought out the books.

Duke sat down at the table and looked through all the books of Duke Ellington Incorporated, the record of his business association with Irving Mills. He looked at almost every page, at some with greater interest than others, at the reports on his best-selling records and those which hadn't sold so well, at the results of this theater booking and that location stand, the Cotton Clubs, East and West, Europe and short stands from coast to American coast.

"Thank you very much," Duke said to the secretary, after better than an hour's poring over the books of Duke Ellington Inc. He got up slowly, adjusted his jacket and tie, put on his hat and overcoat and walked out of the office. He never returned. In the spring of 1939, Duke signed a contract with William Morris, the oldest and greatest of the vaudeville and radio booking agencies, at that time making a belated entrance into the band business.

Duke was uncertain about his business future. William Morris was very new in the field. The firm had engaged Willard Alexander, who, as a minor executive at the Music Corporation of America, had risen to an important position in the trade as a result of his brilliant booking of the Benny Goodman orchestra and his general piloting of other jazz outfits under the MCA banner. MCA was the biggest of the band-booking agencies, the first to enter the field in strength; Willard's experience with MCA was first-rate and his record was impressive. He should be a big help, Duke thought. But Willard was going to build up the William Morris band department. He was bringing over the Count Basie band, his and his friend Benny Goodman's pet outfit. Would Duke again suffer from "lack of attention"?

There was a lack of attention in other spheres of Duke's life.

Mildred. She and Duke had never had very serious words together, "just the normal spats of married couples," Mildred always explained it. But now, with the several strains upon Duke,
there was a serious situation. He and Mildred didn't talk things
over as much as they had. He was so busy with his changing
business affairs, so uncertain about his family life, so generally
mixed up.

Mildred had heard about a girl who was crazy about Duke
and for whom Duke seemed to have some affection. Bea Ellis,
a beautiful showgirl at the downtown Cotton Club, had indeed spent a lot of time at the place with him.

"There's something there," Mildred told Duke one afternoon
at the Apollo.

"I think there is," Duke said.

"Do you love her?" Mildred asked Duke.

"I think I do," Duke said.

"All right," Mildred said, "you do as you think best."

Early in 1939, Mildred gave Duke his freedom and Bea Ellis
became Mrs. Ellington. They moved over to a new apartment at
935 St. Nicholas Avenue. There was something fresh about new
surroundings, something fresh and new and hopeful about a
new life. Duke looked up from his aching years with new interest.

A great adjustment was made all around. Ruth and Mercer
remained at 381 Edgecombe, and Billy Strayhorn, who had just
come in from Pittsburgh, moved in with them. Gradually, Duke
moved his belongings over to his new apartment and Mildred
left for Boston after eleven years with Ellington. Great adjustments to come, too.

Duke sailed for Europe with hope. Just as the last time, this
was to be a reinvigoration, he hoped, a bath in the cultured
waters of the old world. He would come back refreshed, to
start again, with new management, new relations, new music,
never again to say

> Saddest tale told on land or sea
> Is the tale they told
> When they told the truth on me.

CHAPTER FIFTEEN

SMORGASBORD AND SCHNAPPS

T HE SECOND TRIP TO EUROPE TOOK A WEEK, A RELAXING seven days on the cabin-class French liner, the *Champlain*. Duke reiterated his support of champagne and brandy as basic sustenance for life at sea and backed his words with sizable portions of the potion. The *Champlain* carried only seventy-five passengers to Europe, and hundreds of crates of bombers destined for France. This was March, 1939, and no boat left Europe without a bulging load of people bound for America. Six hundred took the place of the seventy-five on the return trip from Le Havre.

At Le Havre, the band was met by hundreds of French Ellington enthusiasts, stomping, shouting their enthusiasm. They escorted all the boys to the special boat train which took them from the seaport to Paris.

"Look at this train," Tricky called to Toby.

"See it," Toby assented.

"Just look," Tricky repeated. "Mmm."

"Mmm what?"

"The design. What streamlining!"

Throughout this European tour of thirty-four days the Ellington musicians were open-mouthed at the tear-drop lines of train design, at the dramatic simplicity of the modern furniture and interior décor in the Scandinavian countries, at the vigorous good taste of the theater design. It was the duality of European theater design which impressed them, the baroque and rococo ornamentation vying with the chaste modern for attention, and both getting plenty.

On their first night in Paris, Friday, March 30, Duke and the boys "cabareted." They were old hands at the forms and fancies of Parisian night-life this time; after all, they'd spent a couple of days more than a week in France in 1933. Once more they were *piliers de cabaret,* the one society of which they cared to be pillars. Once more they suffered from *mal aux cheveux* and *la gueule de bois* the next morning. Sonny entered *les vignes du Seigneur* early in the trip. By the time they got to Sweden the doctors were warning him.

The next day followed the same routine, drinking *comme un trou,* taking *une cuite,* sponging it up, getting baked, plastered. But there was delicacy and taste to their drinking, an art to getting baked which these musicians had mastered over many years. There were some surprises in the bottles; sudden receptions they were not expecting; sometimes more strength than joy; sometimes more joy than strength. It was all very delightful and nobody actually was prostrated by the unexpected or the uninvited effect of some of the new liquors. Duke maintained so even a keel that he was able to handle the press conference that Saturday afternoon with typical, seasoned aplomb. And once more the press was entirely receptive, warm, fascinated.

On Sunday, the band trained to Brussels for matinee and evening concerts. The Palais des Beaux Arts, the Belgian capital's biggest and most beautiful concert hall, was sold out, and the packed auditorium screamed and yelled with excited approval of the music.

Between the matinee and evening performances, the management of the Palais des Beaux Arts gave a reception in the hall's grill room for the band. The grill room was filled with friends, admirers and autograph hounds. For more than an hour, Duke and his musicians picked up drinks with their left hands and fountain pens with their right, returning to the stage with severely cramped digits, but with sufficient enthusiasm to offset the physical discomfort.

Back in Paris for Monday and Tuesday concerts at the Palais de Chaillot, also known as the National Theatre, the Ellington musicians discovered a new type of theater. The Chaillot was the world's only bombproof auditorium, constructed 100 feet below the Paris ground in anticipation of German bombs. The war had not yet started, but the French were apprehensive. In its subterranean confines every modern stage device had been incorporated. Duke stared in awe at its magnificent equipment and listened with delight to its beautifully balanced acoustics as the band ran over a few pieces in rehearsal.

The concerts at the Chaillot were great successes, well-balanced programs which were bound to please every Ellington fan, and did. With no "Hot Dictator" to direct the audience's applause, to determine just which numbers had real concert stature, or in any other way interfere with the musical procedure, Paris audiences, like those later in Belgium, Holland, Sweden, Norway and Denmark, were treated to "the real Duke," to what Ellington himself wanted to play.

The routine stayed pretty much the same. There were the traditional pieces, *Rockin' in Rhythm, Black and Tan Fantasy, Mood Indigo.* There were the concertos, *Echoes of Harlem, Clarinet Lament, Trumpet in Spades,* featuring Cootie and Barney and Rex. Lawrence Brown played *Sophisticated Lady* as a trombone solo and Juan Tizol was presented in his dual role as valve trombonist and composer of *Caravan.* There was the eight-year-old standard jump number, *Merry-Go-Round,* which Europeans had known on records before Duke's countrymen did, and of which they were especially fond. There was the precisely named *Dinah in a Jam,* in which the chords of a very well-known song were subjected to strenuous jazz treatment by improvising soloists. And there was Duke's flag-waver of the moment, his stentorian variations on the theme of Sergei Rachmaninov's Prelude in C sharp minor.

In Paris, the tremendous reception of the audience at the Palais de Chaillot was quickly followed by another of another kind. After the Monday night concert, there was a surprise party for Duke given by the Swedish Countess Inga-Lisa Lewenhaupt in her apartment in the *arrondissement* of Passy, Paris's most swank, most luxuriously developed residential section. The Countess, who was a sport and aviation enthusiast as well as an ardent admirer of the music of the Ellington band, threw a lavish affair with great care and attention paid to the tastes and idiosyncrasies of the musicians. Willie Lewis, expatriate American Negro musician whose little band had been the top jazz outfit in Paris for many years, served as the Countess's assistant.

Willie acted as his own host on the band's remaining nights in Paris, as he and the other American musicians who had been working in France and elsewhere on the continent feted the Ellington musicians. Arthur Briggs, the trumpeter, and Garland Wilson, the pianist, organized parties, both planned and impromptu. Jimmy Monroe, owner of the Swing Club, where most of France's outstanding jazzmen played, gave an Ellington party. So did Gene Bullard, proprietor of the Aviators' Bar and Restaurant. Musicians, French, American, of all the countries on the continent of Europe, thronged to hear the Ellington band and to drink with its musicians. Fans once again besieged the leader and his men.

Immediately after the first Paris concert, a young Frenchwoman rushed backstage. She told Duke how much she had enjoyed his concert. She was very pretty and Duke gave her his utmost attention.

"It was simply wonderful," she said, *"magnifique, extraordinaire, fantastique!"*

"I'm delighted that we pleased you in some small way," Duke acknowledged and bowed in courtly European manner.

The attractive young woman clasped her hands and looked very serious. "I couldn't live without your picture," she said. "If you don't give me one I shall die."

"No, no," Duke said, "not that." He signed a picture for her immediately, with a particularly florid inscription.

"He should receive the Legion of Honor decoration," Tricky commented.

"Why?" Toby asked.

"For saving a woman's life," Tricky answered.

Before leaving Paris, the boys in the band did almost everything. Homesick, some of them made long phone calls to America, to their wives and sweethearts and families.

Rex Stewart and Billy Taylor and Barney Bigard combined trumpet, bass and clarinet with Django Reinhardt's gypsy guitar on four lovely record sides, three originals and one standard for the Swing label of the Hot Club of France. The standard was *I Know That You Know;* the originals were called *Finesse, Montmartre* and *Low Cotton.* When the band got back to the United States, Steve Smith, who was then running the Hot Record Shop and putting out records with the HRS label, borrowed Rex's copies of these sides and dubbed them.

From France, the band went back to Belgium again, playing two concerts in the same evening, Thursday, April 6, at Antwerp. Next night, they played at The Hague in Holland, in the first of three concerts organized by the Dutch jazz magazine, *De Jazzwereld.* After the concert, Johnny Hodges, Sonny Greer and Tricky Sam sat in with Jack de Vries' Dutch jazz band at the Tabaris, and, as the local papers said, "gave Dutch fans the treat of their lives." Valaida, a trumpeter and singer who had made a sizable reputation for herself in England and Europe, was singing at the Tabaris with de Vries, and George Johnson, who had just left the Willie Lewis band, was the band's first alto. Americans both, they were overwhelmed to see such eminent fellow-countrymen and professional confreres. There was joy at the Tabaris, The Hague, on April 6, 1939.

Next day, the band was due for two performances, matinee at Utrecht and evening performance in Amsterdam. In Amsterdam, the large hall was so crowded that there were 1000 people seated on the stage. At the end of the show there was a mad, literally death-defying rush for autographs. The autographing took two hours to complete. Trapping Duke on the chair which he had mounted to give his hands writing freedom, the crowd surrounded him and he was inched, still standing on the chair, down the length of the concert hall. Rescued at last, Duke retired to his dressing room and the musicians went to theirs, but there, too, the demand for autographs was unrelenting and the signing continued. In the confusion attending these ceremonies, a small boy was knocked down and trampled underfoot, very seriously hurt. That incident put an end to what Duke called "the post-concert show."

To get to Denmark, the band had to travel through Germany. There were no bookings in officially anti-Negro, anti-jazz Nazidom. Arriving in Hamburg on Sunday the ninth, the boys looked around for the sleepers to take them up the Danish peninsula. No sleepers. For seven hours the band waited for the train that didn't come. Waiting for the ghost train, the band wandered around the near-by streets. The city was overrun with uniformed members of the *Wehrmacht* and the *Schutzstaffel*, army men and soldiers of the Elite Guard of the Nazis; it was Easter. Though there was no marked tribute to the Resurrection of the Lord, it was a holiday and the spectacle in which the Nazis specialized was colorful, gay and bibulous. The Ellington musicians didn't join in the drinking, but they did go looking for hamburgers. This was Hamburg—must have the best hamburgers in the world.

"*Jawohl,*" Sonny said, beside himself with joy at the opportunity to use his high-school German.

At a small Hamburg restaurant some of the musicians ordered hamburgers. They took a few bites.

"Well, I'll be damned," somebody said.

"*Ach, du lieber,*" Sonny murmured.

They had taken good chunks of what tasted for all the world like burnt wood. Maybe it was burnt wood. It was *ersatz* hamburger. Hamburg did not have the best hamburgers in the world.

After eating and looking around and pacing, twiddling thumbs in exasperated impatience at the train which never showed up, Duke decided to charter a bus to take them to Denmark. He got one and they continued on their way. By the next day they made Malmo, Sweden, after having taken seven trains, two big ferries and a bus.

At Malmo and Helsingbörg and Copenhagen, the acclama-

tion for the band was sensational. In Copenhagen, 10,000 people turned out for two performances and then the band went
back to Sweden and the most intense tour of that country
ever made by a band, dance or brass, American or European or
Swedish. From April 12 to May 1, the Ellington organization played nineteen concerts, in Goteborg and Stockholm twice
each, in Milhaus, Husgvarna, Vasteras, Karlstadt, Orbro, Eskil-
tuna, Strovik, Upsala, Vaxjo, Karlshona, Linhoping, Norhoping,
Varborg, with a one-day excursion to the Norwegian capital,
Oslo, to play and to look.

All over Sweden, as in Denmark, Holland, Belgium and
France eager audiences thronged to hear the band, to grab
the bandsmen by the hand, to be thrilled and to let those who
thrilled them know just how thrilled they were. But the most
exciting event of the trip for Duke was the occasion of his
fortieth birthday, April 29, in Stockholm.

In the morning, Duke was turning over in his sleep, just beginning to feel the effect of daylight, when a strange sound
entered his ears. He sat up in bed to greet a sixteen-piece
jazz-band from the radio station, which entered his rooms and
serenaded him with the Swedish language version of *Happy
Birthday*. All day long flowers arrived at the hotel. During the
intermission of the concert that day at the magnificent Concert-
husen, Duke was presented with bouquet after bouquet of flowers, with the best wishes of hundreds of celebrities and well-
wishers parading to his dressing-room. Then the entire audience
rose to its feet and sang the Swedish *Happy Birthday*, after
which ten little girls dressed in white marched up to the stage
to sing *Happy Birthday* in painful, painstaking English.

That night, a reception was arranged for Duke at Stockholm's
famous Crown-Prinzen Café. At the head of the room, a table
set for forty had been prepared for Duke and his musicians
and their friends. There was a tremendous birthday cake and
everybody stood up while the band played one more serenade
to Ellington and everyone sang a song of celebration. Duke
went to bed "very high' and very happy."

Three days after his birthday, Duke sailed for London with

his band, a trip across the North Sea requiring two days. They couldn't play in London because of the restrictions on foreign artists, but they did have seven hours to renew some old acquaintances and make promises to come back sometime soon, perhaps with the special permission of the Ministry of Labour, to play as well as to party. If, on this trip, the band couldn't play, Duke at least could have the satisfaction of hearing and reading the intense dissatisfaction of Englishmen with their Labour Ministry. "British fans of Duke Ellington, gnashing their teeth because their Harlem idol is not allowed a permit to work in England, are following his barnstorming tour of West Europe with breathless interest," the *Melody Maker* said. "We know it is inevitable that the Duke and his boys will present jazz at its very best," the paper continued. "There is nothing new in hearing that the audience is thrilled to death about it and we are very envious that we can't enjoy the same treat in this country."

A few of the boys really renewed old acquaintances in London: Duke says they "had to be poured on the train," the boat train which was to take the band to Southampton. On the train, Sonny locked himself in the bathroom and promptly fell asleep and nobody could get in. It was a memorable train trip.

They sailed homeward on the *Ile de France,* sticking to the boats of the Compagnie Generale Transatlantique, the French Line, for this European trip. The ship's holds were stuffed with $23,000,000 in gold, $13,000,000 of France's, $10,000,000 of Britain's, destined for the United States and safe keeping. Duke, too, carried a good portion of the precious metal back with him. The tour had been a fabulous success. Sell-outs all over, no unpleasantness anywhere. At no point was there a vestige of prejudice displayed as the people of Western Europe turned out to do homage to Duke Ellington and company. From Sonny at the back of the band to Duke and Ivie in front, the trip had been magnificent.

When the band returned to New York, at early recording sessions, Duke made permanent some of his strong sentiments about the trip. *Smorgasbord and Schnapps* was a tribute to Swedish hors-d'oeuvres and whisky. *Serenade to Sweden* was just that, a lovely melody which expressed Duke's thankful feeling for the country and its people. On the reverse, he took cognizance of the growing war tension with, *The Sergeant Was Shy*, a bright brass fantasy on the chords of *Bugle Call Rag*.

Duke was a changed man as a result of this European trip. Besides, just as everything possible had happened to bring him down in the years before, 1937 and 1938 and early '39, now all the things that were happening cheered him. There was Billy Strayhorn, his new arranger, the brilliant music he was writing and the charm of his person. There was a new home with Bea. And the William Morris arrangement looked good. The band was leaving for an engagement at Boston's foremost hotel, the Ritz-Carlton; good bookings after that, too, Chicago, the Coast. There was a new Victor contract. These were heart-warming things. But above all, that European trip.

"Europe is a very different world from this one," Duke explained. "You can go anywhere and talk to anybody and do anything you like. It's hard to believe. When you've eaten hot dogs all your life and you're suddenly offered caviar it's hard to believe it's true."

CHAPTER SIXTEEN

WEELY

S TRAYHORN WAS THE BIG NEW THING IN DUKE'S LIFE, WHEN he returned from Europe. "Weely," as they called Billy or Willie Strayhorn, was living with Ruth and Mercer at Duke's old apartment. Little (five foot three), sturdily built (135 pounds), Billy was like another member of the family; because of his size, his soft manner, his large, solemn eyes behind thick glasses, he seemed like the youngest, though he is actually four years older than Duke's son, and some months older than his sister.

Strayhorn's background is in the great Negro tradition. His mother's grandmother had been General Robert E. Lee's cook. His father's grandparents had also been slaves. He remembers his great-grandfather, who was part Indian, because that remarkable man was able to pick up anything with his feet that a normal person could with his hands; he would pull something right out of little Billy's hands with his feet, though Billy braced himself and held on with all his young strength. His wife, whom Billy called "Grandma" Craig, though she was actually a generation beyond that, used to sit by the hour in a chair a short distance away from the great fireplace. As an old woman, she arranged things skillfully so that she never had to move; with long tongs she could manipulate any of the food she had cooking over the great fire. When the food was done, if it needed to be kept hot for some time, she would pull out a heap of coals and build a fresh mound on the hearth, then she would set the food on top to wait its turn.

Grandma Strayhorn, Billy's father's mother, was Billy's prime parent until he was ten, when she died. His father had left home when Billy was sixteen. "Wanderlust," he explained, "plain ole wanderlust." Home was Hillsboro, North Carolina; the house was three blocks from the railroad station, but very far from the town's industrial section, not quite the lovely location in which Grandma Craig's house was set down by the river, but attractive. Not attractive enough, however, for Billy's father who had the wanderlust. He settled in York, Pa., then moved on to other towns in Pennsylvania and Ohio, finally sitting down for a while in Dayton, from which he sent for his wife. There Billy was born, second child of the Strayhorns to live: two others had died before Billy; two others died after him; six lived, altogether.

"At five," Billy explains, "I moved in with my Aunt ["Ont," he says] in Montclair, New Jersey. And then I spent the rest of my little years see-sawing." He see-sawed between Montclair and North Carolina and the small suburb outside Pittsburgh where his father finally settled.

Most important of the three homes continued to be Hillsboro, N. C., until Grandma died. Billy's every need and hope and wish were attended to closely. If he woke in the night with a slight croup or a bellowing cough, Grandma Lizzie had the remedy. It was a cool white stuff, something that looked like Noxzema and felt like Menthol. Grandma stuck a hunk of it on her finger and put it on Billy's lips. "Swallow that, William," she said, and he did and he was cured. Mullein syrup was another cough remedy, a delicious oozing syrup that looked like a very pale molasses and tasted even better, made from mullein leaves. Grandma had a remedy for everybody and a wonderful way of doing everything. When she ironed clothing, she always decked the shirts and underwear and dresses with pine needles and ironed the breathtaking scent into the under- and overthings. And she supervised a weekly fete: on Sundays everybody in the house united after church, to make rich ice cream and to eat it. Little Billy strained, heaved all his strength into twisting the ice-cream churner around on its axis. When his strength gave out, Grandpa took over to assure ice cream for the Sunday meal. It was a happy ritual.

Pittsburgh was not the warm, sweet atmosphere that Hillsboro had been. Billy's father was away a great deal, removing his handsome self from the household at irregular intervals, taking away that impressive head, gray-topped with a solid streak of black down the center. The family was large, sprawled all over the house, the houses in Braddock, Ranking, Homewood, the three Pittsburgh districts in which the Strayhorns lived. But for all the crowding any big family in a big city would experience, for all the limitations of this life after the sizable splendor of Hillsboro, Pittsburgh was fun for Billy and an experience of sufficient magnitude to leave him with at least a slight parochial affection for the place.

Billy was born on November 29, 1915; fourteen years later he took up his first career, soda jerk and odd-job boy in a Pittsburgh drug store. His head didn't rise very high above the soda fountain, but he was an able dispenser of the sweetmeats and tendered provender of ice cream and syrup and nuts and whipped cream and fruit. He was good enough to hold his job for eight years, during which time he completed elementary and high school. At high school, he studied harmony, outside school he took piano lessons with a private teacher. By his middle 'teens, Billy was well acquainted with traditional music: he played many of the Chopin Waltzes and Preludes as piano exercises; upon graduation from high school, he played Grieg's A minor Concerto with the school orchestra.

The music of the traditional composers was Billy's first strong interest and his immediate musical background. But jazz was beginning to catch his ear as he rounded the twenty mark. He played some himself and listened to such Pittsburgh contemporaries as Erroll Garner, a brilliant young pianist whose style rambled intriguingly from Debussy to Duke Ellington. He wrote lyrics for songs, one that he occasionally still runs over for friends at parties, a sophisticated song in the Noel Coward manner, pretty far removed from Billy's life in the thirties, but none the less convincing therefor. This song is called *Lush Life*. It was one of several he played for Duke when he got to meet him in December, 1938.

Billy had heard the band a few times on records and on the air, but he'd never been so impressed with it as he was at the Stanley Theatre, Pittsburgh's best. The wide brass voicings, ensemble chords that sounded as full and brash and impressively experimental as Stravinsky and Ravel, these things hit him.

"You know," Billy told a friend who knew Duke, "he's got something."

"Yeah," the friend replied, "I think so, too."

"I'd like to meet him," little Strayhorn said.

Billy was taken backstage by his accommodating friend and introduced to Duke. Billy sat down at a backstage piano and ran over a few tunes, singing the lyrics to some of them as he played.

"I like that," Duke said about one of the songs, and another, and another. "Why don't you leave those with me?" he suggested. "Maybe we can do something with them."

"I can't," Billy said, "I haven't written them down," and he laughed in his own special way, as if he were taking Duke into a delightful confidence. Duke, who has a special liking for eccentrics, and particularly musical eccentrics, laughed with him.

"Maybe we'll see you here again," Duke suggested. "Or maybe you can come and see me in New York. I like your stuff."

Billy figured nothing would ever come of it, but he was heartened by Duke's words. About a month later he told a friend of his, an arranger named Bill Esch, that he was damned if he wasn't going to take advantage of Duke's offer, no matter how tentatively it had been tendered. Bill said, swell, why not go to New York together. Off they went, in February.

Duke had been primarily interested in Billy's lyrics, and when Strayhorn arrived in New York and brought some of them in to Duke, on paper, he was all set. One particularly impressed Duke, a tune of Billy's called *Something to Live for*. It was a perfect vehicle for Jean Eldridge, newly set with the band, Duke figured, and a good tune for him, to arrange. Duke arranged it and Jean sang it and the record was so successful,

musically at least, that Ellington told Billy to go ahead and
write music, words, any damn thing he wanted to. And today,
as yesterday and a few months ago and a couple of years ago,
back to 1939, when the record was made, if you ask Duke what
is his favorite record, he will give you one of two answers.
Either he will say, "My next one," or he will say, "Why, er,
Something to Live for. Yes, *Something to Live for.* Things
kind of went on that record. Song. Singer. Arrangement. Besides, did you know that was Strayhorn's first record for us?"

Billy not only impressed Duke, he got along beautifully with
his son and his sister. Billy moved in with Mercer and Ruth.
He and Mercer began to "cabaret" together, as he called it,
touring Harlem's late spots and those downtown on 52nd Street,
drinking, talking, listening to music and debating its controversial qualities. He and Duke talked about music. He and
the boys in the band talked about music, and both Duke and
they suggested he try a hand at making small band arrangements.

"I was scared," Billy recalls.

"Come on, ole man," Duke suggested, "don' worry. Just
write."

"C'mon, Weely," the Rabbit encouraged, "make something
for me."

Billy made a number of small band sides, first for Johnny
Hodges, then for the other Ellington unit leaders. For Johnny he
did *Like a Ship in the Night,* an ordinary pop tune which assumed
real majesty under the mellifluous trappings of Hodges' alto
sax. As in his first big band record, Billy was given a firm assist
by Jean Eldridge's lovely voice. Everybody was very pleased,
pleased with this record and *Savoy Strut* and *You Can Count on
Me,* with *Barney Goin' Easy* and the *Minuet in Blues,* which he
did for a Bigard date. The *Minuet in Blues* was a genuine
minuet and a genuine blues, a delicate combination of the
rhythmic character of the minuet and the chord changes which
make the blues.

While Duke was in Europe, Billy fashioned a soft bit of

music, named with exquisite exactness, *Day Dream*. He scored it for full band, but, like hundreds of other Ellington and Strayhorn arrangements, it never achieved a permanent place in the band's books. As the first side made by Johnny Hodges' small band on Bluebird, however, it was an enormous success. It has been scheduled for some time for the commercial "refresher" process which has made, successively, *Never No Lament (Don't Get Around Much Any More)*, *Concerto for Cootie (Do Nothing Till You Hear from Me)* and *Sentimental Lady (I Didn't Know about You)* into smash hits as popular songs.

After Duke returned, Billy really brought his living materials, his luggage and person, over to the band. He traveled with the Ellington musicians, listened intently to each of them, those who played in the section only, those who soloed. He pored over Duke's scores and took apart his writing and arranging technique, his ensemble chords, his melodic line, his characterization of the various soloists, the growlers (Cootie and Tricky Sam), the sweet voices (Lawrence Brown and Johnny Hodges and Juan Tizol), the comic sounds (Rex above all, then Tricky and Cootie), the depth of the band (Harry Carney) and its purest, most legitimate voice (Barney Bigard). He "dug" the doubling of Toby's lead alto and Harry's anchor baritone, in the saxes, and he understood quickly how important all of these colors were in the Ellington manner and method and mode. For years musicians have wondered at the inability of other arrangers and composers in jazz to imitate Duke with any fidelity. After Strayhorn, they wondered at his astonishing similarity to Duke, so great a similarity that it was more often than not impossible to tell who had written what. Since Billy's advent, other bands have imitated Duke, but without the fidelity which marks his work. They have been able to duplicate Ellington harmonies—those are objective and susceptible to mathematical analysis. They have not been able to capture his colors and textures, his moods, as Billy has.

Billy's secret is really no secret at all. Much of it lies in his close study of the man and his band, the music and the musicians. A lot lies in his affinity with Duke, the way he lives and talks and, consequently, the way he writes. When the band returned from Europe, Billy went along on its summer trip to Boston, to play the Ritz-Carlton Hotel Roof. On the way, sitting with Duke, talking over men and music, women and music, the band, Ivie Anderson, Duke suggested a lyric for *Barney Goin' Easy*. *I'm Checkin' Out, Goom-bye*, Duke said should be the title. Billy picked it up from there, wrote a lyric; Duke did the arrangement and the band recorded it for Columbia, the re-named Brunswick label (the Columbia Broadcasting System had bought the American Record Company, its assets, good will and labels). They repeated on *A Lonely Co-Ed*, in which the two men who had never been to college, had hardly ever been near one, caught the misery of a campus solitude. While in Boston, Billy did a full arrangement for Ivie, on the currently popular *Jumpin' Jive*, and it jumped. He did some others, then did the full arrangement for *Killin' Myself*, one of Ivie's most successful records, a blowzy confession of a knocked-out "chick,' with band background which jumped the way the words and Ivie's voice and the tune itself did. That did it. Billy was all set with the band.

From his very first work for the small bands, it was obvious that Strayhorn was adept in the jazz chamber forms. He took over all the small unit dates, displacing Duke not only as arranger but as pianist on many. Neither he nor Duke remembers accurately who played on which date, and it isn't always possible to tell from their playing which of the two men is at the keyboard. As Billy picked up Duke's florid arpeggios, Duke picked up his bright skipping notes, so much like Art Tatum's runs, and both have ringing piano tones and thoroughly original chordal imaginations. It is Billy, definitely, on the Cootie Williams' *Blues a Poppin'*, *Toasted Pickle* and *Give It Up*. He is on Johnny Hodges' *Tired Socks*, *Skunk Hollow Blues* and *Your Love Has Faded*. He speaks the responses on *Killin' Myself*.

As the band moved along, after the 1939 European trip, playing the Boston Ritz, the Chicago Sherman, California, it moved more and more into Strayhorn's groove. In the early years of his association with Ellington, he was influenced by Duke: that was primary. Later on, the influence became mutual, and Ellington and his band moved into their third and most formidable musical phase, that of carefully planned scores, a phase that led inevitably to Carnegie Hall in 1943, to works of the magnitude of *Black, Brown and Beige,* of *New World A-Comin'* and the *Perfume Suite.*

Billy did almost all of the band's pop tunes, the first records with singer Herb Jeffries, who joined the band in 1940, and the last with Ivie Anderson in 1942. He collaborated on arrangements with Duke, and then, in 1940 and 1941, he began to contribute his brilliant original compositions to the Ellington library.

First there was *Take the "A" Train,* still the best known of his original instrumentals for the band. He had long been interested in writing something along Fletcher Henderson lines, the kind of thing which had formed the musical base for Benny Goodman's huge success. Unison saxes would carry the main theme; brass in cup mutes would punctuate the sax figures; it would go at a medium-fast tempo. Because he completed the rough outline of the score riding on the Eighth Avenue express which goes straight from 59th Street, in midtown Manhattan, to 125th in Harlem, Billy named it after that train, "the 'A' Train." It was one of the most successful riff instrumentals of that or any other time. As bands had earlier played *Christopher Columbus* and later did *Jersey Bounce,* in 1941 they all performed Billy Strayhorn's *Take the "A" Train,* relaying its blithe figures very slowly (Glenn Miller) or pretty fast (Cab Calloway), but getting them across.

Chelsea Bridge followed, a sensitive mood-piece, in harmonies more than faintly reminiscent of Ravel. As a matter of fact, its main figure is a passing phrase in one of the French composer's *Valses Nobles et Sentimentales.* Until it was played for Billy, however, about a year after he wrote *Chelsea Bridge,* he'd never heard the French composer's ironic waltz. Like Duke, like Will Vodery, like most of the alert young composers and arrangers of our time, Strayhorn has leaned an attentive ear

in Ravel's direction. He has accepted the harmonic dicta of the
French impressionists, combining the chromatic invention of
their music with the chord and key changes of the blues, the
rhythmic structure of jazz and the colors and textures and
delicate assaults upon pitch which characterize the music of
Ellington.

Another piece, much like the *Bridge,* is *Passion Flower,* in
which the languorous twists and turns of pitch are performed
by Johnny Hodges with insinuating efficiency. The *Bridge* was
inspired by a Whistler painting, though the English reviewers
assumed that Billy had somehow dreamed a walk across London's
Chelsea Bridge and had communicated his vicarious experience,
with "astonishing fidelity," they said, "to the atmosphere and
mood of the bridge itself and its surroundings." *Passion Flower*
is a kind of summing-up of Strayhorn's aesthetic, of the atmosphere and mood of his "salon." It earned him still another nickname. By one of his close friends, Billy is called P.F.

The Strayhorn salon suffers no physical boundaries. It may be
a stretch of ten blocks in Harlem on Lenox Avenue or Edgecombe or Seventh. It may be a segment of South Parkway in
Chicago, Central Avenue in Los Angeles or Greenwich Village
in New York. It may be a bar in any part of town in any town
in the United States. It may be a private house, a park, a barber
shop or a hot dog stand. Wherever Billy is, wherever there are
some people he knows, and in his six years with Duke he has
come to know some people almost wherever there are people,
there he sets up his salon.

Talk at the salon wanders from music, by way of clothing,
drinks and drinking, a new novel, a new word, a French idiom,
a new friend, a moment of autobiography, to music.

"Thing about Tatum," Billy will say, "even a nothing becomes a something. *Begin the Beguine,* now you don't like
that," he will admonish a friend, "but you jus' listen a few
ow-uhs [a typical Strayhorn pronunciation] and it'll make sense.
Runs in place. Chord changes. Everything." And he will wave
his hands in the air over his head, as if he were conducting
semaphore conversation instead of oral.

"Tatum was so wonderful the other night," Aaron Bridgers will amplify. Aaron is Billy's roommate, a non-professional but a talented pianist whose long body sprouts long fingers to make the stretch of a thirteenth as easy for him as an octave for the rest of us. Aaron is a close friend of Art Tatum's, close enough so he can gain admission to the battles of music which follow Art's completion of the job, at four of a morning. These battles are the great proving-grounds for the new ideas of Tatum, generally regarded as the most brilliant of jazz pianists and one of the most accomplished technicians on his instrument in or out of jazz. "Tatum was wonderful," Aaron will continue. "To hear him play stride. Like Fats or James P. Only funnier."

"Funniest thing I ever saw," Billy comments, "funniest . . ." He can't continue: thinking of the funniest thing he ever saw, he begins to laugh, a soft little laugh that finally gathers enough power to stay Strayhorn speech entirely.

"Well?" Aaron asks.

"Well?" Bernard asks. Bernard is another of Billy's close friends, a gentle man, just about between Billy's shortness and Aaron's tallness. "Well?"

But Billy is too far gone. "Never mind," he says, "you probably wouldn't think it was funny anyway." He takes off his glasses, wipes them, and thinks of the funniest thing he ever saw again. He starts laughing, even more uproariously than before. He almost drops his glasses. But no matter how Aaron and Bernard press him, Billy never tells them what is so damned funny.

"I wish I could express myself," Billy confesses. "I can't tell you because I can't describe it."

"You express yourself," Bernard comforts.

"Not like Koestler," Billy says sadly. "Did you read *Arrival and Departure?*" He asks Bernard.

"No."

"You mus'," Billy insists. "Psychological mess of our time. Very much to the point. I was impressed." He stares at Bernard's tie. "I'm impressed by your tie, too," he says. "What a lovely color. What is it, a kind of blue, hm?"

"Azure," Aaron identifies, "azure as I'm alive."

"Oh, my God!" Billy comments.

"Let's go," Bernard comments.

"Enough said," Aaron admits. "I'll go quietly."

"*Quel drôle,*" Billy describes Aaron. "*Il est fou à lier, un hurluberlu.*" Billy smiles. "Oooh," he says, "I've been waiting to use that idiom. Mmm," he mouths with self-satisfaction.

"Are you all *fou?*" Aaron asks.

"I told you we oughtta go," Bernard says.

"*Je suis de votre avis,*" Billy agrees. Fluent in the casuals of French conversation and devoted to the language, he has the seemingly inevitable failing of Americans who've learned their French in the schools: he addresses all his remarks, even to his intimates, in the second person plural. The distinction between *tu* and *vous, ton* and *votre,* has somehow eluded him. But the idioms have not. When he is feeling blue, he says that he is mixing black paint, *broyant du noir.*

Billy, Aaron and Bernard will go downtown to eat a snack at the Turf, on Broadway, maybe. Perhaps they will wander over to a party at a friend's house in the Village, or pay a long call to the bar at Café Society Downtown. The Downtown Café is likely to get them on a Sunday, when there isn't much else open. Then they will stand at the bar, Billy just barely reaching above it, and sip Zombies, those treacherous rum and brandy combinations. Two Zombies are guaranteed to annihilate the sipper and spring his emotional zipper. But Billy has stood up to the beverage equivalent of trinitrotoluene and he'll be damned if he'll be annihilated, and he isn't.

There are times, of course, when the intense drinking schedule and concomitant light eating catch up with Strayhorn. About three of a morning of a long and arduous party Billy has been known to fall suddenly asleep, sitting in a chair which literally envelops him, as any upholstered chair does, clutching his glass. Billy can sleep anywhere from a half hour to four in that position, clutching the glass, never tipping it, no matter how full it is. Billy never tips liquor out of a glass; it's too valuable. He's just as proud of that accomplishment as he is of his ability to hold a cigarette between his fingers until it is within a quarter-inch of extinction. He holds the cigarette up so the ash doesn't drop and at the same time doesn't burn him.

Of his drinking and cigarette-balancing, of his cabareting proclivities and proficiencies, Billy is proud. Of his deft manipulation of controversial conversation so that, as in his holding of the burning cigarette, he isn't burned (and neither is his opponent), he is proud. Of his close association with Duke and the Ellington musicians, Billy is proud, but he is little concerned with his personal musical accomplishment. He is much more concerned with the self-education which he inaugurated a few years ago and which he takes up and puts down with starts and turns which startle even him, and he isn't much startled by irregularities of any kind. But suddenly a book or a piece of music or a new art gets to him and he must pursue it. One of the benefits of this liberal education, so very different in its boundlessness from the St. Johns Hundred Great Books, so very liberal, one of its strongest benefits has been the intensification of his friendship with Lena Horne.

Lena met Billy right after *Jump for Joy*, Duke's musical, finished its run on the Coast in 1941. Billy was no longer Weely or Billy, though he was occasionally called Strayhorn. He was addressed by almost everybody as "Swee' Pea." Toby Hardwick had given him the name. Walking down the aisle of a train on the way to a one-nighter, Toby grabbed Billy.

"Your new name is Swee' Pea," Toby said. A new name from Toby was pretty sure to stick. He'd named Joe Nanton Tricky Sam, and Roy Eldridge had become Little Jazz under his spell. Billy was ready to accept the new name, but he wanted to know why.

"Why?"

"Because you look like him."

"Who?"

"Swee' Pea."

"Who?"

"Popeye's baby."

"Oh." Billy thought a moment. "Oh," ne said again, as he laughed. Popeye in the comic strip of the same name. "Oh."

Lena called Billy Swee' Pea immediately. The name fitted him so well. The smallness and cuteness of the comic strip baby and the sweetness of the flower and anyway you had to call this phenomenon by some name other than his given. Swee' Pea was excellent.

In the making of *Cabin in the Sky*, movie version of the Vernon Duke–Lynn Riggs–John Latouche musical comedy which won the name of "Uncle Tom's Cabin in the Sky" because of its handkerchief-head conception of Negroes, Lena and Rochester and Ethel Waters and Duke and the band were employed. M-G-M was going to have *the* all-Negro movie. Louis Armstrong was signed for a minor role. Buck and Bubbles cavorted through a scene. Veteran "Tom-actors," Hollywood's own, moved through scenes with self-respecting colored entertainers. It was inevitable that Lena and Duke and Billy, a bulwark of good taste in a land of bigoted waste, would get together. Lena and Duke exchanged somewhat more than polite words. But it was with Billy that the beautiful singer really talked. During the making of the movie, she broke her ankle, and she and Billy moved their discussions from the Metro-Goldwyn-Mayer lot at Culver City to Brother's, a fabulous after-hours place in L.A.

If Brother did not consider you a brother, you didn't get into Brother's. It was one of those places. Upstairs, all the lushness and sleekness and comfort for the lush and sleek of Hollywood was seriously rivaled by Brother's lily pool. The lily pool was in the center of the room with a glass table over it, pillows all over the floor and low blue light to set it all off. There Lena and Billy went.

"Will he let us in?" Billy asked.

"He's very 'hincty,' " Lena admitted of Brother, "but he likes me, so he'll let us in." Lena and Billy were a natural couple: one or the other was liked by everybody.

"And so," Lena thinks back to 1941 at Brother's in Los

Angeles, "we looked into the lily pool and learned about life."

Lena's leg was heavily bound in a plaster cast and it stuck out 'way beyond the table. Her crutches, laid beside her, were just below the line of most people's vision and their sounds of annoyance or desperation as they tripped over them were the only interruptions in Billy's and Lena's speculations and reveries beside Brother's lily pool. Lena wore a black and white cowboy outfit a lot; Swee' Pea liked it.

"You know, Swee' Pea, until I really struck out on my own, I was terribly dependent," Lena told Billy.

"I guess I was, too."

"When I was singing with Charlie Barnet," Lena explained, "Mother went everywhere with me. But then Café Society, the movies, my own life. I've gotta do something with it now."

"Look down into the lovely faces on the Lotus Flowers," Billy said, "they can teach you so much." They called the lilies Lotus Flowers.

Billy suggested some of the things that Lena could learn. He made her listen to music she had never heard before or to which she hadn't paid attention. *Iberia. La Mer. Alborada del Gracioso. Rhapsodie Espagnole*. Ravel and Debussy were easy conquerors. Stravinsky was more difficult. "But I like the *Dance of the Virgins* from the *Sacre* when I'm a little juiced," Lena admits.

When the band was out on the Coast in January, 1945, to play a concert at which Duke received his award as the leader of the best jazz organization in the world, in the opinion of the country's leading jazz critics as polled by *Esquire* magazine, Billy spent a lot of time with Lena. He was to receive an award at the concert, too. Duke had been elected top arranger, Billy second favorite. It was logical, since movie stars were making most of the presentations of "Esky" statuettes, that Lena present Billy with his. And so on the coast-to-coast Blue Network Lena Horne acknowledged that she was "presenting this award not only to one of my favorite musicians but to one of my favorite friends."

Billy accepted the statuette and said slowly, haltingly, "I can't imagine anything more wonderful than receiving this award from the gracious hands of the mos' favorite of my mos' favorite people." Lena leaned down and kissed him and both she and he broke down; she cried and he forgot to announce the next number, which was one of his most skillful originals, *Midriff*. The millions of listeners to the show heard an unusual jazz piece, in which a few figures are skipped blithely along from complex brass voicings to simple unison scorings for three saxes, one that is named with remarkable accuracy, since its principal theme is just beyond riff size, just short of full-length. But the listeners didn't know that it was named with remarkable accuracy because Strayhorn was too moved and Lena was too moved and the best they could offer was a kiss to each other and dead air to the country.

When, shortly after the *Esquire* concert, Duke opened at Ciro's, the most chic of Hollywood's band stands, Billy was rarely to be found at Ciro's.

"It's utterly, utterly glamorous," Billy explained to Lena, "but I prefer your apartment."

Ellington was rather chilled by the glamour, too, and he would phone Billy at Lena's and ask wistfully what they were doing, and no matter what answer Billy or Lena would give, "talking," or "eating," or "drinking," or "thinking," Duke would reply, "Gee, that sounds awfully good. Wish I was there."

When Lena played the Capitol Theatre in New York, in the spring of 1945, Billy sent ahead a picture of himself taken the previous fall, in Toronto. Eleven by fourteen, the photo was remarkably clear and remarkably true; the smile on his face was just the bright smile that friends of Strayhorn look for, the dreamy look in his eyes, behind the thick lenses of his glasses, the accustomed dreamy look. Lena couldn't resist saying, "Hello, Swee' Pea," every time she came into her dressing room, and several times during the day, friends of Strayhorn who visited her there made similar salutation and obeisance to the little man on the make-up table. Telling the story of her experience at an army camp in the South, Lena made several references to the picture. "He would have been mad at that, even little Swee' Pea," she said. Or, "Even Swee' Pea would have bristled."

Lena had been set for a three-day engagement at Camp Robinson, Arkansas, but she quit after the first day when camp officials allowed Nazi prisoners of war to attend her performances at the post theater, because they were white, but excluded the Negro soldiers from the audience. After indignant protest, she finally got permission to give a show for the Negroes in a mess hall and then she left the camp. When she went to New York a few months later, she was interviewed by Shirley Eder, who conducts a radio column. Asked about the Camp Robinson incident, Lena spoke straightforwardly about it. In all the mail the program drew that week, only one letter protested Lena's frank comments. It was from a sailor who said he knew what he was fighting for and it wasn't for Lena. "Go back to Africa," he told Shirley Eder, "and take Lena Horne with you." Lena told the broadcaster how to answer him.

"Tell him," Lena smiled, "that the Africans wouldn't take trash like me. I'm too mixed up with whites." Which was precisely the sort of answer Billy would have made to that sort of suggestion and Lena was delighted that she had made an answer he might have made.

"I've grown so, knowing him," she says. "Certain people make you happy. That's Swee' Pea. I suppose I was supposed to know somebody like him. I'm very honest with him, you know," Lena explains, carefully, "most others don't know what I'm like at all." She pauses a moment. "You know how it is. Most people who know Swee' Pea get that feeling for him."

Most people do and did and will get that feeling for him. When Jimmy Blanton joined the band at the Coronado Hotel in St. Louis in December, 1939, Strayhorn was almost his first warm contact. Blanton was a twenty-one-year-old bass player from St. Louis, a replacement for Billy Taylor. Blanton was an eager young man, anxious to please, worried about making good with the greatest of all bands. Billy helped him over some of the first hesitancies, the rough moments inevitable in any man's first days with a social unit as tight as a dance band. And Blanton made good.

Jimmy Blanton, in his three years with the Ellington band, revolutionized the art of bass playing for the art of jazz. He took the bass out of the doghouse to which it had been traditionally assigned in jazz, for which it had been named among jazzmen ("doghouse" is the name bassmen used to call their instrument in the twenties and thirties). The bass was, before Blanton, a rhythm instrument, limited, for the most part, to playing four notes, the four beats of the measure, or just as many beats as the measure contained, eight, if the four quarters were broken up into eighth-notes, but rarely more, even if the trumpets or reeds were playing triplets, twelve notes to a bar, or running sixteenths, sixteen to a measure. It played the basic rhythm, one, TWO, three, FOUR. Or ONE, two, THREE, four. Or, one, two, one, two: the steady oompah of Dixieland jazz. Blanton changed all that. He made the bass a legitimate solo instrument. He played as much on the bass as could be played on a single-noted melody instrument, emphasizing the tricky syncopations typical of the jazz of our time, just the triplets and sixteenths which had been proscribed for the bass in previous years. Blanton's skipbeat bass playing was picked up by almost every bass player of any technique or taste or sensitivity in the business. Duke was so taken with him that he made three records accompanying Blanton's bass, *Plucked Again* and the *Blues* on Columbia, *Pitter Panther Patter, Sophisticated Lady, Body and Soul* and *Mr. J. B. Blues* on Victor. All out of print, now, these are prime collector's pieces.

Jimmy Blanton was a weak boy, physically, a victim of congenital tuberculosis. But he wasn't seriously aware of his fragile lungs until overcome by the racking pain of coughing fits in California in the spring of 1942. He went off to a sanitarium at Monrovia near Los Angeles, high enough up in the hills to guarantee fresh air for his tired, emaciated lungs. But it was too late, and, as everybody in the band knew was inevitable, though they had hoped and prayed it wouldn't happen, Jimmy Blanton succumbed. The greatest bass player jazz had ever known, one of its giants, died at twenty-four. His death affected Billy strongly, Ben Webster even more. Ben, one of the revered tenor saxophonists today, after his years with Ellington, joined Duke just before Blanton did. When Jimmy died, Ben cried so bitterly on the stand at the Hotel Sherman in Chicago, that he had to leave for the evening. Strayhorn went out with him.

"Don't let it hit you so hard, Uncle Benny," Billy suggested. "He was jus' too great, that's all."

"That's right," Ben said. "But that's not right."

"I know it isn't right," Billy admitted, "but that's the world. Not only do the good die young, but they're tortured while they're alive. Anyway, Benny, we'll live to be very, very old."

Ben smiled at Billy, his first smile in a long time. But that smile and his subsequent return to work did not erase the ugly feeling Blanton's death left him with. It added to an ingrained cynicism one of the most formidable philosophies of original sin in the music business. It added, too, to Billy's presentiments of inevitable evil, but he leavened his bitterness, his conviction of a fundamental inequity in the world, with a nature which made the name of Swee' Pea as hard to evade as evil.

Billy's philosophy is a simple dualism, compounded of his sense of evil and of his aesthetic hedonism. Music should give pleasure, he believes. He listens to music expecting pleasure and composes and arranges it expecting to give pleasure. He doesn't quite accept Duke's dictum about catering to the whims and fancies of audiences, which may usually be expected to have lush tastes. "If it's milk they want," Duke says, "it'll be heavy cream." Billy gives them what *he* wants, sometimes skim milk. sometimes extra heavy cream, and Duke contradicts official Ellington doctrine in a headlong rush to welcome whatever beverage Strayhorn has provided.

"If Strayhorn likes it," Duke says, naming his final arbiter, "then it's all right." Billy sits in the control room at all Ellington record sessions to give final okays or turn masters down. Duke respects his taste above all others and lives by it musically. It is a good taste to live by, it is catholic, and though shaped by the pleasure principle, it doesn't eschew wry and arid sounds,

it doesn't avoid the downright ugly. Billy likes Stravinsky and
Rachmaninov, gets his kicks from the piano *Capriccio* and the
four piano concertos of Sergei. He likes Ravel and Milhaud and
Schubert. He likes Billie Holiday and Mildred Bailey, singers
who give notes even inflection and those who bend and twist
them with rhythmic regularity. In the vastness of his musical
tastes he is much like Duke, who, asked whom he prefers—Delius
or Sibelius or Ravel or Debussy or Stravinsky—answers in-
variably, "I like music."

To Billy's influence may be ascribed Duke's switch from
catch-as-catch-can composing to disciplined preparation of man-
uscripts. There are legends galore about Duke's mode of composition, about the number of pieces he has composed on his
shirt sleeves, on scraps of paper, hurrying to a rehearsal or record
session in a taxi, waiting outside a record studio. Some of these
are true: there certainly was a time when Duke did much of his
composing in that helter-skelter way. And even today he will
snatch inspiration from the spiral of a roadway through a city's
park or the sound of a train's wheels as they clatter along the
steel tracks. But the bulk of his work, as of Strayhorn's, is now
done at home in the privacy of his own room, or at a hotel, if
he is quartered out of town for any length of time. It is organized composition, as carefully put together as the movements
of a symphony or the arias of an opera in the classical tradition.
There may be last-minute changes at a record session; Duke
will not relinquish the spontaneity of improvised solos or the
wealth of ideas of his soloists. The basic pattern of Ellington
composing today, however, is self-control, musical certainty,
knowledge of what is being done, what can be done in music.
Billy Strayhorn can be credited for bringing much of this certainty into Ellington's life.

Duke accepted Billy's cultivated musical pen, his tie with the
musical past, though he had rejected Rimsky-Korsakov and any
serious immersion in traditional music for himself. The explanation is easy and it is important. He was still wary of forced
discipline, still worried about losing the spontaneous character
of his music, if he yielded to these influences; he still is. But in

Billy he found a wonderful balance of the traditional and the contemporary revolt against it, a background in the classics and a solid participation in the world of jazz. He found a musicianship and a personality admirably mixed, one which could borrow materials from Ravel, perhaps consciously, perhaps not, and produce a *Chelsea Bridge* and a *Passion Flower* and dozens of scorings for pop tunes with the same magic atmosphere. He found an elf who wrote gentle music, in character, like *After All* and *Day Dream* and *Minuet in Blues,* and jump stuff, like *"A" Train* and *Clementine, Raincheck* and *Johnny Come Lately* and *Midriff,* which turned out to be just as much in character. He found a co-worker, with whom he could turn out large groups of music, such as the *Perfume Suite,* "which is not intended to describe the various labels of the commercial perfumes but rather to delineate the character a woman takes on under the influence of." It is in four parts. *Sonata,* inaccurately named but not imprecise in its description of what Duke calls the "serenade or under-the-balcony type of love": that is Strayhorn's. Billy and Duke collaborated on *Strange Feeling,* which describes "violent love." *Dancers in Love* is Duke's alone and almost his alone in the playing: it's for piano and rhythm section, with the rest of the band tapping out the beat with their feet, playing "hot floor." This section is about "naïve love." Duke subtitles it "a stomp for beginners." The Suite closes with *Coloratura,* "sophistication in love, representative of the person who feels over and above everything just frightfully grand." This is Duke's—he gets the required sound from the trumpet of William "Cat" Anderson, the new man in his band who can actually play "over and above everything," up to a G above C above high C with absolute ease and to a B flat above that with a little more difficulty.

Billy unfortunately has dropped work on his own large-scale compositions as he has inspired Duke to finish his or collaborated with him. Duke did *Black, Brown and Beige* and *New World A-Comin'* and *Blutopia,* works continually on materials for musical comedies and suites and revues now. But Billy has allowed the shavings and scrapings of musical idea and develop-

ment which he has gathered toward the shaping of a piano
concerto to gather dust in his rented room in an apartment at
545 Edgecombe Avenue. His routine is well established now: he
cabarets all night and often through the early morning, drinks,
talks, sometimes eats; after a brief sleep he will get up to work
or to play piano battles with Aaron or to come down to an
Ellington rehearsal or record session. He doesn't have time between the cabareting, the sleeping and his actual assignments
for Duke, to get much other work done. He can be quite late in
turning in those assignments, and he usually is, following a
pattern set by Duke himself. Duke will forgive him anything,
for, after all, when he feels the strength of God within him and
the sense of doom evanescing without, he writes such magnificent music or goes over to Duke's apartment, at five in the
morning, to talk about it. And he is still the remarkable little
man who, after an evening's "sashaying" around the town of
Buffalo, eating here, drinking there, got "jus' loaded enough"
so he wasn't quite sure what had happened to his drinking companion, gathered hat and coat and found where the band was
playing. He walked, slowly, with all the dignity he could
muster, up to the stage, carefully placed his coat on the back
of the chair, his hat on the back of his head and went to sleep,
right on the stage. Through better than an hour and a half
Strayhorn slept on the stage in full view of the audience. But
neither Duke nor any of the musicians would disturb him.

Once, recently, Duke and Peaswee', as Ellington calls him,
shared a roomette together, Strayhorn taking the upper berth,
Duke the lower. Several hours after they had retired Strayhorn's
pillow fell down.

Duke inclined his head outside his berth and looked up at
Strayhorn. "What was that?" he asked Billy.

"That was my pillow," Billy said.

"Oh," Duke said, "I thought it was a cloud."

CHAPTER SEVENTEEN

JUMP FOR JOY

"I'VE GOT THE GIRL," DUKE SAID. "SHE'LL SUN-TAN THE FIRST ten rows."

This was in the early summer of 1941. Duke and the movie writers who formed the American Revue Theatre were talking over possible stars and featured players for a new type of revue. It was to atone for the guilt feelings of the movie writers. It was to atone for the serious mistakes and grievous errors, of omission and commission, in the treatment of Negroes in the American theater. It was to feature the Ellington band and such talent as Duke thought fitted with it. But the advice of these movie writers had to be listened to. They were putting up much of the money. They were writing the skits and the lyrics. They were bright men.

"Who is she?" one of the advisory council asked.

"Lena Horne," Duke answered.

"Good girl," somebody confirmed.

"She'll cost too much," somebody denied. Lena wasn't a big name then, but she was enough of a singer on records and at spots in New York and Hollywood so she could command a fair salary.

"No go," somebody else added. Lena was out. Nonetheless, a good share of sun-tanning was effected. There were some very pretty girls in the cast finally arrived at, notably Dorothy Dandridge, who is getting a good career as a movie actress under way. There were good comedians and good dancers and good singers and the Ellington sections and soloists. During the show's run, it impressed the "hip," confirmed Duke's conception of the validity of honest Negro theater and got a number of excellent

239

careers under way. And it was the vehicle for the finest show score Duke ever wrote.

When George Gershwin's *Porgy and Bess* was produced by the Theatre Guild in 1935, Duke was asked to comment on the first American opera by the *New Theatre,* a leftist monthly. Duke was not at all loath to comment.

"Grand music and a swell play, I guess, but the two don't go together," he said. "I mean that the music did not hitch with the mood and spirit of the story. Maybe I'm wrong, or perhaps there is something wrong with me, but I have noted this in other things lately too . . . I am not singling out *Porgy and Bess."*

Duke listed a bill of particulars. It is about Negroes but "it does not use the Negro musical idiom. It was not the music of Catfish Row or any other kind of Negroes." The music was grand, Duke said, because it was in the spirit of the "grand" composers and the composers of grand opera, too much in their spirit, as a matter of fact. "Gershwin didn't discriminate. . . . It [the music] was taken from some of the best and a few of the worst. . . . He borrowed from everyone from Liszt to Dickie Wells' kazoo band." Ellington demonstrated the way Gershwin borrowed, showing the derivation of some passages from *Rhapsody in Blue* in *Where Has My Easy Rider Gone?,* a Negro blues. His own music, Duke explained, was truly "in the Negro idiom." And he played what he called a "gutbucket waltz," still a waltz, still Negro. "I have not stolen or borrowed."

He objected strongly to much of the music in *Porgy and Bess* which did not characterize the scenes it set. "The actors," he said, "had to make their own characterizations . . . There was a crap game such as no one has ever seen or heard. It might have been opera, but it wasn't a crap game. The music went one way and the action another. . . . Still, the audience gasped: 'Don't the people get right into their parts?' and 'Aren't they emotional!' "

In any honest Negro musical play, Duke said, there would have to be social criticism. Talking of a projected movie short on which he was working, Duke gave an example of what he

meant: "I have an episode which concerns the death of a baby
. . . I put into the dirge all the misery, sorrow and undertones
of the conditions that went with the baby's death. It was true
to and of the life of the people it depicted. The same thing cannot be said for *Porgy and Bess*."

The *New Theatre* interviewer, Edward Morrow, summed up
well for Ellington as well as himself. "No Negro could possibly
be fooled by *Porgy and Bess*. . . . The production is cooked
up, flavored and seasoned to be palmed off as 'authentic' of the
Charleston Gullah Negroes—who are, one supposes, 'odd beasts.'
But the times are here to debunk such tripe as Gershwin's
lamp-black Negroisms, and the melodramatic trash of the script
of *Porgy*. . . . There will be fewer generalized gin-guzzling,
homicidal maniacs, and more understanding of rotten socio-
economic conditions. . . . There will be fewer wicked, hip-
swinging 'yellow-gal hustler' stereotypes. . . . The music will
express terror and defiance in colorful Negro musical idioms
which have remained melodious despite a life of injustices.
They will compose and write these things because they feel the
consequences of an existence which is a weird combination of
brutality and beauty."

Morrow was overoptimistic perhaps. A few years later along
came *Mamba's Daughters* and *Cabin in the Sky* (stage and
movie versions), which once again bowed handkerchief-heads.
Bill Robinson continued to play the arch Uncle Tom character.
Billy Rose produced a mildly syncopated version of Bizet's
Carmen, with the modern counterparts of the Spanish liquor-
guzzling, homicidal maniacs found, naturally, of course, among
Negroes. He used also the usual exaggerated "dese, dem, dose,
I'se gwine" diction, and had that last line spoken by the colored
equivalent of Don José (Joe)—that immortal sentence, "String
me high to a tree," an incredible line to hear a Negro speak,
with his people's tragic history of lynching.

Duke has the permanent answer to these stereotypes and caricatures of Negroes. It is as well a deft parry of the thrusts of
amateur anthropologists who refer to all Africans of darker
color as savages. It's a musical comedy called, tentatively, *Air-*

Conditioned Jungle. The opening scene sets mood and clime
and theme. In a particularly chic living-room, decorated in the
best of urbane good taste, but not given to flamboyant extrav-
agances, sit the King and Queen of one of the ancient African
tribes. She's dressed in a gown by Schiaparelli; he in a sleekly
fitted dinner jacket. They are drinking their after-dinner
brandy and coffee in relaxed comfort: the house is air-conditioned. A muffled bell rings. The King picks up the telephone.

"Yes," he says, "yes, yes. Mmm-hmm. Oh, bother. Well, if
there's nothing we can do about it." He slams the receiver down
on its cradle and turns unhappily to his consort.

"What is it, darling?" she asks.

"There's another of those expeditions coming over from
America. Trying to discover the original sources of their jazz,
you know?"

"Oh, damn," the Queen curses.

"Yes, my dear," the King says, "we shall have to get out our
leopard skins again."

The story goes on from there to inquire, not too politely,
but without inflammatory wrath either, into the castes and
molds of Negro culture in Africa and America, those which are
true and those which are false, the whole structure of myth
and legend about the colored people. It isn't too likely that this
ironic inquiry will ever reach Broadway or Hollywood production. Its subtleties will not be understood; its stratagems will
probably not be appreciated.

Much of *Jump for Joy* was above people's heads, too. But
there was so much warmth and humor and musical enjoyment
in that revue that most people who came to see it couldn't help
loving it. Almena Davis, Editor of the Los Angeles *Tribune*,
one of the most exacting and most able of Negro journalists,
caught its mood and named its character. *"Jump for Joy,"* she
said, "gawky and as unaware of its real charm as an adolescent,
is new and exciting. It's a new mood in the theatre, reflecting
truly the happy satire of colored life. In *Jump for Joy* Uncle
Tom is dead. God rest his bones."

The title song of the musical announced its point of view

with great good humor. Paul Webster, who wrote the lyrics for most of the songs, did very well by Duke's social philosophy in these words:

> Fare thee well, land of cotton,
> Cotton lisle is out of style, honey chile,
> Jump for joy.
>
> Don't you grieve, little Eve,
> All the hounds, I do believe,
> Have been killed, ain't you thrilled,
> Jump for joy.
>
> Have you seen pastures, groovy?
> Oh, *Green Pastures* was just a technicolor movie.

It goes on from there to its last eight measures, more typical show-song stuff about stepping up to Pete when you stomp up to Heaven and giving Pete some skin. To "give skin" is pretty basic social exchange among musicians, especially colored musicians today. Instead of shaking hands, you pat or slap palms. There are many "skin" variations: some involve touching little fingers, some thumb and pinky, some go from rump to elbow to little finger to thumb to palm. Generally you take the skin you've been given and deposit it, in an elaborately formal pantomime gesture, in a pocket. Tricky Sam has a lovely way of giving skin, preferably to a pretty girl. He takes her hand, rolls the skin together from wrist and fingers, as if he were gathering tobacco to fill a home-made cigarette; then he closes her fingers slowly over the skin gathered so carefully in the center of her palm, takes the fist which results and kisses it with surpassing elegance.

Jump for Joy was "hip." People gave skin. They were, upon occasion, dressed in "zoot" suits. As a matter of fact, the first extensive treatment of the "zoot suit with a drape shape and a reet pleat" was in this revue. Pot, Pan and Skillet, whom Almena Davis called "the unholy triumvirate," danced deadpan through a tailor-shop scene in which the zootiest suit ever was draped about one of their shapes. The language, the costumes, the dancing, the singing in *Jump for Joy* were the real thing, music with a beat, talk with an understanding, bodies moving with unpretentious grace across the stage of the Los Angeles Mayan Theatre.

The sketches and skits followed the lines of the title song lyric. "Cotton lisle was out of style." "*Green Pastures* was just a technicolor movie." The first half opened with an explanation of the place and position of *The Sun-Tanned Tenth of the Nation.* It closed with a little serenade entitled *Uncle Tom's Cabin Is a Drive-In Now.* The second act spotted Rex Stewart in his *Concerto for Klinkers,* one of his several engaging cornet chop sueys in which wrong notes, humbug notes, notes just a hair's breadth sharp or flat, are paraded amusingly across the valves and through the bell of his capricious horn. And then Joe Turner, the great blues singer, turned up dressed as a policeman in a skit called *Ssh! He's on the Beat!* Joe came on every night about 9:30, and his fans turned up every night about that time. They listened to him shout the blues for fifteen minutes and then left. Joe himself left, went to a near-by gin-mill and played his own records on the juke-box, singing duets with his recorded voice.

Marie Bryant and Paul White cavorted through *Bli-Blip,* a bright Ellington jump-piece, and Marie came back to do her parody of Katharine Hepburn. Marie and Paul and an exotic dancer named "Garbo" kept toes on a high level. "Garbo," whose body, Almena Davis said, "was like strawberry mousse . . . interpreted Ellingtonia like it cries to be interpreted." Marie swung her hips intriguingly in a *Chocolate Shake* to one of Duke's catchiest tunes. The show used Strayhorn's *"A" Train* and Duke's *I've Got It Bad and That Ain't Good,* perhaps the most touching of Ellington's torchy ballads. Ivie's singing of its melancholy strains stopped the show and sold hundreds of thousands of records. In contrast, she "kicked" the slightly raucous plaint, *Rocks in My Bed,* which was also a record success. Herbie Jeffries sang several of Duke's songs, none better than he did *The Brownskin Gal in the Calico Gown* and the title tune. Herbie's tall, lithe figure, trained in all-colored Western films, strode a stage with some magnificence, and his soft voice, excellently disciplined by Duke, made more than ordinary sense of Paul Webster's lyrics. Dorothy Dandridge was lovely to look at, and Wonderful Smith and Willie Lewis and Udell Johnson were very funny to listen to. The show was jammed with specialties: the bands' soloists, Rex and Johnny and Ben Webster and Ray Nance, another newcomer, Lawrence and Tricky and Barney and Carney, got some opportunities to display their capacious talents; the writing was fresh and its delivery invigorating.

Each night, for twelve weeks, as soon as the curtain was down, the collective which ran the show met to discuss that night's performance. The material was always in flux.

"You're sure, now, that the point of that first act curtain gets across?" somebody, one of the writers, perhaps Sid Kuller or Paul Webster or Hal Borne or somebody, would ask Duke. "People won't think we're 'Tomming,' will they?"

"No, no, baby," Duke would assure them, individually. "It isn't 'Tom' stuff." They were worried about the white-haired Uncle and his millions of followers more than anything else. In this show he was to be killed dead.

Jump for Joy lasted less than three months. It didn't go anywhere from Hollywood, just dragged itself out as a little bit of this stage show and that in theaters in Boston, Chicago, and so on. But it left enough of an impression so that most of those who saw it and are concerned with a vigorous and honest Negro theater continually refer to it as *the* Negro musical. It was probably the only employment of colored singers and dancers and comedians which really didn't lapse into crude caricature of the Negro at some point, which didn't pander to the white man's distorted idea of colored singing and dancing and comedy. It was ahead of its time and presented on the wrong coast of America for theatrical success, but it made its valorous point.

Duke's plans for opera and operetta and musical comedy and revue have never crystallized, since the demise of *Jump for Joy*. He's always working on three or four or half a dozen at once. One was an idea based on modernizing *Aesop's Fables* in jump time. Another was the *Air-Conditioned Jungle,* which ended up as a title for a piece written for clarinetist Jimmy Hamilton. But Duke has not entirely relinquished the hope of doing that bright satire. He wants to do a show for Lena, because "she's got a soul." And he's talked with Paul Robeson about one. He's got a complex rhythmic pattern worked out for a dance-drama, which may end up as a ballet or a scene in a musical, utilizing the polyrhythms of African drumming, music set in two against that set in three against four to the bar, and motions to follow the twists and turns of the beats against each other. Once, in the time when Duke made so many plans for large-scale expression and did not carry them out, even in part, it would have been possible to dismiss these ideas as verbal blueprints, which would always remain at the nebulous plane of conversation pieces. But Duke has *Jump for Joy* behind him, "gawky and unaware of its real charm" as it was, which demanded and extracted from him a brilliant score and ingenious casting and matching of cast and music. He wrote and helped to direct a musical which cast out some of the devils from the Negro entertainment world. With that achieved, it is certain that other shows will follow. They will follow as *Black, Brown and Beige* followed *Jump for Joy* a year and a few months later.

Jump for Joy, though it spun no narrative, told a story, the story of Negroes in the entertainment world, what they looked like and how they acted and danced and sang and made fun. Unlike *Porgy and Bess,* its music did "hitch with the mood and spirit of the story." "It was true to and of the life of the people it depicted." There was no heartless lampooning of Negroes, as in the country-club scene in *Carmen Jones.* Here was a happy show which still had dignity. Duke had done what he'd always wanted to do. With that accomplished, the success and the rich articulation of ideas which followed were inevitable. Since the trip to Europe in 1939, everything, work and play, thinking and acting and composing and performing, seemed to fit into a pattern of achievement. *Black, Brown and Beige* was the proper next step, as Duke confronted his twentieth anniversary in popular music.

CHAPTER EIGHTEEN

BLACK, BROWN
AND BEIGE

WHEN THE BAND CAME BACK EAST IN THE WINTER OF 1942; there were great cheers from its supporters up and down the Atlantic Coast. Duke had stayed in California, with just short excursions away, for almost two years. Listeners in the East had heard the band on the air, had spun his records on their turntables, but had not heard the Ellington musicians in person. The personnel of the band had changed greatly. Everybody was interested. Loyal supporters of the band were anxious.

The first big change in the band had taken place in October, 1940. Cootie Williams left Duke to join Benny Goodman's Sextet. Benny offered him more money than Duke could pay him, to play in his Sextet and to take spotlighted solos before the band. The figure was good, the stardom sounded good. Cootie left. Dire were the predictions of the Ellington's band's future. Duke was finished. If not finished, he was on his way out. Nobody could replace Cootie. That distinctive growl sound, that remarkable open trumpet tone could not be elicited from any other horn. Raymond Scott composed a dirge to accompany the sad shaking of heads, *When Cootie Left the Duke*, which was one of his band's most successful jazz instrumentals. But Cootie was replaced and the replacement, bruited about in the trade press as just "temporary," turned out to be happily permanent. The man who replaced Cootie became one of Duke's greatest stars, one of the most versatile performers ever to hit jazz.

Duke brought Strayhorn to hear Ray Nance at Joe's De Luxe, a South Side spot in Chicago, where he was featured as trumpeter, violinist, singer and dancer. Duke was impressed with him, amazed at his freshness and versatility, and Ray was hired. Ray was a Chicago boy, born in 1913, brought up on the South Side. He was taught violin by a friend of his mother's, a photographer and musician named Charlotte Page. After eight years with her, he studied under her teacher, Max Fisher, at the Chicago Musical College for another four. And during his years of study, he peppered his education along traditional musical lines with gigs and some longer engagements fronting small and large jump bands. He played opposite Nat "King" Cole's band in battles of music, then got jobs with Earl Hines and Horace Henderson, and, as a single, at the 5100 and other clubs in Chicago.

From the first number Nance played with Duke, his ebullient, infectious personality was clear. When he jumped up to play a solo, only sheer sparkle made his short little figure apparent behind the broad shoulders of the trombonists who sat in front. Like Freddy Jenkins before him, Ray was a "Posey," a natural showman. When he came down to stage front to play fiddle solos, he fenced an imaginary opponent with his violin bow. He danced brightly, short nervous steps alternating with great twirls and swirls. He sang, as do most singing trumpeters, with a rhythmic rip in his voice. On the band's record of *Bli-Blip*, from *Jump for Joy*, his fetching, slightly raucous singing was heard. On *Take the "A" Train*, his trumpeting, more tasteful than anybody else's in the band at that time (1941) could be apprehended. Singing, dancing, fiddling through such very different pieces as *Moon Mist* and *C Jam Blues*, blowing bright horn on *Brown Suede* and *"C" Blues*, for Barney's small unit, Ray was in. Cootie had been brilliantly replaced; that gloomy gossip had been scotched.

Next big loss was Barney Bigard. He left in July, 1942, to join Freddy Slack, a white band, on the West Coast, later to form his own little band. Nobody could replace him. Chauncey Haughton, a veteran of the Chick Webb band, took over his

chair for a year, playing the clarinet parts with legitimate exactness, but without distinction. Later, more successful substitutes
were found, but Barney's particular brilliance on his instrument was his own alone. In the growth of Jimmy Hamilton as
a clarinetist of stature, another sort of musician is being developed in his place, but it is true beyond cavil that Barney is
missed.

By the time Duke got to New York, he was carrying four
trumpets. Rex was the veteran, now playing cornet, preferring
the shorter, stubbier horn's brilliance to the more reliable, full
tone of the trumpet. Wallace Jones, who had taken Whetsol's
place, was next oldest in length of service. Then came Ray
Nance and Harold Baker. Baker was an added starter, a fourth
of surpassing brilliance. He had been a mainstay in the Andy
Kirk band for some years. Before that he had played with
Teddy Wilson's big band and, briefly, with Louis Armstrong.
Harold was everybody's idea of how to play lead trumpet. His
big singing tone carried a melody as nobody else could, and his
conception, so important in shaping a jazz phrase, was rhythmic.
There was some dyspeptic talk about his not fitting Ellington,
but one hearing of his choruses of *Stardust* and *Body and Soul,*
later of his parody performance of *Paper Doll* in the olden
manner, was sufficient to allay that querulous discussion.

The vocalists had changed, too. Ivie Anderson had wanted to
leave for some time. She wanted to get back to California and
tend to her cooking: Ivie's Chicken Shack was a successful Los
Angeles restaurant and Miss Anderson was anxious to supervise
the roasting and the toasting, the drying and the frying of the
legs and wings and breasts which were her delectable specialties.
She gave fair warning, and Duke replaced her over some months,
an interesting process. First, Joya Sherrill, a seventeen-year-
old Detroit schoolgirl, came in, with Betty Roche, to pick up
some of Ivie's tricks, her showmanship, her fine understanding of song lyrics and her remarkable feeling for the way
this band thought and felt and acted and played. But the
tall girl with the bright eyes and the eager manner was still very
young in the summer of 1942. She needed more schooling,

both formal education and band experience: Joya went back to school after four months with Ellington, and Betty Roche stayed.

Betty had sung with the Savoy Sultans and other little outfits. She'd gigged around, played all kinds of spots and was a trained blues singer with something of the manner of Billie Holiday. She bent notes and carried measures along in cadenced groups much like the magnificent Billie. In addition, she had her own specialties, an infectious *Body and Soul,* with her own added lyrics ("Take it all, Take it all, Take it all, Body and Soul") at up tempo, lots of blues. Duke wrote a salacious set of blues choruses for her, *I Love My Lovin' Lover,* which Betty sold with delicious gesture and rowdy shout. It was all about taking her man to his wife's front door and his wife turning out to be as big as Joe Louis ("I ain't gonna do that no more"). Betty was still new when the band hit New York in the winter of 1942 and Ellington fans crowded the bandstand at a one-nighter in the Royal Windsor Ballroom in uptown Manhattan to "dig" her and the other new additions to the band.

Jimmy Britton was new, too. He replaced Herbie Jeffries, who went back to the Coast to start his own café and make records for small companies, records which revealed all his melodramatic defects, unfortunately, and none of the charm which he had displayed with Duke. The balancing musicianship of Ellington and his musicians was sadly missed on those sides, but even on them some of Herbie's rich voice and tender feeling could be heard. He was easily the best ballad singer Duke ever had. Jimmy Britton was the pride of St. Louis, a boy in his early twenties who never quite "got with" Ellington's music. But he did sing an occasional song beautifully; Strayhorn wrote naturally for soft voices like his and in such arrangements as Billy's *Just As Though You Were Here,* score and singer matched perfectly and set exquisite moods. Jimmy was cut out of the finale of *Black, Brown and Beige* at the dress rehearsal performance at Rye High School the night before the Carnegie Hall concert, and he was a broken-hearted boy. The cut was inevitable: he had been assigned some gaudy flag-waving lyrics in the patriotic splurge with which *BBB* concluded. They had to go. But Jimmy didn't last long after that.

January 17 to 23, 1943, Ellington Week was proclaimed in the music business and among Negroes. It was the anniversary, roughly, of Duke's New York debut, twenty years earlier, and the week before his first Carnegie concert. All up and down New York, jazzmen were discussing a coming event. It was to be a benefit for Russian War Relief and the committee in charge of the affair had done a good job in getting word around that Duke was going to do a concert for them. Musicians to whom Duke was an idol were excited. They came in large number to hear rehearsals for the concert at Nola Studios, where all bands in New York rehearse, in the Hollywood Theatre building on Broadway between 51st and 52nd Streets. There was talk about a forty-five-minute work, something symphonic in conception and dimension.

Rehearsals were devoted almost entirely to this forty-five-minute work, called *Black, Brown and Beige.* Duke stood before the band with the great score before him, rehearsing it piecemeal, section by section, sometimes in sequence, more often out of it. The hangers-on, who came from every part of the music business, "sidemen" (members of bands), bandboys, young fans, music publishers, friends of those in the band, critics, were disappointed.

"Doesn't sound like much," a musician commented.

"Awfully choppy," another agreed.

Don Redman, who was listening with intense interest, turned to the disappointed musicians. "You're so wrong," he said. After the concert they agreed that they had been wrong.

There were a lot of fine performances at that first Ellington concert at Carnegie, on Saturday evening, January 23, *Black, Brown and Beige* was preceded and followed by a distinguished number of Ellington compositions, but it was the long work that held primary interest.

The concert opened with *Black and Tan Fantasy* and *Rockin' in Rhythm,* Ellington classics. Then came two pieces of son Mercer's, *Moon Mist* and *Jumpin' Punkins,* two of his first ambitious efforts: the first a beautiful example of Nance's fiddling; the second a swing exercise, with Sonny's cheerful drumming its highlight. This formed the first section of the concert. The second comprised three of Duke's *Portraits,* tone pictures of Bert Williams, "Bojangles" (dancer Bill Robinson, of course) and singer Florence Mills. The Florence Mills tribute was a scantily rescored version of Bubber's old *Black Beauty,* with Harold Baker carrying its heavy solo. Rex played perky cornet through the first two *Portraits,* with nimble assistance from Tricky Sam in the impression of the great Negro comedian and from Ben Webster in the sketch of the tap dancer. Missing from this group was Duke's charming *Portrait of the Lion,* pianist Willie Smith, which he had written several years earlier.

Black, Brown and Beige, which followed, was the centerpiece of the concert; it in turn was followed by the brief intermission, after which the listeners, eagerly discussing the merits and faults of *BBB,* were hastily summoned back into the hall to watch and hear the presentation of a plaque in honor of Duke's twenty years in the music business. Movie actor Dennis Morgan made the presentation, stumbling unhappily through lines which were written for him. But his stumbling and the hastiness and roughness of the whole ceremony were forgotten in the rush of emotion which the Ellington musicians, the Ellington friends and fans and Duke himself felt as the names of the thirty-two musicians on the plaque were read. These were the men who congratulated Duke Ellington, who tendered him gratitude and admiration and respect for his formidable musical achievement, men from both sides of the musical tracks, who were anxious to break down every line of musical snobbery, from the social to the aesthetic. A baton was fitted into the top of the plaque. Under it were the signatures.

"Leopold Stokowski," Dennis Morgan read. That was the first name. A man who had given jazz and Ellington great support. "Walter Damrosch," George Gershwin's first sponsor. "Edward Johnson," the Metropolitan Opera impresario. The other names followed, all well known in music, from every branch of music. John Charles Thomas, William Grant Still, Deems Taylor, Earl Hines, Marian Anderson, Paul Robeson, Lawrence Tibbett, Marjorie Lawrence, Artur Rodzinski (he had not then decided boogie-woogie was the cause of juvenile delinquency), Roy Harris, Count Basie, Albert Coates, Fritz Reiner, Eugene Ormandy, Morton Gould, Kurt Weill, Aaron Copland, Paul Whiteman, Benny Goodman, Jerome Kern, Cab Calloway, Artie Shaw, Max Steiner, Dean Dixon, Allen Wardwell, L. E. Behymer.

After a short wait the air was broken with the searing sounds of *Ko-Ko,* an excerpt from the incomplete score for Duke's opera, *Boola,* which had also yielded much of the material for *BBB.* The names of both the opera and the excerpt are African, but the music is simply Ellington. Tumultuous brass writing, with brilliant accenting by piano and bass and Tricky Sam's growling trombone, carries all before it.

Then it was Strayhorn's turn. A *Dirge, Nocturne* and *Stomp* were announced, but only the first and last were played. The *Stomp* was the jump piece, *Johnny Come Lately.* The *Dirge* was something new, played at that concert and since dropped by the band. It is fit only for concerts, and somehow, by its nature, not fit, Duke feels, for his concerts. It is jazz only in its colors. Its scoring, for valve trombone, two trumpets and saxes, out of tempo, implements its dry, acrid figures: it really is a dirge. The audience was nonplused by what it heard, music that sounded more like Milhaud and latter-day Stravinsky than Ellington, with only a bent note here and slow syncopation there to remind them whose concert it was. But for all these difficulties, most musicians at the concert listened attentively and were deeply moved by Billy's somber chant for jazz instruments.

Next, a flock of concertos featured various men in the band. Chauncey Haughton on clarinet did Barney Bigard's *Are You Sticking?* (which is a word-play in Harlemese on "licorice stick"). Juan Tizol was featured, along with Ray Nance, in his own Turkish delight, *Bakiff,* exotically near-Eastern in harmonies and rhythms. *Jack the Bear* (ain't nowhere—to complete

the couplet well known as a description of a Harlem character)
spotted Junior Raglin on bass. Then *Blue Belles of Harlem*,
which featured, as Duke said, "the pianist in the band." Johnny
Hodges elicited screams with his tortuous unveiling of Strayhorn's *Day Dream*, and Lawrence Brown played jump trombone, unusual for him in the forties when most of his assignments were of a lusher sort, in *Rose of the Rio Grande*, the one
number on the program not written by Duke or one of the boys
in the band. *Boy Meets Horn*, Rex's half-valve love story, concluded this section of the concert.

The concert itself was concluded with a trilogy: *Don't Get
Around Much Any More*, then enjoying great popularity as a
pop tune; *Goin' Up*, which appeared in an abortive version in
Cabin in the Sky, but here gave blowing space to Tricky and
Johnny and Lawrence and Ben Webster and sixteen impassioned
bowing measures to Ray Nance; and *Mood Indigo*, which until
quite recently was Ellington's inevitable closing piece, a soft
end to an evening which had missed none of the dynamics
from *pp to ff*.

When the audience left the hall that night it was buzzing
with talk about the various soloists, about the works of Duke
and Billy and Tizol, but those buzzes skirted the louder roars
of approval or condemnation which greeted Ellington's long
work, *Black, Brown and Beige*. One listening, most people felt,
was not enough. Unfortunately, only a privileged few were ever
to hear the complete work again.

Duke introduced each of the three sections of *Black, Brown
and Beige* verbally. He explained first of all that it was "a
tone parallel to the history of the American Negro." This was
the suite he had been talking about since the middle thirties.
It had much in it of the opera he had been preparing for an
even longer period. It was the story of his people.

Black, the first section, is the longest, built around work
songs and spirituals, driving deeply into the Negro past for its
thematic material, musical, social and literary. Sonny Greer's
timpani smashes out the opening sounds of Negroes working
on the railroad, in road gangs of all sorts, on the levee, in cotton

fields. Harry Carney's baritone saxophone announces the secondary theme after the first has been stated imperiously by the ensemble. Then comes Tricky Sam's growling of still another work song. Toby leads the way into *Come Sunday*, the spiritual theme which is the second section of *Black*. The Sabbath is portrayed by the various members of the orchestral community in spirited solos, Nance's fiddle, the valve trombone, muted trumpet. Then the full glory of the spiritual theme appears as Johnny Hodges at his most mellifluous sings against the strong chording of Freddie Guy's guitar and the bass in stunning contrast. In a final recapitulation, the several themes of this section are restated and Duke's opening scene ended, the dominant motifs of early Negro life not finished, either historically or in the music, but temporarily abandoned.

Brown, part two, chronicles the various wars of the past in which Negroes have participated and the great nineteenth-century influences among the colored people. There are the American Revolution, then the West Indian Influence, in which musical representation is given to the migration to the United States of Negroes from the Bahamas and Puerto Rico and Jamaica and other islands in the Caribbean by Duke's piano and Tricky's trombone and two trumpets in vigorous plunger playing. *Swanee River* and *Yankee Doodle* call the Confederate and the Union armies to Civil War, and Rex Stewart joyously proclaims Emancipation with Tricky, after the older folks, whose lives have been uprooted by the war, have had their mournful say in the voices of baritone and tenor saxes in duet. The Spanish-American War cues the end of the century and introduces the urbanization of the Negro in the twentieth century. Our time suggests the Blues, and the Blues are played and sung, in exposition of the lives and experiences of the people colored *Mauve*. An unmeasured Blues is sung (at the concert Betty Roche sang, later Marie Ellington took over) with obbligato by Toby Hardwick in the early portions and a tenor solo between those and the end. The words and the music follow an intriguing pattern of build-up and break-down:

> The Blues. . . .
> The Blues ain't. . . .
> The Blues ain't nothin'. . .
> The Blues ain't nothin' but a cold gray day
> And all night long it stays that way.
>
> 'Tain't sump'n' that leaves you alone,
> 'Tain't nothin' I want to call my own,
> 'Tain't sump'n' with sense enough to get up and go,
> 'Tain't nothin' like nothin' I know.
>
> The Blues. . . .
> The Blues don't. . . .
> The Blues don't know. . . .
> The Blues don't know nobody as a friend,
> Ain't been nowhere where they're welcome back again.
> Low, ugly, mean blues.

The whole band interrupts, almost viciously; then there is a tenor saxophone solo of the kind of reedy virility of which that instrument alone is capable. The brass introduces the work's only orthodox twelve-bar blues, and the singer comes back for the sorrowful bridge and the conclusion:

> The Blues ain't sump'n that you sing in rhyme;
> The Blues ain't nothin' but a dark cloud markin' time;
> The Blues is a one-way ticket from your love to nowhere;
> The Blues ain't nothing but a black crepe veil ready to wear.
> Sighin', cryin', feel most like dyin'. . . .
> The Blues ain't nothin'. . . .
> The Blues ain't. . . .
> The Blues. . . .

And with an anguished chord the movement ends.

Beige, the third movement, depicts the contemporary Negro, the United States between two world wars and during the second. It is Ellington's own story and beautifully told, skipping from the fast ensemble statement of the theme of the twenties to that of the thirties and the forties. The twenties meant gin-mills, the pseudo-African movement, the Charleston, the party life. The ensemble spins that tale, quickly, lightly. Then Duke's

piano enters in the lonely plaint of the single drinkers, the sad
tinkle of a people sad beneath the temblors of their night life.
Here is a new dignity, the serious side of Negro life. In exposition of this theme, Duke says, "After all, there are more
churches in Harlem than gin mills." First ensemble, then in
beautiful open trumpet (at the concert this was Harold Baker's
most entrancing contribution) there is a change to waltz time,
and a lovely little tune marks the Negro's striving for sophistication. Tenor saxophone, the band, Duke and Carney present several themes: yearning for education, the shouts of the underfed
and poorly clothed and miserably housed, the kept woman in a
Sugar Hill penthouse (Harry Carney's clarinet tops the saxes
in this gently mordant melody). Finally, a brief patriotic motto,
"The Black, Brown and Beige are Red, White and Blue," sig-
nifies Duke's awareness of the war and the Negro's participation in his country's destiny and brings the movement and the
whole work to a conclusion.

There was a lot to be said about the work. The critics on the
daily newspapers went right to work. Paul Bowles, of the *Herald Tribune,* the most knowing of the classical arbiters at the
concert and generally the most sympathetic to jazz, was displeased because: "Between dance numbers there were 'symphonic' bridges played out of tempo. . . . If there is no regular
beat there can be no syncopation, and thus no tension, no jazz.
. . . Nothing emerged," was Paul's sad verdict, "but a gaudy
potpourri of tutti dance passages and solo virtuoso work."

John Briggs in the New York *Post,* Douglas Watt in the
Daily News and Robert Bagar in the *World-Telegram* generalized their disapproving impressions: Briggs curtly, "Mr. Ellington had set himself a lofty goal, and with the best of intentions
he did not achieve it"; Watt snidely, ". . . Such a form of
composition is entirely out of Ellington's ken"; Bagar kindly,
"If you ask me, Mr. Ellington can make some two dozen brief
air-tight compositions out of *Black, Brown and Beige.* He
should." Henry Simon in *PM* was more appreciative. He felt
that the first movement "all but falls apart into so many
separate pieces." But he was impressed by "the extraordinary

melodic fertility of the Duke, his genuinely subtle rhythms and some harmonic experimentation." He thought *BBB* "showed, better than any of the shorter pieces, how well and how far Mr. Ellington has emancipated himself from the straitjacket of jazz formulas. He has taken a serious theme and treated it with dignity, feeling and good humor." Irving Kolodin in the *Sun* was most appreciative. "The sheer talent that has gone into it," he said of the large work, "the number, variety and quality of the ideas, certainly affirm again that Ellington is the most creative spirit that has worked this field." He had a mild demur. "Only a very great amount of talent could sustain the interest bowed down by the limitations of a dance band, its rhythmic conventions and clichés. One can only conclude that the brilliant ideas it contained would count for much more if scored for a legitimate orchestra, augmented by the solo instruments indicated for certain specific passages."

Metronome and *Down Beat,* the leading trade magazines in popular music, and *Billboard* and *Variety,* the entertainment world's news weeklies, were whole-heartedly enthusiastic. The latter organs were impressed by the tremendous box-office returns (ELLINGTON, AT B.O. AND MUSICALLY, NIFTILY IN GROOVE AT CARNEGIE HALL CONCERT, said *Variety*), and the former were more taken by the impact of the music upon its reviewers and the audience (DUKE KILLS CARNEGIE CATS, said *Metronome*).

The *BBB* controversy brought to a head the whole problem of vital expression in the small jazz forms, the place of Duke among contemporary composers and the validity of his art judged by universal standards. Constant Lambert, who had been a constant supporter of Ellington before and during his trip to England in 1933, a year after that visit reappraised Duke and jazz in a section of his provocative and admirably organized panorama of contemporary music, *Music Ho! A Study of Music in Decline.* Though he knew "of nothing in Ravel so dextrous in treatment as the varied solos in the middle of the ebullient *Hot and Bothered* and nothing in Stravinsky more dynamic than the final section"; though he found "the exquisitely tired and four-in-the-morning *Mood Indigo* . . . an equally remarkable piece of writing of a lyrical and harmonic order," he nonetheless decided that Ellington was "definitely a *petit maître*. . . . But that, after all," he said, "is considerably more than many people thought either jazz or the coloured race would produce." He amplified this judgment. "Ellington's best works are written in what may be called ten-inch record form, and he is perhaps the only composer to raise this insignificant disc to the dignity of a definite genre. Into this three and a half minutes he compresses the utmost, but beyond its limits he is inclined to fumble."

There is no question that *Black, Brown and Beige* is not traditional symphonic writing: it is essentially a series of solos linked together by orchestral bridges; its themes are not developed, changed and restated in accordance with the rules of sonata form. It is, too, clearly programmatic writing which is heightened by an understanding of the program and an appreciation of the sociological, psychological and musicological significance of various of the phrases introduced in the long suite. The fact that it is not written in the sonata form and therefore is not a symphony, the fact that it is programmatic, these are not limitations from Duke's point of view or from that of sympathetic auditors whose listening experience in some large way duplicates Ellington's. Duke, contrary to the arrogant dismissal of his musical equipment and knowledge, could have written a symphony and would have if that were the form which best expressed his ideas and emotions about his people. He would have written a symphony or string quartet or oratorio or opera; he chose, instead, to write a "tone parallel," in which jazz virtuosi, in solo and in section and in band ensemble, gave vigorous interpretation to his phrases, some rough, some tender, all colorful and all directed to a narrative point.

It is not easy for those of us who have had a traditional musical education to listen to music with an idea of a program in mind. We have long been taught that the association of imagery with musical phrases is a banalization of them, that we are not to hear Cervantes' hero fighting windmills in Richard

Strauss' *Don Quixote,* nor specific birds in a thunderstorm in
Beethoven's Pastoral Symphony, but simply the music itself.
But the fact is that Strauss and Beethoven and countless other
composers had these images, these stories, in mind when they
wrote their music, and like artists of stature in any art, they
communicated the images and stories with an unassuming directness. Certainly it is not necessary to see Don Quixote's lance
hurtling through the air toward the windmill nor is it vital to
limn the outlines of a cuckoo and a rain cloud to appreciate
the tone poem of Strauss or the symphony of Beethoven, but
neither is it necessary to strain oneself to obliterate those images
from one's mind. In *BBB* there is a similar relationship of picture and tale to the music: you can take it or leave it alone as a
story. Your understanding and appreciation of the work will,
however, be considerably heightened if you bear Duke's program in mind while listening to this music.

There are both the obvious and the subtle in *BBB.* The
gradation of color, black to brown to beige, as the Negroes were
assimilated in America, mixed with the whites and changed in
character as well as appearance, are obvious. The paradoxical
mourning of the old folks for the old way of life which they
had fought against, from which they had been freed by the con-
quest of the Confederate armies by the Union, this is subtle,
subtle on every level, the social, the psychological, and the musical. In the second section of the suite, *Brown,* Duke gives exquisite voice to these people, in the baritone and tenor saxophone duet, answered in enthusiastic stridency by another duet,
trombone and trumpet in plunger mutes. The old Negroes
were free but bewildered, insecure; their progeny were happy,
Emancipation was literal for them, unshackling, it held out
hope for the hopeless. This difficult, this subtle conflict is in the
music.

Though anthropologists and sociologists and psychologists
have been unable to adduce any statistical evidence of any inherent musical superiority among Negroes over members of
other races, evidence even of any rhythmic understanding different from or greater than whites', they cannot and have not

denied the vital role of music in the lives of colored people. To Duke especially, of course, but to most of his people as well, there are musical symbols for all the great moments in American Negro history. To these, Duke has given expression in a structure as loose as the flow of events in *Black, Brown and Beige*. It may give offense to those oriented in traditional music, but it gives a people with very different orientation and traditions a powerful voice. The least those interested in the people can do is to listen to the music with some awareness of the meaning of *Black, Brown and Beige* to Duke and to Negroes. In its apparent formlessness listeners may find a greater awareness, an understanding of the main lines of Negro experience and thinking. They may or may not discover great music. They will surely find a great people.

CHAPTER NINETEEN

SOMETHING
TO LIVE FOR

"JONES!" DUKE BAWLED DOWN THE CORRIDOR OF THE DRESS-ing-room floor of the Cleveland Music Hall. It was a familiar sound, well known backstage at a few hundred theaters and just as many night clubs and many more ballrooms and civic auditoriums and concert halls from coast to coast. Duke was calling for his valet. Richard Bowdoin Jones, the man in question, shuffled up to Duke's dressing room, a broad smile on his dark face.

"Did you call me?" he asked Duke.

"Did I call you?" Duke turned around to ask a rhetorical question of friends and musicians gathered in his dressing-room. "Did I call him?" He picked up his shirt and threw it down in front of him. Jones caught it dexterously within an inch of the floor. "Jones," Duke accused, "you're trying to make me look trampier than you. Look at that shirt, look at it." Unperturbed, Jones went happily about the task of getting Duke together in fresh clothing. When he was all dressed, Duke took a look at himself in the mirror. He caught what looked like a spot on the back of his coat. "Is there a spot there?" he asked Jerry Rhea.

"Yes," said Jerry, "there sure is."

"Damn," Duke said, "you're trying to make a damned wood-chuck out of me, Jonesy. Look," he continued, facing his full audience, "he puts green spots on the back of my coat, in the middle, at the bottom, where I can't find them." Jones just grinned as Duke worked himself up into roaring mock anger. In the middle of the storm, he sneaked out of the room to get about his business of packing the music and clothes and instrument trunks and getting them aboard the trucks which would transfer them to the train.

Jones is very close to Duke. Since 1927, when Duke found him at the Cotton Club, a newly-wed bus-boy, he's been in constant attendance upon him, a valet, factotum, friend. Once, in 1938, Duke found himself the prisoner of some hoodlums who were holding him for ransom at a restaurant. The first person he thought of was Jonesy. He caught a waiter's attention and slipped him a note he had scrawled on a menu along with the doodling which was ostensibly holding all his attention. The note was addressed to Jonesy and asked him to get a couple of guns and come and get him right away. Reached quickly by the waiter, Jonesy hopped a car and got to the restaurant within a few minutes.

Jonesy looked around for Duke. He spotted the table. Rushing to it, he menaced the hoods as he slipped Duke a gun. The two of them, Duke and Jonesy, left the place shooting in the air, and when they got into the car waiting for them outside, Jonesy continued to threaten from the running board, at nothing in particular, just making fearsome noises in the manner of Western and gangster films.

At various times in his career, Duke has faced personal danger and at various times he, or somebody in his entourage, has "packed a heater," carried a gun, usually of .38 caliber. Al Celley, who joined Duke in 1944 as road manager, was faced that same year with such an emergency in Toronto. A good share of the band's instruments was stolen, and after one performance upon borrowed horns it became obvious that the musicians' own trumpets and saxes would have to be found and returned to them. Al, well trained by previous band-managing experience in the wiles and lairs of the underworld, tracked down the gang which had stolen the instruments in the Canadian city. He caught three of the men and got them together in his hotel room.

"Now look, guys," he said, "either you produce those instruments or I'm gonna hang one or all of you out of this window by the thumbs until you tell me." He looked and talked as if he would; the mild Celley, with glasses so thick one can barely make out his eyes behind them, could sometimes sound and act menacing. After a few routine denials of any complicity in the crime and a few more horrifying suggestions of punishment from Al in return, the criminals took Celley to where they had placed the instruments.

Al carries innumerable papers around with him, contract forms, filled out or about to be, railroad tickets, hotel bills, all the complex paraphernalia of a man who is the active business head of an enterprise which grosses over a half-million dollars a year.

The Ellington reputation has grown amazingly. After surmounting the swing craze, Duke went on to top any of his previous achievements, musical or financial. The first Carnegie concert led to two more within a year and a string of concert dates all over the United States, Boston, Philadelphia, Cleveland, Chicago, Los Angeles, and a lot of smaller cities. Fans and musicians and critics all confirmed his unchallengeable position at the top of the band heap by electing him their favorite of all jazz leaders for three years running in the *Down Beat* poll, again in 1944 in the newly revived *Metronome* balloting, and in the same year in the *Esquire* poll.

One instrumental after another has been turned into a huge money-making song hit by the addition of clever lyrics. Under publisher Jack Robbins' aegis, lyric-writer Bob Russell put *Never No Lament* to work as *Don't Get Around Much Any More,* revamped *Concerto for Cootie* as *Do Nothing Till You Hear from Me* and *Sentimental Lady* as *I Didn't Know about You.* Russell's writing was bright, highly singable and framed by good song narratives: the collaboration paid off. So did several songs written directly with lyric-writer Don George, *I'm Beginning to See the Light* and *Ain't Got Nothin' but the Blues.* Duke has formed effective song-writing combinations, tasteful on the aesthetic level and lucrative on the financial.

Most of Duke's biggest hits have been farmed out to different publishing houses, to Jack Robbins, biggest of them, with whom he used to have an exclusive contract, to Harry James' publishing firm (with Harry's name added to the list of writers), to the firm founded by songwriters Johnny Burke and Jimmy Van Heusen. But he's saved some and Strayhorn has saved more for his own outfit, Tempo Music. Tempo is run by Duke's sister Ruth and her husband, Danny James. It is as yet a comparatively small publishing house, but Ruth and Danny, who are the center not only of their own business but of an active circle of vigorous minds in arts and politics, are building it into some eminence in the field. It concentrates on such distinguished instrumentals as *Take the "A" Train, Chelsea Bridge, Perdido, Things Ain't What They Used to Be* and *Moon Mist* (the last two written by Duke's son, Mercer). It owns the parts of *Black, Brown and Beige* which have been chopped from the big work. And Danny and Ruth are contemplating the publication of large-scale works, those turned out by young writers of their acquaintance who are original thinkers in the traditional forms, sonata, string quartet, symphony. Duke takes rather a paternalistic attitude toward this family offshoot of his business enterprises. To his surprise, perhaps, Tempo has turned into a publishing organization of distinction, with a good catalogue, a much better than average set of cover designs for its sheet music and stock arrangements and widespread progressive plans for the future.

With both his parents gone, Duke has become paternalistic, of necessity, to all of his family. He is more than unusually generous, to friends, relatives, causes. When Mercer started a band of his own in 1941, Duke delegated Weely Strayhorn to provide his son with manuscript and rehearsal aid, and he himself did more than pat his pianist-arranger son upon the head in the way of encouragement. The coming of war sent Mercer into the Army, too soon after starting his own band and stopping it and starting again to know whether or not he has a future as a leader. But Father Duke did not, at least, stand in his way.

Father Duke is Grandfather Duke now. Mercer, married, has a son, Edward Kennedy Ellington II. This, as well as the sprightly activities of his nephew Michael, Ruth and Danny's son, delights Duke, who sees a new family growing up about him. The family, and an interest in his own home, have tended to make Duke increasingly conservative in his spending and more interested in investing his money. He remains profligate in the spending of money upon an enormous wardrobe, food, the luxuries of life generally, but he is casting about him for more permanent ways of investing his considerable income and of passing it on.

Endurance, if not permanence, has long interested Duke, the greatest possible endurance for his music, a greater endurance for himself. After his parents' death, Duke began to pay more attention to his physical condition. He developed a vigorous hypochondria that was, perhaps, always latent in him. In Arthur Logan, he found a young doctor who was not only able as a medical man but whose thinking and personality were markedly sympathetic to his own. Whether it is an itch or a stomach-ache, or a serious ailment, such as the tonsil trouble with which he has suffered for years, Duke sends for Arthur at the first wince. From out of town, Duke phones Arthur whenever he is troubled. On one memorable occasion, he had the doctor fly out to Chicago to look after him.

Arthur is one of the inner circle of Ellington intimates which meets irregularly in sessions of what Duke calls the "Expounders." Meeting in living room, between drinks, and kitchen, between nibbles, men like Arthur and his brother-in-law, painter "Spinky" Alston, and Duke kick around their ideas, important and unimportant, frivolous and serious. Spinky may talk about the length of service of Duke's musicians, absolutely unheard of and without parallel in jazz.

"Sure have had those men a long time," Spinky says, "and they get better all the time." He pauses. "Whatcha going to do with all that talent, Duke?"

"I have goals, Spink, goals," Duke answers.

Duke is working hard toward goals which are almost immeasurable. He has seen his band grow not only in public esteem but in musicians' and his own until it is the vehicle for formidable large-scale musical expression. For a while, there were musicians just passing through his saxophone section. Ben Webster, one of the great names among tenor saxophonists, left in 1943 after four years with Duke, and Skippy Williams took his place at the Hurricane in the first of the band's two sojourns at the Broadway night club. Skippy was quickly replaced by Al Sears, who, though capable enough before joining Duke, never exhibited the drive and originality he has evidenced with Ellington. When Barney left, the clarinet chair was reduced to an unimportant adjunct of the reeds. Then, at the Hurricane in '43, when Toby was out briefly, two clarinetists came in, one to replace Chauncey Haughton, one to replace Toby. Jimmy Hamilton took Chauncey's place; Nat Jones came in for Toby. Nat didn't last, though he turned in some sensitive Bigardian solos. Jimmy did last, and, after two years with Ellington, added to the technical skill he exhibited earlier with Teddy Wilson and Lucky Millinder an understanding for Duke's use of his instrument and a creative vitality that makes some of his solos really go.

The brass section really suffered when Harold Baker left to join the Army, in 1944, but it had already been enriched by the addition of Taft Jordan in '43, and Shelton Hemphill, who took Harold's place, is a big-toned first trumpeter—Louis Armstrong calls him "the first lead trumpet of our race." Taft came in for Rex, who left the band for a while when it first came into the Hurricane. Jordan, the former Chick Webb trumpeter, showed what listeners to Chick's band had known for years, that he was a brilliant disciple of Armstrong, good as a blasting open trumpeter, just as good playing tightly-muted horn. He had ample opportunity to play the latter during Duke's memorable Sunday night series of radio shows over the Mutual Broadcasting System, during the six-month Hurricane stay in 1943. The show was called *Pastel Period:* it was music at the piano or pianissimo volume, music that set the soft, sensitive mood Duke calls "pastel." When he wants to set that kind of gentle, genuinely soul-stirring mood, Duke not only writes with the lower dynamics in mind, he also calls to his men: "This is pastel," he says, and they blow accordingly. In the summer of 1943, listeners were treated to a remarkable series of radio programs in which that medium was employed at its mechanical best to give bright but not extravagant amplification to elusive sounds which are more often than not lost in the night club or even the concert hall.

When Rex returned to the band, Duke kept Taft, of course, and Hemphill (known as "Scad" rather than by the more dignified Christian name of Shelton, which just doesn't suit his smiling round face and stumpy figure), who, along with Nance and Cat Anderson, added shortly before the December, 1944, Carnegie concert, filled out the trumpets to a quintet. Cat's fabulous command of the altissimo register of his instrument, hitting notes which it is hard to imagine anyone but a dog hearing, was the big kick of that concert for the audience, which received his work in that register, as well as lower down, with frenzied applause. Juan Tizol left Duke earlier in 1944, to take a place with Harry James as valve trombonist. Claude Jones, who replaced him, is a veteran on his instrument and has played with most of the great colored bands at one time or another. He isn't as imaginative a musician as Tizol, nor has he quite the purity of tone which Juan produces on the valves, but he is an excellent musician. Duke calls an anaemic man a "tapioca Tarzan." Tizol was a "tapioca Tarzan" as a soloist; his greatest contribution to the band was as creator and arranger of exotica, the jazz rondos a la Turque, *Caravan, Bakiff, Moon Over Cuba,* music which reflected his native Puerto Rican rhythms. But neither these nor his unquestionably able section work made him as valuable, objectively, as the intensity with which Duke deplores his loss would lead one to believe.

Tizol did not leave only for the obvious reasons, the greater money and prominence he and his music would receive with one of the country's two or three most successful white bands. He wanted to stay in California, where Harry spends most of his time working in the motion pictures and playing radio commercials. At one time or another most of the veterans of the Ellington band have expressed a desire to settle down, preferably in California, and several have taken vacations which threatened to turn into retirement. The one-nighter schedule which all bands play is tough on musicians; colored bands play more one-nighters than the white, even the big colored bands, because the line against them is so firm in over 90 per cent of the country's leading locations, hotels or night clubs, where they might be able to play long runs. Playing one-nighters is a grueling experience, four-hundred mile jumps in coaches by day or even sleepers by night, sometimes by rocking, tossing busses. It involves every kind of sleeping accommodation, and in the case of colored musicians these are often not too comfortable. And there are the eating problems which a colored musician must face away from home.

When Richard O. Boyer wrote his three-part Profile of Duke for the *New Yorker* magazine in 1944, he told a story about the Ellington musicians' eating problems. In the story, Jack Boyd, then the road manager of the band, was at a saloon near the Fox Theatre in St. Louis, from which you could see the stage door. The boys in the band had been trying to get food sent in to them, because the theater was in the white section of town, where they would not be waited upon. They had sent a white man out to try to get sandwiches for them from a drugstore but had gone hungry when the store proprietor found that the sandwiches were for a Negro band. The musicians were hungry, angry. The theater manager admitted that they had to eat and he arranged for food to be sent to the theater. One of the men left the theater to get something for himself. He left by the stage door and got into a taxi.

"Did you see that?" asked a woman seated on a stool near Boyd at the saloon.

"See what?" Boyd said.

"See that nigra get into that cab?"

"Well, he's a pretty nice fellow. He's a member of the Ellington band. Some people think he's a very great artist."

"A very great artist? Well, I don't know what you think, but I always say that the worst white man is better than the best nigra."

Actually, the experience happened to Boyer, not to Boyd. Boyer was shocked throughout his travels with the band to dis-

K*

cover the intolerance and bigotry which even Negroes of the stature of Duke and his musicians must face. The desire of men to get off the road, when they have been facing those odds for over twenty years, is quite understandable.

How long Duke will continue with this routine is hardly predictable. The money is pretty good and he has an astonishing capacity for enjoying himself in almost any surroundings. The days of depression, of personal gloom and *Weltschmerz*, are over for Duke. When something is unpleasant, he turns it away with a smile or a joke. Somebody hollers overbearingly in or near his dressing room. "Don't yell so loud," Duke says. "You always try to act so mannish!" Jonesy or Jerry Rhea, who is often in attendance upon Duke, may forget to pull down the shades of his dressing-room windows when giving him a massage. Lying there nude, his huge body visible through the windows, Duke spies the raised shades. "Pull those shades down," he says. "I'm not giving this kind of a show at these prices."

Duke's business affairs are in good hands: William Morris handles his bookings; he has a personal accountant to keep his books. He is on good terms with song publishers, songpluggers, most of the men of little or great significance in popular music. He has found a good deal of the peace and calm he told Mildred he wanted so badly.

"I'm a train freak," Duke says, explaining another of the reasons he is so little bothered by the turmoil and discomfort of one-nighters. "I love everything about a train, from the caboose up to the little tender behind." Duke laughs a minute after his explanation. "Ooh," he says, "I'm funny!

"You see," he continues, "I don't worry any more. Everybody thinks those great circles under my eyes are the result of worry. No, no. My bags are the accumulation of virtue and a few hearty laughs. I don't worry."

Duke has a great love of eccentrics and it delights him to watch anybody with any peculiar trait, with any sort of idiosyncrasy whatever, perform. When a man eats more than he does (which is eating a great deal) or drinks a great deal (which is much more than Duke does) or talks with an extensive vocabulary, perhaps, Duke looks on with wonder. "He's a tough man," he will say in compliment, "he waltzes on the two-steps and fox-trots on the waltzes."

On the long train rides, Tricky Sam reads *Time* or any other magazine of fact. He has a head full of statistics and odd facts, and he is continually gathering more. Toby Hardwick may engage somebody in conversation about the inequities of this world. "Take the scales of justice," he says, "have you ever noticed that one side is always lower than the other? Just like the world, just like the world." If Strayhorn is around, he may join Toby to add a few words of cheerful doom to the picture of gloom. A lot of the musicians, but particularly Johnny Hodges and his wife and Taft and Cat and the other newcomers and Freddie Guy and Carney, will play cards. They play "Red Dog" a lot, a gambling game which Juan Tizol learned in the Harry James band and taught to his old bandmates. It looks simple at first glance, but it involves complicated bidding and a great turnover of the accumulated pot. Duke plays cards with Al Sears, "a gentleman," Duke explains, "a gentleman always, from whom it is a pleasure to take money." Duke usually beats Al. Lawrence Brown reads or thinks. Junior Raglin, who replaced Blanton, reads comic books. Somebody may have a drink.

"The slush you got to flush," Tricky says and adds, "Don't mind if I do," as he helps himself to a drink. "The slop you've got to mop," he concludes.

When Jerry Rhea is along, he and Toby and Sonny will get together and discuss old times in Washington. "Little Willie from Long Branch," Jerry says, slapping his side and howling as he looks at Sonny. Sonny will go away in mock anger to listen to one of singer Joya Sherrill's amusing tirades at somebody who has been trying to make a pass at her.

"You haven't lived," Joya barks, "until you've known me. I hope you *die* with that thought on your lips."

Joya rejoined the band in 1944, along with three other girl singers. They were Duke's replacements for Wini Johnson, the very beautiful girl who replaced Betty Roche in 1943. Wini left to marry a Cleveland doctor, taking a lovely face and figure from the organization but not depriving it of any great voice. Joya, who had been with the band earlier, was out of school. She had developed into a good jazz singer with a delightful personality, fresh, vivacious, always on the go, a perfect complement for her pert figure. Kay Davis, who holds a Master of Arts degree from Northwestern University, has a trained lyric soprano voice, which Duke used for a while only to sing humming obbligatos in one old work, *Creole Love Call*, and one new one, *Ain't Got Nothin' but the Blues*. Her limited assignment elicited the comment that she was "the only her that's a hmmmmmm." On the Saturday afternoon following President Roosevelt's death, April 15, 1945, when Duke's was the only dance band on the networks during a seventy-two-hour period, Kay sang again. She sang the Negro spiritual, *City Called Heaven*, and sang it with such beautiful quality of voice and feeling that listeners wrote and wired and phoned to ask if Marian Anderson had been singing with Duke. After that Kay got more to do. Rosita Davis did not stay with the band very long, and Marie Ellington (no relation of Duke's) combined Rosita's duties with her own. Though all the duties didn't add up to much, it was enough to show Marie as an able girl who did as much as possible with meager assignments, usually with a pronounced New England accent. Like Kay and Joya, though in a very different way, Marie is unusually attractive. All are fair, Kay with light, Marie and Joya with black hair. Kay's is a kind of baby face, bright and cute; Joya's much like that, though more mischievous-looking; and Marie's is one that shows a sophistication matching her clothing.

Al Hibbler is the other Ellington singer. Al, who has been blind since birth, first auditioned for Duke in his native Little Rock, Arkansas, in 1935. Duke liked him and told him to come and meet him at his train later the same day. Al was so amazed and delighted at being taken by the great Ellington that he immediately went to a bar and got high. He showed up at the train, but Duke was disinclined to take him when he saw his state. A few years later Hibbler turned up in New York with another band, Jay McShann's. When that amazing jump crew broke into a few parts in 1942, with Jay's departure for the Army, Al took jobs as a single around New York. One night at the Hurricane in 1943, Ben Webster spotted him at a table. He insisted that he sing with the band, brought him up to the stand, thrust him before a microphone and said, "Now sing." Al sang *Summertime* and was hired on the spot.

When Duke hears criticism of Al's tone-shoveling and tendency to forget the meaning of a song's lyrics for a great power dive into his gorgeous lower register, he answers it deftly. "Hibbler's no singer," Duke says, "he's a tone-pantomimist. What other singer creates such tonal drama?"

There has been a lot of criticism of Duke for carrying four singers, the three girls and Hibbler, in addition to Taft and Nance, who sing occasionally. It comes mostly from those who admire the unquestionable talents of the two trumpeters, who are first-rate rhythm singers, but find the girls and Al less attractive because they are less obviously "groovy"—that is, that they sing with less interest in the beat. That is as Duke wants it. On his series of Saturday afternoon programs for the Treasury Department, during most of 1945, he introduced the girls and Hibbler singing in new arrangements of such Ellington evergreens as *Solitude* and *It Don't Mean a Thing*. Here they are used as vocal instruments, singing parts in a vocal section which has been added to the band as one might add violins or French horns. The effect is astonishing: it is another example of Duke's ability to keep going forward, to keep from doing the hackneyed and the stereotyped.

What Am I Here for? Duke asked in one of his 1942 compositions, an instrumental statement of the metaphysical inquiry. Sometimes Duke finds the question puzzling, though it rarely upsets him. He has an unquestioning religious faith which leaves him without serious worries or speculation, a cross of his father's Methodism and his mother's Baptist beliefs. He says Grace before most meals and prayers at night and recites a little verse from the Bible before retiring. A gold cross, a gift from his sister, is always about his neck. "My religion," Duke says, "gives me an edge. It makes me feel I have the edge over my opponents, over opposition of any kind. Beyond a certain point I have nothing to worry about. I have a certain power as a result of my faith."

Duke doesn't worry "beyond a certain point," but he can be concerned about criticism of his music. When most of the New York critics were so severe in their reviews of *Black, Brown and Beige,* he quickly accepted their criticism. He broke the long work into a series of excerpts of less than half the length of the original and introduced them at the Carnegie Hall concert of December 11, 1943. He played them again at the concert at Carnegie a year later, on December 19. He recorded *BBB* in excerpt form, too, killing whatever chances might have remained for future performances of the complete work. When the critics dismissed the most ambitious of his new works introduced at the December, 1943, concert, a composition for piano and orchestra, *New World A-Comin',* he dropped it. The title of the twelve-minute work was taken in optimistic gratitude from Roi Ottley's best-selling book about Negro life, but Duke did not accept the courageous spirit of the book.

Duke knows that his band has improved, that, for all the dissatisfaction and the ruptures and the breaks' in morale as it became more of a disciplined organization and less of a co-operative social unit, its musical excellence has steadily increased. He has watched with satisfaction the intense imitation of his orchestral colors by almost all the distinguished white bands of the late thirties and the forties, most notably and most successfully by Charlie Barnet, Hal McIntyre and Woody Herman, in chronological order. But with all the public admiration, the flattering imitation and the clear advances of his band, he has not found absolute musical security. This explains the lack of courage behind the whittling-down of *BBB* and the dropping of *New World A-Coming.* It also explains his unrelenting activity in both his careers.

"I have two careers," Duke says, "and they must not be confused, though they almost always are. I am a bandleader and I am a composer. Sometimes I compose for the band; sometimes I compose for other organizations; sometimes I compose in a vacuum. What I'm trying to do with my band is to win people over to my bigger composing ideas. That's why I pared down *B, B and B*. You gotta make 'em listen first, listen to things like *Don't Get Around Much* and *Do Nothin'*. Then, when they've heard that, maybe they'll say, 'Gee, this guy isn't so bad at all,' and they'll listen to the longer and more ambitious works and maybe even enjoy them. Yes, *I'm Beginning to See the Light* is the new work song."

It is almost impossible to determine whether or not his audiences understand and appreciate and enjoy Duke's longer, more ambitious works. But the audiences are larger than ever before, and more and more of them are coming to be dedicated to the cause of his music as his fellow jazz musicians have been since 1927, when he went into the Cotton Club. There is every reason for Duke to take music in hand and play anything he wants for the receptive audiences which await him from coast to American coast, in Europe and anywhere else he wants to go. If he lacks courage to do so, if he does not have an absolute sense of security in his music, it is because of many things. It is because of the complexity of his career. It is because of the streak of penitential masochism in him which will not permit him to enjoy anything too much. It is because of a great sense of humility. "I have talent," Duke says. "If only I could apply myself!"

Duke's humility and penitence have provided him with an incalculable amount of the drive which keeps him and his musicians working and progressing. The churchman might praise both; the psychiatrist would surely disapprove of the second, but, more than likely, if a moral judgment is in place here, both are vital to this man. And, fortunately for him as a member of a persecuted minority, he has rarely succumbed either to a sense of racial inferiority or to an acceptance of the underdog role for which America seemed for so long to destine people of his color. He did accept some of the narrow racial doctrine by which he determined that his was Negro music and not jazz or any other differently named art form. But, significantly, as he found expression for his beliefs and experiences as a Negro, and those of his people, in his music, he became less and less of a chauvinist in the arts. Today, Duke Ellington speaks of his band as American. "It is an American band, because it is a democratic band," Duke says. "Each man is an individual with a personality and a voice." And he speaks of his music as American. He gives voice to the sound and rhythm of Negroes in his music, but only as part of the greater sound and still more driving tempo of the United States as a whole. Taking a typically dissonant chord he has constructed for a composition, he will play it on the record or at the piano. "That's the Negro's life," he explains. "Hear that chord. That's us. Dissonance is our way of life in America. We are something apart, yet an integral part."

As the Negroes fight for equality, for recognition on every plane of human activity in America, Duke's music fights with them. To some, this gives his work greater sociological meaning than musical, which is the height of praise or the depth of scorn, depending on the aesthetic philosophy. To others, this music has social value without losing the musical: to them, it can be judged equally well with either set of standards or both. However it is judged, this is the music of our time, the music of America, music which has crossed both the color line and the equally formidable barriers of traditional musical rules.

A COMPLETE
DUKE ELLINGTON
DISCOGRAPHY

The section dealing with the Ellington records from 1925 to 1936 has been specially revised for this edition by ALBERT J. McCARTHY, *who wishes to acknowledge the able assistance of Charles Fox.*

ON THE FOLLOWING PAGES you will find a complete list of Duke Ellington's records. It is as complete as the researches of discophiles working on both sides of the Atlantic, over a period of more than a decade, have been able to make it. These include Charles Delaunay in France, John Hammond and John Reid in the United States. Reid, as an employee of the RCA-Victor Company, prepared a discography of all the Ellington records made for Victor, listing their master numbers and personnels and the dates of recording. There isn't any similar information available for the OKeh and Vocalion and Brunswick and Columbia and countless smaller labels for which Duke recorded. Perhaps, some day, a record scholar, driven mad for want of this information, will demand access to the files of the Columbia Record Corporation and those of Brunswick before 1931, now in Decca's keeping, and will match Reid's effort. In the meantime, we are able at least to name the years in which just about all of Duke's records were made, and that is really sufficient to chart the musical progress of the Ellington band and its composer-arranger-leader.

The titles of the records have considerable significance. Some are obvious, stimulated by the location of the band *(Washington Wobble, Harlem River Quiver, Dallas Doings, Serenade to Sweden,* for example). Others cite the night spot in which the band had been playing *(Cotton Club Stomp, Sherman Shuffle).* Others are dances, all kinds of stomps *(Jubilee, Double Check, Stevedore).* The blues, a significant source of early inspiration, pops up time and again, either directly as a noun *(Rent Party Blues)*, or in adjectival description *(Blue Ramble)*. Some titles tell stories all by themselves *(Lament for a Lost Love, When a Black Man's Blue, Saddest Tale)*. Some titles are reflections of the musicians' vocabulary at the time they were recorded : *Hip Chic* is a young woman who knows her way around ; *Buffet Flat* refers to an after-hours place. Some titles don't seem to make any sense, but they have meaning to Duke at least—that's why they were chosen: *Old King Dooji*, for example, refers to an African King. There are mood-pieces by the dozen *(Dusk* and *Dusk in the Desert, Blue Light, Blue Serge, Misty Mornin', Warm Valley)* which describe clime or time or place or simple space. There are abstractions of feeling and straightforward narratives. Taking up each of Duke's records, one could fill a book twice as long as this one, just in identifying the mood, naming the musical form and the soloists and explaining the meaning of the title.

It is not really necessary, in any of these shorter works of Ellington, to make literary contact with the thought in Duke's mind, or in Strayhorn's or Tizol's or the soloists', when they were written and recorded. Like most good short works of art, they communicate those feelings and programs directly. It helps to be able to tell the difference between a blues chorus (12 measures) and a regular song chorus (32 measures) and thus to note Duke's departures from and variations upon those forms. It helps to be able to spot modulations from key to key and the expertness with which melody and rhythm are varied and organized harmonically. It helps to know anything about the technique of jazz, which is as reasonable and as susceptible to analysis as that of traditional music, from which it springs. To know this technique, to appreciate the vitality of the jazz scale, essentially the blues scale with its flattened third and seventh, is to hear more than just lively rhythm and attractive colour in the music. But whether or not you know and understand these things, listening to his records will carry you beyond enjoyment to recognition of the orchestral devices of Ellington and the characteristic tones and ideas of his soloists. To make the acquaintance of this extraordinary group of musicians is a sizable experience. It is nothing less than a direct introduction to the mainspring of America's most original contribution to the arts, jazz, the major source of its great ideas and the greatest influence upon those who have realized those ideas.

DUKE ELLINGTON'S WASHINGTONIANS

Personnel uncertain. (*Trumpet; Trombone; two Reeds;* Ellington, *Piano; Banjo; Tuba*).

Late 1925

I'M GONNA HANG AROUND MY SUGAR (106250-1)	Pe 14514
TROMBONE BLUES (106251-1)	Pe 14514

As last, plus one *Trumpet,* one *Trombone, Drums.*

Late 1925

GEORGIA GRIND (106729)	Pe 104, Pat 7504
PARLOUR SOCIAL STOMP (106730)	Pe 104, Pat 7504

Harry Cooper, Leroy Rutledge, *Trumpet;* Charlie Irvis, Jimmy Harrison, *Trombones;* Otto Hardwicke, Don Redman, George Thomas. Prince Robinson, *Reeds;* Duke Ellington, *Piano;* Fred Guy, *Guitar;* Bass Edwards, *Bass;* Sonny Greer, *Drums.*

1926

JIG WALK	Ge ——
ALABAMA BOUND	
YOU'VE GOT THOSE WANNA GO BACK AGAIN	
BLUES	Ge 3291, Bu 8010
IF YOU CAN'T HOLD THE MAN YOU LOVE	Ge 3291, Bu 8010

Bubber Miley, Charlie Johnson, *Trumpets;* Charlie Irvis, *Trombone;* Otto Hardwicke, Prince Robinson, *Reeds;* Rhythm section as last.

1926

ANIMAL CRACKERS (355)	Ge 3342
LI'L FARINA (19471)	Ge 3342

Probably same personnel as last.

1926

CHOO CHOO (2005)	Blue-Disc 1002
RAINY NIGHTS (2006)	Blue-Disc 1002
DEACON JAZZ (2007)	Blue-Disc 1003
OH HOW I LOVE MY DARLING (2008)	Blue-Disc 1003

DUKE ELLINGTON AND HIS KENTUCKY CLUB ORCHESTRA

Bubber Miley, Louis Metcalfe, *Trumpets;* Joe " Tricky Sam " Nanton, *Trombone;* Otto' Hardwicke, Harry Carney, *Alto and Baritone Saxes;* Rudy Jackson, *Tenor Sax and Clarinet;* Duke Ellington, *Piano;* Fred Guy, *Guitar;* Bass Edwards, *Bass;* Sonny Greer, *Drums.*

Late 1926

EAST ST. LOUIS TOODLE-OO (E 4110)	Vo 1064
BIRMINGHAM BREAKDOWN (E 4114)	Vo 1064
IMMIGRATION BLUES	Vo 1077
THE CREEPER	Vo 1077

Same Personnel.

1927

NEW ORLEANS LOWDOWN	Vo 1086
SONG OF THE COTTON FIELD	Vo 1086
BIRMINGHAM BREAKDOWN	Br 3480, 6801, 80000, BrE 02299
EAST ST. LOUIS TOODLE-OO	Br 3480, 6801, 80000, BrE 02299
EAST ST. LOUIS TOODLE-OO (143705)	Co 953, PaE R 2202
HOP HEAD (143706)	Co 953, PaE R 2202
DOWN IN OUR ALLEY BLUES (143707)	Co 1076, CoE 4562
BLACK AND TAN FANTASY	Br 3526, 6682, BrE 01540
	BrE 02306

June Clark, *Trumpet,* replaces Miley on the following side.

1927

SOLILOQUY	Br 3526, 6804

DUKE ELLINGTON AND HIS ORCHESTRA

Bubber Miley, Louis Metcalfe, *Trumpets;* Joe " Tricky Sam " Nanton, *Trombone;* Otto Hardwicke, *Alto Sax and Clarinet;* Harry Carney, *Alto and Baritone Saxes;* Rudy Jackson, *Alto Sax and Clarinet;* Duke Ellington, *Piano ;* Fred Guy, *Banjo ;* Wellman Braud, *Bass;* Sonny Greer, *Drums;* Adelaide Hall, *Vocal.*

New York City, October 26, 1927

CREOLE LOVE CALL (39370)	Vi 24861, 21137, HMV B 6252, 4895
THE BLUES I LOVE TO SING (39371)	Vi 21490, 22985, HMV B 6343, B 4966
BLACK AND TAN FANTASY (40155)	Vi 21137, 24861, HMV B 6356, B 4869
WASHINGTON WOBBLE (40156)	Vi 21284, Bb 6782, HMV B 8652, B 4929

Jabbo Smith, *Trumpet,* replaces Miley, November, 1927.

WHAT CAN A POOR FELLOW DO (81775)	OK 40955, 8521, PaE R 1549
BLACK AND TAN FANTASY (81776)	OK 40955, 8521, PaE R 2211
CHICAGO STOMP DOWN (81777)	OK 8675

DUKE ELLINGTON AND HIS COTTON CLUB ORCHESTRA

Bubber Miley, *Trumpet*, returns in place of Jabbo Smith.

New York City, December 19, 1927

HARLEM RIVER QUIVER* (41244)	Vi 21284, 22791, HMV B 4946, B 8528
EAST ST. LOUIS TOODLE-OO (41245)	Vi 21703, 20-1531, HMV B 4958, B 8649
BLUE BUBBLES (41246)	Vi 21490, 22985, Bb 6415, HMV B 4915

Late 1927

RED HOT BAND	Vo 1153
DOIN' THE FROG	Vo 1153

Early 1928

SWEET MAMA (145488)	Ha 577, Di 2577
STACK O'LEE BLUES (145489)	Ha 601, Di 2601
BUGLE CALL RAG (145490)	Ha 577, Di 2577

Barney Bigard, *Clarinet*, replaces Rudy Jackson.

Early 1928.

TAKE IT EASY (400030)	OK 41013, Br 7670, PaE R 144, R 2304
JUBILEE STOMP (400031)	OK 41013, Br 7670, PaE R 144, R 2523
HARLEM TWIST (400032)	OK 8638
EAST ST. LOUIS TOODLE-OO	Ca 8182, Pe 14962, Pat 36781
JUBILEE STOMP	Ca 8182, Pe 14962, Pat 36781
TAKE IT EASY	Ca 8188, Pe 14968, Pat 36787

New York City, March, 26, 1928

BLACK BEAUTY (43502)	Vi 21580, Bb 6430, HMV B 6166, B 4872
JUBILEE STOMP (43503)	Vi 21580, Bb 6415, HMV B 6262, B 4859
GOT EVERYTHING BUT YOU (43504)	Vi 21703, Bb 6531, 10244, HMV B 4958

Early 1928

BLACK BEAUTY (3411)	Ca 8352, Ro 775
TAKE IT EASY	Br 4009, 6803, BrE 01778
JUBILEE STOMP	Br 4044, 6804, BrE 3878
BLACK BEAUTY	Br 4009, 6803, BrE 01512, 02306
YELLOW DOG BLUES (E 27771)	Br 3987, 6802, 80049, BrE 02650
TISHOMINGO BLUES (E27772)	Br 3987, 6802, 80049, BrE 02503
DIGA DIGA DOO (400859)	OK 8602, 41096, PaE R379, R 2336
DOIN' THE NEW LOW-DOWN (400860)	OK 8602, 41096, PaE R379, R 2550

*Issued as BROWN BERRIES on all but Vi 21284.

Duke Ellington (piano solos).

New York City, October 1, 1928.

BLACK BEAUTY (401172)   OK 8636, PaE R 571
SWAMPY RIVER (401173)   OK 8636, PaE R 582

Previous Full Band Personnel plus Lonnie Johnson, *Guitar*, and Baby Cox, *Vocal*, for this session only.

New York City, October 1, 1928

THE MOOCHE (401175)   OK 8623, Br 8241, PaE R 1615
MOVE OVER (401176)   OK 8638
HOT AND BOTHERED (401177)   OK 8623, PaE R 582

Probably the same personnel as before.

Late 1928.

HOT AND BOTHERED (3528)   Ca 9023, Ro 827
MOVE OVER (3529)   Ca 9025, Ro 829, Pe 15080, Pat 36899
THE MOOCHE (3530)   Ca 9032, Ro 836, Pe 15080, Pat 36899

Ozzie Ware, *Vocal*, accompanied by the Ellington Band.

HIT ME IN THE NOSE (3532)   Ca 9039, Ro 843
IT'S ALL COMIN' HOME TO YOU* (3533)   Ca 9039, Ro 843

DUKE ELLINGTON'S COTTON CLUB ORCHESTRA

Personnel as before.

Late 1928

AWFUL SAD (E 28341)   Br 4110, 6805, 80050, BrE 01616, 02307
THE MOOCHE (E 28359)   Br 4122, 6812, 80002, BrE 1235
LOUISIANA (E28360)   Br 4110, 6805, BrE 02650

Personnel unknown.

New York City, October 30, 1928

THE MOOCHE   Vi 38034, 24486, 20-1531, HMV B 6354, B 4920
   (47799)
I CAN'T GIVE YOU ANYTHING   Vi 38008, Bb 6280, HMV B 4959
   BUT LOVE (48102)
NO PAPA NO (48103)   Vi 26310, HMV B 9253

*Accompanied by Ellington *(Piano)* only.

Arthur Whetsel, Bubber Miley, Freddy Jenkins, *Trumpets;* Joe Nanton, *Trombone;* Johnny Hodges, Otto Hardwicke, Barney Bigard, Harry Carney, *Reeds;* Duke Ellington, *Piano;* Fred Guy, *Banjo;* Wellman Braud, *Bass;* Sonny Greer, *Drums.*

New York City, November 15, 1928

BANDANNA BABIES (48166)	Vi 38007, Bb 7182, HMV B 4957, B 8652
DIGA DIGA DOO (48167)	Vi 38008, Bb 6305, HMV B 4949
I MUST HAVE THAT MAN (48168)	Vi 38007, Bb 7182, HMV B 4957, B 8649

Otto Hardwicke, *Alto,* absent. Lonnie Johnson, *Guitar,* added.

November, 1928.

BLUES WITH A FEELING (401350)	OK 8662, Co 35955, PaE R 2258
GOIN' TO TOWN (401351)	OK 8675
MISTY MORNING (401352)	OK 8662, Co 35955, PaE R 2258

As last without Lonnie Johnson.

Early 1929

DOIN' THE VOOM VOOM (E 28939)	Br 4345, 6807, BrE 02365
TIGER RAG—Part 1 (E 28940)	Br 3956, 4238, 80048, BrE 1338
TIGER RAG—Part 2 (E 28941)	Br 3956, 4238, 80048, BrE 1338

Same Personnel.

January 16, 1929.

FLAMING YOUTH (49652)	Vi 38035, 24057, Bb 10243, HMV B 4942, B 6528
SATURDAY NIGHT FUNCTION (49653)	Vi 38036, 24674, HMV B 4956, B 8404
HIGH LIFE (49654)	Vi 38036, Bb 6269, HMV B 4956, B 6269
DOIN' THE VOOM VOOM (49655)	Vi 38035, 24121, Bb 7710, HMV B 4942, B 6404

THE WHOOPEE MAKERS

Probably similar personnel.

1929.

HOTTENTOT (3563)	Pe 15104, Pat 36923, Ro 840
MISTY MORNING (3564)	Pe 15104, Pat 36923, Ro 840
DOIN' THE VOOM VOOM (4062)	Pe 15240, Pat 37059, Ro 1101
FLAMING YOUTH (4063)	Pe 15240, Pat 37059
SATURDAY NIGHT FUNCTION (4064)	Ro 1101

DUKE ELLINGTON AND HIS ORCHESTRA

Similar Personnel.

New York City.   February 18, 1929

JAPANESE DREAM (48373)   Vi 38045, HMV B 6353, JF 54
HARLEMANIA (48374) Vi 38045 Bb 6306, HMV B 6351, B 4966, B 8505

Cootie Williams, *Trumpet*, replaces Miley.   ˙

Early 1929.

RENT PARTY BLUES   Br 4345, 6807, BrE 02365
PADUCAH   Br 4309, 6806, BrE 02003
HARLEM FLAT BLUES   Br 4309, 6806, BrE 02003

Same Personnel.

New York City.   March 7, 1929

THE DICTY GLIDE (49767) Vi 38053, Bb 6269, HMV B 4920, B 6356
HOT FEET (49768)   Vi 38065, Bb 6335, HMV B 4865, B 6343
SLOPPY JOE (49769)   Vi 38065, Bb 6396, HMV B 4865, B 6352
STEVEDORE STOMP (49770)   Vi 38053, Bb 6306, HMV B 6106

NOTE : Duke Ellington and His Orchestra are present on the following record.

WARREN MILLS AND HIS BLUES SERENADERS

GEMS FROM BLACKBIRDS OF 1928   Vi 35962
ST. LOUIS BLUES   Vi 35962

Same Personnel.

Early 1929.

I MUST HAVE THAT MAN (148170)   CoE 5486
FREEZE AND MELT (148171)   Co 1813
MISSISSIPPI MOAN (148172)   Co 1813, Co 36157

Same Personnel.

May 3, 1929.

COTTON CLUB STOMP   Vi 38079, Bb 10242, HMV B 4872,
  (51971)   B 6292
MISTY MORNIN' (51972)   Vi 38058, Bb 6565, HMV B 8828
ARABIAN LOVER (51973)   Vi 38079, Bb 6782, HMV B 4895
SARATOGA SWING*   Vi 38058, Bb 6565, 10245, HMV B 6929,
  (51974)   B 8828

*Last side by Williams, Bigard, Hodges and rhythm section only.

Same personnel.

May 28, 1929

THAT RHYTHM MAN (148640)	Co 36157
BEGGARS BLUES (148641)	Co 2833, Vo 3012, CoE DB 5033
SATURDAY NIGHT FUNCTION * (148642)	Co 2833, Vo 3012, CoE DB 5033

Personnel probably as before.

1929

SARATOGA SWING (3713)	Ca 9175, Ro 977
WHO SAID " IT's TIGHT LIKE THAT " (3714)	Ca 9195, Ro 997

Ozzie Ware, *Vocal*, acc. Ellington Orchestra (as The Whoopee Makers).

HE JUST DON'T APPEAL TO ME (3715)	Ro 1042

Previous personnel.

Mid 1929

BLACK AND BLUE	Br 4492, 6809, BrE 02701
JUNGLE JAMBOREE	Br 4492, 6809, BrE 02701

THE HARLEM FOOTWARMERS

Same personnel.

Summer, 1929

JUNGLE JAMBOREE (402551)	OK 8720, PaE R 1946
SIX OR SEVEN TIMES (402552)	Unissued
SNAKE HIP DANCE (402553)	OK 8720, PaE R 2305

DUKE ELLINGTON AND HIS ORCHESTRA

Arthur Whetsel, Freddy Jenkins, Cootie Williams, *Trumpets ;* Joe Nanton, Juan Tizol, *Trombones;* Johnny Hodges, Harry Carney, Barney Bigard, *Reeds;* Rhythm section as before.

Autumn, 1929

JOLLY WOG	Br 4705, 6810, 80035, BrE 02299
JAZZ CONVULSIONS	Br 4705, 6810, 80050, BrE 01827, 02309

*Last side by Whetsel, Nanton, Bigard, Hodges and rhythm section only.

Teddy Bunn, *Guitar*, added.

September 16, 1929

MISSISSIPPI (55845)	Vi 38089, 24057, HMV B 6355, B 4943
THE DUKE STEPS OUT (55846)	Vi 38092, Bb 6727, HMV B 6292, B 4960
HAUNTED NIGHTS(55847)	Vi 38092, Bb 6727, HMV B 4960
SWANEE SHUFFLE (55848)	Vi 38089, 24121, Bb 6614, HMV B 6328, B 4943

Bunn leaves.

November 14, 1929

BREAKFAST DANCE (57542)	Vi 38115, Bb 10243, HMV B 6230, B 4905
JAZZ LIPS (57543)	Vi 38129, Bb 6396, HMV B 6351, B 8505, B 4939
MARCH OF THE HOODLUMS (57544)	Vi 38115, HMV B 6404

Note : SIX JOLLY JESTERS :

Recorded late 1929

SIX OR SEVEN TIMES	Vo 15843
OKLAHOMA STOMP	Vo 1449

May be an Ellington record.

Same personnel.

November 20, 1929

LAZY DUKE (403286)	OK 8760, PaE R 1549
BLUES OF THE VAGABOND (403287)	OK 8746, PaE R 1535
SYNCOPATED SHUFFLE (403288)	OK 8746, PaE R 1535

Same personnel.

Late 1929

SWEET MAMA	Br 4760, 6811
WALL STREET WAIL	Br. 4887, 6813, 80013, BrE 01886

THE TEN BLACKBERRIES

Same Personnel.

Early 1930

ST. JAMES INFIRMARY (9319)	Pe 15272, Ba 0594, Ro 1209
WHEN YOU'RE SMILING (9320)	Pe 15272, Re 8941, Ro 1862
RENT PARTY BLUES (9321)	Ba 0594, Or 1849, VoE C 0006
JUNGLE BLUES (9322)	Ba 0598, Or 1854, VoE C 0006

English VoE issues as Duke Ellington and his Orchestra.

DUKE ELLINGTON AND HIS ORCHESTRA

Same personnel.

Early 1930

WHEN YOU'RE SMILING	Br 4760, 6811, BrE 02671
MAORI	Br 4776, 6812, BrE 02671
ADMIRATION	Br 4776, 6812

Probably same personnel as before.

1930

SING YOU SINNERS	HOW 1045
ST. JAMES INFIRMARY	HOW 1046

Issued as HARLEM HOT CHOCOLATES.

Same personnel.

April 11, 1930

DOUBLE CHECK STOMP	Vi 38129, Bb 6450, HMV B 6277, B 4939
(59692)	
MY GAL IS GOOD FOR NOTHING	
(59693)	Vi 38130, HMV B 4961
I WAS MADE TO LOVE YOU	Vi 38130, HMV B 4961, B 8653
(59694)	

Joe Cornell, *Accordeon*, and Dick Robertson, *Vocal*, added for this session only.

Mid 1930

DOUBLE CHECK STOMP	Br 4783, 6846, 80035, BrF 500170
ACCORDEON JOE	Br 4783, 6846
COTTON CLUB STOMP	Br 4887, 6813, BrE 01186

Personnel probably as before.

Mid 1930

THE MOOCHE	Ve 7072, Di 6046
EAST ST. LOUIS TOODLE-OO	Ve 7072, Di 6046
SWEET MAMA	Ve 7088, Di 6062
HOT AND BOTHERED	Ve 7082, Di 6056
DOUBLE CHECK STOMP	Ve 7088, Di 6062
BLACK AND TAN FANTASY	Ve 7082, Di 6056

Arthur Whetsel, Freddy Jenkins, Cootie Williams, *Trumpets;* Joe
Nanton, Juan Tizol, *Trombones;* Johnny Hodges, *Alto Sax;* Barney
Bigard, *Tenor Sax and Clarinet;* Harry Carney, *Alto and Baritone Saxes;*
Duke Ellington, *Piano;* Fred Guy, *Banjo;* Wellman Braud, *Bass;*
Sonny Greer, *Drums.*

New York City, June 4, 1930

SWEET DREAMS OF LOVE (62192)	Vi 38143, HMV B 6277, B 4915
JUNGLE NIGHTS IN HARLEM	Vi 23022, Bb 6335, HMV B 6328, B4836
(62193)	
SWEET JAZZ O' MINE (62194)	Vi 38143, HMV B 6106
SHOUT 'EM AUNT TILLIE (62195)	Vi 23041, Bb 10242, HMV B 4853

Personnel as before with THE RHYTHM BOYS (Bing Crosby, Al
Rinker, Harry Barris) *Vocal Trio.**

Summer, 1930

RING DEM BELLS (61011)	Vi 22528, 25076, 20-1530, HMV B 5945
OLD MAN BLUES (61012)	Vi 23022, Bb 6450, HMV B 6353, B 4888
THREE LITTLE WORDS* (61013)	Vi 22528, 25076, HMV B 5945

Same personnel.

October 2, 1930

HITTIN' THE BOTTLE (63360)	Vi 23116, HMV B 4888
THE LINDY HOP (63361)	Vi 23116, HMV B 6335, JF 51
YOU'RE LUCKY TO ME (63362)	Vi 23017, HMV B 5954
MEMORIES OF YOU (63363)	Vi 23017, HMV B 5954, Bb 6280

Arthur Whetsel, *Trumpet;* Joe Nanton, *Trombone;* Barney Bigard,
Clarinet, and Rhythm section only.

Late 1930

BIG HOUSE BLUES (404482)	OK 8836, Co 14670, 35682, PaE R 1044
ROCKY MOUNTAIN BLUES	OK 8836, Co 35682, PaE R 1449
(404483)	

Previous Full Band personnel.

Late 1930

RUNNIN' WILD	Br 4952, 6732, BrE 1068
MOOD INDIGO	Br 4952, 6732, BrE 1068
HOME AGAIN BLUES	Br 6003
WANG WANG BLUES	Br 6003, BrE 1088
RING DEM BELLS (404519)	OK 41468, PaE R 849
OLD MAN BLUES (404521)	OK 8869, PaE R 942

SWEET CHARIOT (404522)   OK 8840, PaE R 1615
MOOD INDIGO* (480023)   OK 8840, PaE R 866
THREE LITTLE WORDS† (480028)   PaE R 883

Same personnel.
November 21, 1930
NINE LITTLE MILES FROM TEN (64812)   Vi 22586, HMV B 6293
I'M SO IN LOVE WITH YOU (64813)   Vi 23041

Same personnel.
November 26, 1930

BLUE AGAIN (64379)   Vi 22603

Same Personnel.
December 10, 1930
MOOD INDIGO (64811)   Vi 22587, 24486, 20–1532, HMV B 6354
WHAT GOOD AM I WITHOUT YOU (64378)   Vi 22586
WHEN A BLACK MAN'S BLUE (64380) Vi 22587, HMV B 4842, B 6294

Same personnel.
Early 1931

I CAN'T REALISE YOU LOVE ME (404802)   Ha 1377, Ve 2455
I'M SO IN LOVE WITH YOU (404803)   Ha 1377, Ve 2455
ROCKIN' IN RHYTHM (404804)   OK 8869, PaE R 924
THEM THERE EYES   Pe 15418, Ro 1556, Or 2191, Re 10244
ROCKIN' CHAIR   Pe 15418, Ro 1556, Or 2191, Re 10244
I'M SO IN LOVE WITH YOU   Pe 15649, Or 2528
ROCKIN' CHAIR (35800)   Br 6732, BrE 01727, 02308
ROCKIN' IN RHYTHM (35801)   Br 6038, 80001, BrE 1105, 02309
TWELFTH STREET RAG (35802)   Br 6038, 80001, BrE 1573, 02307

The first six sides were issued as by the WHOOPEE MAKERS.

Same Personnel.
January 16, 1931

THE RIVER AND ME (67798)   Vi 22614, HMV B 4884, B 6160
KEEP A SONG IN YOUR SOUL   Vi 22614, Bb 6305, HMV B 4884,
   (67799)   B 8653
SAM AND DELILAH (67800)   Vi 23036, HMV B 6175
ROCKIN' IN RHYTHM (67401)   Vi 26310, HMV B 9253

*Arthur Whetsel, *Trumpet ;* Joe Nanton, *Trombone ;* Barney Bigard, *Clarinet,* and
Rhythm section only.
   †Issued as by the PHILADELPHIA MELODIANS.

Same personnel.

Early 1931

THE PEANUT VENDOR	Me 12080
CREOLE RHAPSODY—Part 1	Br 6093, 80047, BrE 1145
CREOLE RHAPSODY—Part 2	Br 6093, 80047, BrE 1145
IS THAT RELIGION ?	Me 12080, BrE 1226

Me issues as by Earl Jackson and his MUSICAL CHAMPIONS.

Same personnel.

New York City, June 11, 1931

CREOLE RHAPSODY—Part 1 (12″) (68231)	Vi 36049, HMV C 4870
CREOLE RHAPSODY—Part 2 (12″) (68232)	Vi 36049, HMV C 4870

Same personnel.

June 16, 1931

LIMEHOUSE BLUES (68237)	Vi 22743, HMV B 6066
ECHOES OF THE JUNGLE (68238)	Vi 22743, HMV B 6066

Same personnel.

June 17, 1931

IT'S A GLORY (68239)	Vi 22791, Bb 10245, HMV B 6293, B 4946
THE MYSTERY SONG (68240)	Vi 22800, Bb 6614, HMV B 6133

DUKE ELLINGTON AND HIS FAMOUS ORCHESTRA

Arthur Whetsel, Freddy Jenkins, Charles " Cootie " Williams, *Trumpets ;* Juan Tizol, Joe "Tricky Sam" Nanton, *Trombones ;* Johnny Hodges, *Alto and Soprano Saxes;* Harry Carney, *Alto and Baritone Saxes and Clarinet;* Barney Bigard, *Tenor Sax and Clarinet;* Duke Ellington, *Piano ;* Fred Guy, *Guitar ;* Wellman Braud, *Bass ;* Sonny Greer, *Drums ;* Ivie Anderson, *Vocal.* *

February 2, 1932

MOON OVER DIXIE (B11200)	Br 6317, BrE 01827
IT DON'T MEAN A THING *	Br 6265, BrE 1292, VoE S 65,
(B 11204)	PaE R 2813
LAZY RHAPSODY (B 11205)	Br 6288, BrE 1299, PaE R 2890

Same personnel.

February 3, 1932

Medley—MOOD INDIGO, HOT AND BOTHERED,	
CREOLE LOVE CALL (71812)	Vi L 16006 (33 1/3 R.P.M.)

Same personnel.

February 4, 1932

BLUE TUNE (B 11223)	Br 6288, BrE 1299
BABY, WHEN YOU AIN'T THERE	Br 6317, 8241, BrE 01681,
(B 11224 A)	PaE R 2813
BABY, WHEN YOU AIN'T THERE (B 11224 B)	Co 35835

Same personnel.

February 9, 1932

Medley—EAST ST. LOUIS TOODLE-OO, LOT O'
FINGERS, BLACK AND TAN FANTASY

(71836)	Vi L 16007 (33 1/3 R.P.M.)
DINAH (71838)	Vi 22938, HMV B 6175
BUGLE CALL RAG (71839)	Vi 22938, HMV B 6188, B 4905

Same personnel. Bing Crosby,* *Vocal.*

February 11, 1932

*ST. LOUIS BLUES	Br 20105, Co 55003, BrE 116, CoE DX 898
(BX 11263)	
CREOLE LOVE CALL	Br 20105, Co 55003, BrE 116, CoE DX 898
(BX 11264)	
ROSE ROOM (B 11265)	Br 6265, BrE 1292

Same personnel, plus Lawrence Brown, *Trombone;* Otto Hardwick, *Alto Sax.*

May 16, 1932

BLUE HARLEM (B 11839)	Br 6374, BrE 1377, PaE R 2925
THE SHEIK (B 11840)	Br 6336, BrE 1337

May 17, 1932

SWAMPY RIVER (B 11850)	Br 6355, BrE 01727
FAST AND FURIOUS (B 11851)	Br 6355, BrE 1367
BEST WISHES (B 11852 A)	Co 35836
BEST WISHES (B 11852 B)	Br 6374, BrE 1377

May 18, 1932

BLUE RAMBLE (B 11866 A)	Br 6336, BrE 1337
BLUE RAMBLE (B 11866 B)	Co 35834

Same personnel.

September 19, 1932

DUCKY WUCKY (B 12333 A)	Co 35683
DUCKY WUCKY (B 12333 B)	Br 6432, BrE 1426

September 21, 1932

JAZZ COCKTAIL (B 12343)	Br 6404, BrE 1399
LIGHTNIN' (B 12344 A)	Br 6404, BrE 1399
LIGHTNIN' (B 12344 B)	Co 35835
STARS (B 12345)	BrF 9331

September 22, 1932

SWING LOW (B 12346 A)	Co 35683
SWING LOW (B 12346 B)	Br 6432, BrE 1426

Personnel as before, except that Barney Bigard is absent.

December 21, 1932

ADELAIDE HALL (vocal) accompanied by Duke Ellington and his Famous Orchestra

I MUST HAVE THAT MAN (B 12773)	Br 6518, BrE 01519
BABY (B 12774)	Br 6518, BrE 01519

DUKE ELLINGTON AND HIS FAMOUS ORCHESTRA

ANY TIME, ANY DAY, ANYWHERE (B 12775)	Br 6467, BrE 1462

Personnel as for December 21.

December 22, 1932

THE FOUR MILLS BROTHERS accompanied by Duke Ellington and his Famous Orchestra

DIGA DIGA DOO (B 12781)	Br 6519, BrE 01520

ETHEL WATERS (Vocal) accompanied by Duke Ellington and his Famous Orchestra

I CAN'T GIVE YOU ANYTHING BUT LOVE (B 12783)	Br 6517, 6758, BrE 01518, 01731
PORGY (B 12784)	Br 6521, 6758, BrE 01522, 01731

DUKE ELLINGTON AND HIS FAMOUS ORCHESTRA

Personnel as before, but with Barney Bigard back.

January 7, 1933

EERIE MOAN (B 12855)	Br 6467, BrE 1462

Same personnel.   Ivie Anderson,* *Vocal.*

February 15, 1933

MERRY-GO-ROUND (265049–1)	Co 35387
MERRY-GO-ROUND (265049–3)	CoE CB 591, FB 2821
SOPHISTICATED LADY (265050)	CoE CB 591, FB 2821
*I'VE GOT THE WORLD ON A STRING (265051)	CoE CB 625

February 16, 1933

DOWN A CAROLINA LANE (265052)	CoE CB 625

February 17, 1933

SLIPPERY HORN (B 13078)	Br 6527, BrE 01540, PaE R 2925
BLACKBIRDS MEDLEY, PART 1 (B 13079)	Br 6516, BrE 01517
BLACKBIRDS MEDLEY, PART 2 (B 13080)	Br 6516, BrE 01517
DROP ME OFF AT HARLEM (B 13081 A)	Br 6527, BrE 01512, PaE R 2876
DROP ME OFF AT HARLEM (B 13081 B)	Co 35837

Joe Garland *Tenor Sax,* replaces Barney Bigard ; Ivie Anderson, *Vocal.*

May 9, 1933

HAPPY AS THE DAY IS LONG (B 13306)	Br 6571, VoE S 64
RAISIN' THE RENT (B 13307)	Br 6571, BrE 02076
GET YOURSELF A NEW BROOM (B 13308)	Br 6607, BrE 01527

Barney Bigard, *Tenor Sax and Clarinet,* replaces Joe Garland.

May 16, 1933

BUNDLE OF BLUES (B 13337 A)	Br 6607, BrE 01573, PaE R 2880
BUNDLE OF BLUES (B 13337 B)	Co 35836
SOPHISTICATED LADY (B 13338)	Br 6600
STORMY WEATHER (B 13339)	Br 6600, BrE 01527

Same personnel.

London, England, July, 1933

HYDE PARK (GB 6038)	DeE M 439, De 323
HARLEM SPEAKS (GB 6039)	DeE M 438, De 800, 3944
AIN'T MISBEHAVIN' (GB 6040)	DeE M 439, De 323, 3516
CHICAGO (GB 6041)	DeE M 438, De 800, 4203

Same personnel.   Recorded in U.S.A.

August 15, 1933

I'M SATISFIED (B 13800)	Br 6638, BrE 01973
JIVE STOMP (B 13801)	Br 6638, BrE 01778

L

HARLEM SPEAKS (B 13802)   Br 6646, Co 36195, BrE 02004
IN THE SHADE OF THE OLD APPLE TREE   Br 6646, Co 36195,
   (B 13803)   BrE 01616

DUKE ELLINGTON AND HIS ORCHESTRA

Arthur Whetsel, Freddy Jenkins, Charles " Cootie " Williams, *Trumpets;* Louis Bacon, *Trumpet and Vocal;* Lawrence Brown, Juan Tizol, Joe " Tricky Sam " Nanton, *Trombones;* Otto Hardwick, *Alto Sax;* Johnny Hodges, *Alto and Soprano Saxes;* Harry Carney, *Alto and Baritone Saxes and Clarinet;* Barney Bigard, *Tenor Sax and Clarinet;* Duke Ellington, *Piano;* Freddy Guy, *Guitar;* Wellman Braud, *Bass;* Sonny Greer, *Drums.*

Chicago, September 26, 1933

RUDE INTERLUDE (77025)   Vi 24431, HMV B 6449
DALLAS DOINGS (77026)   Vi 24431, HMV B 6449

Same personnel, except that Juan Tizol, *Trombone,* is absent.

Chicago, December 4, 1933

DEAR OLD SOUTHLAND (77199)   Vi 24501, HMV B 6468, BD 5766
AWFUL SAD (77200)   Unissued
DAYBREAK EXPRESS (77201)   Vi 24501, HMV B 6468, BD 5766

Chicago, January 9, 1934

DELTA SERENADE (80144)   Vi 24755, HMV BD 183, JF 20, B 9345
STOMPY JONES (80145)   Vi 24521, 201533, HMV B 4992, B 6502

Chicago, January 10, 1934

SOLITUDE (80149)   Vi 24755, HMV B 8410, JF 20
BLUE FEELING (80150)   Vi 24521, HMV B 6502, B 4992

Personnel as for September 26, 1933, but minus Louis Bacon, Juan Tizol and Otto Hardwicke. Ivie Anderson,* *Vocal,* added.

Hollywood, April 12, 1934

*EBONY RHAPSODY (79155)   Vi 24622, 24674, HMV B 6528, X 4316
COCKTAILS FOR TWO (79156)   Vi 24617, HMV B 6497
LIVE AND LOVE TONIGHT (79157)   Vi 24617, HMV B 6497

Otto Hardwicke, *Alto Sax,* and Juan Tizol, *Trombone,* added.

Hollywood, April 17, 1934

I MET MY WATERLOO (79169)   Vi 24622, 24719, HMV X 4316

Personnel as above minus Otto Hardwicke and Freddy Jenkins.

Hollywood, May 9, 1934

*TROUBLED WATERS (79211)   Vi 24651, HMV B 8410, JF 54, X 4593
*MY OLD FLAME (79212)   Vi 24651, HMV B8404, JF 51

Otto Hardwicke and Freddy Jenkins return.

New York City, September 12, 1934

SOLITUDE (B 15910)   Br 6987, BrE 02007, VoE S 40, CoE DB 5041
SADDEST TALE (B 15911)   Br 7310, BrE 01901, PaE R 2880
MOONGLOW (B 15912)   Br 6987, Co 36317, BrE 01901
SUMP'N 'BOUT RHYTHM (B 15913)   Br 7310, BrE 01973, PaE R 2884.

Probable personnel : Charlie Allen, Charles " Cootie " Williams, *Trumpets;* Rex Stewart, *Cornet;* Lawrence Brown, Juan Tizol, Joe " Tricky Sam " Nanton, *Trombones;* Otto Hardwick, Johnny Hodges, Harry Carney, Barney Bigard, *Reeds;* Duke Ellington, *Piano;* Fred Guy, *Guitar;* Hayes Alvis and/or Billy Taylor, *Bass;* Sonny Greer or Fred Avendorf, *Drums.*

Chicago, January 9, 1935

ADMIRATION (C 883)   Unissued
FAREWELL BLUES (C 884)   Unissued
LET's HAVE A JUBILEE (C 885)   Unissued
PORTO RICAN CHAOS (C 886)   Unissued

Same personnel.

March 5, 1936

MARGIE (B 16973)   Br 7526, BrE 02096, PaE R 2884
PORTO RICAN CHAOS (B 16974)   Unissued
TOUGH TRUCKIN' (B 16975)   Unissued
INDIGO ECHOES (B 16976)   Unissued

Arthur Whetsel, *Trumpet,* and Sonny Greer, *Drums,* return.

April 20, 1935

†IN A SENTIMENTAL MOOD (B 17406)   Br 7461, Co 36112, BrE 02038
†SHOWBOAT SHUFFLE (B 17407)   Br 7461, Co 36112, BrE 02038
MERRY-GO-ROUND (B 17408)   Br 7440, BrE 02030
ADMIRATION (B 17409)   Br 7440, BrE 02030

†Re-issued on PaE R 2898 and R 2904 respectively.

Ben Webster, *Tenor Sax*, added.

August 19, 1935

COTTON (B 17974)	Br 7526, BrE 02080
TRUCKIN' (B 17975)	Br 7514, BrE 02080, Co 36317
ACCENT ON YOUTH (B 17976)	Br 7514, BrE 02096

Webster leaves.

September 12, 1935

REMINISCING IN TEMPO—PART 1 (B 18072)	Br 7546, Co 36114, BrE 02103
REMINISCING IN TEMPO—PART 2 (B 18073)	Br 7546, Co 36114, BrE 02103
REMINISCING IN TEMPO—PART 3 (B 18074)	Br 7547, Co 36115, BrE 02104
REMINISCING IN TEMPO—PART 4 (B 18075)	Br 7547, Co 36115, BrE 02104

Same personnel.

January 3, 1936

COOTIE'S CONCERTO (C 1195)	Unissued
JUMPY (C 1196)	Unissued
BARNEY'S CONCERTO (C 1197)	Unissued
FAREWELL BLUES (C 1198)	Unissued
I DON'T KNOW WHY I LOVE YOU (C 1199)	Unissued
DINAH LOU (C 1200) .	Unissued

Same personnel.

February 27, 1936

ISN'T LOVE THE STRANGEST THING ? (B 18734)	Br 7625, BrE 02194
NO GREATER LOVE (B 18735)	Br 7625, BrE 02194
CLARINET LAMENT (Barney's Concerto) (B 18736)	Br 7656, BrE 02222, PaE R 2876
ECHOES OF HARLEM (Cootie's Concerto) (B 18737)	Br 7656, BrE 02222, PaE R 2904
LOVE IS LIKE A CIGARETTE (B 18738)	Br 7627, VoE S 64
KISSING MY BABY GOODNIGHT (B 18739)	Br 7627, BrE 02268
OH BABE, MAYBE SOMEDAY (B 18740)	Br 7767, BrE 02268

Same personnel. Hayes Alvis only on *Bass*.

July 17, 1936

SHOE SHINE BOY (B 19562)	Br 7710, VoE S 22
IT WAS A SAD NIGHT IN HARLEM (B 19563)	Br 7710, VoE S 22
TRUMPET IN SPADES (B 19564)	Br 7752, VoE S 113, PaE R 2890
YEARNING FOR LOVE (B 19565)	Br 7752, VoE S 50

Ben Webster, *Tenor Sax*, added for this session only.

July 29, 1936

IN A JAM (B 19626)	Br 7734, VoE S 31
EXPOSITION SWING (B 19627)	Br 8213, VoE S 50
UPTOWN DOWNBEAT (Black Out) (B 19628)	Br 7734, VoE S 31

DUKE ELLINGTON (Piano Solos)

1937

MOOD INDIGO—SOLITUDE	Br 7990, Co 36312
SOPHISTICATED LADY—IN A SENTIMENTAL MOOD	Br 7990, Co 36312

Previous orchestra personnel. Ivie Anderson,* *Vocal.*

I'VE GOT TO BE A RUG CUTTER (M 179)	Ma 101, Br 7989
(Ivie Anderson, Harry Carney, Rex Stewart, Hayes Alvis, *Vocal*).	
THE NEW EAST ST. LOUIS TOODLE-OO (M 180)	Ma 101, Br 7989
*THERE'S A LULL IN MY LIFE	Ma 117
*IT'S SWELL OF YOU	Ma 117
SCATTIN' AT THE KIT KAT	Ma 123, Br 7994
NEW BIRMINGHAM BREAKDOWN	Ma 123, Br 7994
YOU CAN'T RUN AWAY FROM LOVE	Ma 124, Br 7995
THE LADY WHO COULDN'T BE KISSED	Ma 124, Br 7995
CARAVAN	Ma 131, Br 7997, Co 36120
AZURE	Ma 131, Br 7997, Co 36120
*ALL GOD'S CHILLUN GOT RHYTHM	Ma 137, Br 8001
ALABAMY HOME	Ma 137, Br 8001

DUKE ELLINGTON AND HIS FAMOUS ORCHESTRA

Cootie Williams, Rex Stewart, Danny Baker, *Trumpets;* Joe Nanton, Lawrence Brown, Juan Tizol, *Trombones;* Johnny Hodges, *Alto and Soprano Saxes;* Otto Hardwick, *Alto Sax;* Barney Bigard, *Tenor Sax and Clarinet;* Harry Carney, *Baritone Sax;* Duke Ellington, *Piano;* Fred Guy, *Guitar;* Billy Taylor, *Bass;* Sonny Greer, *Drums;* Ivie Anderson,* *Vocal.*

1937–1938

CRESCENDO IN BLUE (M 649)	Br 8004
DIMINUENDO IN BLUE (M 648)	Br 8004
DUSK IN THE DESERT (M 651)	Br 8029
CHATTER-BOX (M 646)	Br 8029
BLACK BUTTERFLY (LO 376)	Br 8044
HARMONY IN HARLEM (M 650)	Br 8044
STEPPING INTO SWING SOCIETY (M 713)	Br 8063
THE NEW BLACK AND TAN FANTASY (M 715)	Br 8063

RIDING ON A BLUE NOTE (M 751)	Br 8083
LOST IN MEDITATION (M 752)	Br 8083
*SCROUNCH (M 771)	Br 8093
*IF YOU WERE IN MY PLACE (770)	Br 8093
BRAGGIN' IN BRASS (M 773)	Br 8099
CARNIVAL IN CAROLINE (M 774)	Br 8099
I LET A SONG GO OUT OF MY HEART (M 772)	Br 8108
THE GAL FROM JOE'S (M 753)	Br 8108
I'M SLAPPIN' SEVENTH AVENUE	Br 8131
SWINGTIME IN HONOLULU	Br 8131
PYRAMID (M 834)	Br 8168
WHEN MY SUGAR WALKS DOWN THE STREET (M 835)	Br 8168
YOU GAVE ME THE GATE (M 832)	Br 8169
DINAH'S IN A JAM (M 811)	Br 8169
LA DE DOODY DOO (M 847)	Br 8174
THE STEVEDORE'S SERENADE (M 846)	Br 8174
ROSE OF THE RIO GRANDE (M 833)	Br 8186
A GYPSY WITHOUT A SONG (M 845)	Br 8186
WATERMELON MAN (M 844)	Br 8200
LOVE IN SWINGTIME (M 881)	Br 8200
LAMBETH WALK (M 833)	Br 8204
PRELUDE TO A KISS (M 834)	Br 8204
I HAVEN'T CHANGED A THING	Br 8213

Wallace Jones, *Trumpet*, in place of Danny Baker.

A BLUES SERENADE (M 800)	Br 8221
HIP CHIC (M 885)	Br 8221
MIGHTY LIKE THE BLUES (M 899)	Br 8231
BUFFET FLAT (M 886)	Br 8231
PLEASE FORGIVE ME (M 882)	Br 8256
PROLOGUE TO BLACK AND TAN FANTASY (M 714)	Br 8256
JAZZ POTPOURRI (M 947)	Br 8293
BATTLE OF SWING (M 949)	Br 8293
BLUE LIGHT (M 958)	Br 8297
SLAP HAPPY (M 961)	Br 8297
BOY MEETS HORN (M 960)	Br 8306
OLD KING DOOJI (M 959)	Br 8306
SUBTLE LAMENT (MW 998)	Br 8344
PUSSY WILLOW (MW 997)	Br 8344
JUST GOOD FUN (MW 990)	Unissued
INFORMAL BLUES (MW 991)	Unissued
PORTRAIT OF THE LION (WM 1006)	Br 8365
SOMETHING TO LIVE FOR (WM 1007) (Jean Eldridge, *Vocal*)	Br 8365

SMORGASBORD AND SCHNAPPS (WM 1000) (arr. Brick Fleagle)	Br 8380
SOLID OLD MAN (WM 1008)	Br 8380
COTTON CLUB STOMP (WM 1030)	Br 8405.
IN A MIZZ (WM 1038)	Br 8405
YOU CAN'T COUNT ON ME (W M1041)	Br 8411
WAY LOW (WM 1032)	Br 8411

DUKE ELLINGTON AND HIS FAMOUS ORCHESTRA

Cootie Williams, Wallace Jones, *Trumpets;* Rex Stewart, *Cornet;* Joe Nanton, Lawrence Brown, Juan Tizol, *Trombones;* Johnny Hodges, *Alto and Soprano Saxes;* Otto Hardwick, *Alto Sax;* Barney Bigard, *Tenor Sax and Clarinet;* Harry Carney, *Baritone Sax;* Duke Ellington, *Piano;* Fred Guy, *Guitar;* Billy Taylor, *Bass;* Sonny Greer, *Drums;* Ivie Anderson,* *Vocal.*

1939

DOIN' THE VOOM VOOM (WM 1031)	Co 35208
*I'M CHECKIN' OUT—GOOM-BYE (WM 1039)	Co 35208
THE SERGEANT WAS SHY (WM 1063)	Co 35214
SERENADE TO SWEDEN (WM 1033)	Co 35214
BOUNCING BUOYANCY (WM 1062)	Co 35240
*A LONELY CO-ED (WM 1040)	Co 35240
LITTLE POSEY (WM 1091)	Co 35291
LADY IN BLUE (WM 999)	Co 35291
TOOTIN' THROUGH THE ROOF (WM 1094)	Co 35310
GRIEVIN' (WM 1093)	Co 35310
I NEVER FELT THIS WAY BEFORE (WM 1092)	Co 35353
WEELY (WM 1095)	Co 35353
*YOUR LOVE HAS FADED (WM 1107)	Co 35640
*KILLIN' MYSELF (WM 1106)	Co 35640
COUNTRY GAL (WM 1108)	Co 35776

New York City, February 14, 1940

Same personnel plus Ben Webster, *Tenor Sax*, and Jimmy Blanton, *Bass*, in place of Billy Taylor.

*MOOD INDIGO (WM 1137)	Co 35427
*SOLITUDE (WM 1135)	Co 35427
STORMY WEATHER (WM 1136)	Co 35556
SOPHISTICATED LADY (WM 1138)	Co 35556

DUKE ELLINGTON AND HIS FAMOUS ORCHESTRA

Cootie Williams, Wallace Jones, *Trumpets;* Rex Stewart, *Cornet;* Joe Nanton, Lawrence Brown, Juan Tizol, *Trombones;* Johnny Hodges, *Alto and Soprano Saxes;* Otto Hardwick, *Alto Sax;* Ben Webster. *Tenor Sax;* Barney Bigard, *Tenor Sax and Clarinet;* Harry Carney, *Baritone Sax;* Duke Ellington, *Piano;* Fred Guy, *Guitar;* Jimmy Blanton, *Bass;* Sonny Greer, *Drums;* Ivie Anderson,* Herbie Jeffries,† *Vocals.*

1940

MY GREATEST MISTAKE (054624)	HMV B 9129, Vi 26719
*AT A DIXIE ROADSIDE DINER (054607)	HMV B 9129, Vi 26719
HARLEM AIR-SHAFT (054606)	HMV B 9135, Vi 26731
SEPIA PANORAMA (054625)	HMV B 9135, Vi 26731
*FIVE O'CLOCK WHISTLE (053429)	HMV B 9153, Vi 26748
†THERE SHALL BE NO NIGHT (053427)	Vi 26748
RUMPUS IN RICHMOND (054609)	Vi 26788
IN A MELLOTONE (053428)	Vi 26788

PIANO AND BASS DUETS

Duke Ellington, *Piano;* Jimmy Blanton, *Bass.*

New York, 1939

BLUES (WM 1120)	Co 35322
PLUCKED AGAIN (WM 1121)	Co 35322

Chicago, October 1, 1940

PITTER PANTHER PATTER (053504)	HMV B 9179, Vi 27221
SOPHISTICATED LADY (053506)	HMV B 9179, Vi 27221
BODY AND SOUL (053505)	HMV B 9211, Vi 27406
MR. J. B. BLUES (053507)	HMV B 9211, Vi 27406

Previous orchestral personnel.

Chicago, October 17, 1940

THE FLAMING SWORD (053552)	Vi 26797
WARM VALLEY (053450)	Vi 26797

1940

ALL TOO SOON (054608)	Vi 27247
†I NEVER FELT THIS WAY BEFORE (053581)	Vi 27247

Chicago, October 28, 1940

ACROSS THE TRACK BLUES (053579)	HMV B 9171, Vi 27235
CHLO-E (053580)	HMV B 9171, Vi 27235

Chicago, March 6, 1940

JACK THE BEAR (044888)	HMV B 9048, Vi 26536
MORNING GLORY (044890)	HMV B 9048, Vi 26536
†YOU, YOU DARLIN' (044887)	HMV B 9068, Vi 26537
SO FAR, SO GOOD (044891)	HMV B 9068, Vi 26537
KO-KO (044889)	HMV B 9078, Vi 26577

Chicago, March 15, 1940

CONGA BRAVA (049015)	HMV B 9078, Vi 26577
CONCERTO FOR COOTIE (049016)	HMV B 9104, Vi 26598
*ME AND YOU (049017)	HMV B 9104, Vi 26598

Hollywood, May 4, 1940

*COTTON TAIL (049655)	HMV B 9090, Vi 26610
NEVER NO LAMENT (DON'T GET AROUND MUCH ANY MORE) (049656)	HMV B 9090, Vi 26610

Chicago, May 28, 1940

BOJANGLES (053021)	HMV B 9085, Vi 26644
A PORTRAIT OF BERT WILLIAMS (053022)	HMV B 9085, Vi 26644
DUSK (053020)	HMV B 9115, Vi 26677
BLUE GOOSE (053023)	HMV B 9115, Vi 26677

DUKE ELLINGTON AND HIS FAMOUS ORCHESTRA

Rex Stewart, *Cornet;* Ray Nance, Wallace Jones, *Trumpets;* Lawrence Brown, Juan Tizol, Joe Nanton, *Trombones;* Johnny Hodges, *Alto and Soprano Saxes;* Otto Hardwick, *Alto Sax;* Ben Webster, *Tenor Sax;* Barney Bigard, *Tenor Sax and Clarinet;* Harry Carney, *Baritone Sax;* Duke Ellington, *Piano;* Fred Guy, *Guitar;* Jimmy Blanton, *Bass;* Sonny Greer, *Drums;* Ivie Anderson,* Herbie Jeffries,† *Vocals;* Billy Strayhorn, *Piano,* on some sides.

Chicago, December 28, 1940

†FLAMINGO (053781)	HMV B 9206, Vi 27326
†THE GIRL IN MY DREAMS TRIES TO LOOK LIKE YOU (053782)	HMV B 9206, Vi 27326
THE SIDEWALKS OF NEW YORK (053780)	HMV B 9235, Vi 27380

Hollywood, February 15, 1941

TAKE THE "A" TRAIN (055283)	HMV B 9235, Vi 27380
JUMPIN' PUNKINS (055284)	HMV B 9196, Vi 27356
BLUE SERGE (055286)	HMV B 9196, Vi 27356
JOHN HARDY'S WIFE (055285)	HMV B 9345, Vi 27434
AFTER ALL (055287)	HMV B 9386, Vi 27434

L*

DUKE ELLINGTON (Piano Solos)

New York City, May 14, 1941

DEAR OLD SOUTHLAND (065604)	HMV B 9284, Vi 27564
SOLITUDE (065605)	HMV B 9284, Vi 27564

Hollywood, June 5, 1941

BAKIFF (061283)	
(featuring Ray Nance, *Violin*)	HMV B 9254, Vi 27502
THE GIDDYBUG GALLOP (061286)	HMV B 9254, Vi 27502
ARE YOU STICKING ? (061284)	HMV B 9277, Vi 27804
JUST A-SETTIN' AND A-ROCKIN' (061285)	HMV B 9268, Vi 27587

Hollywood, June 26, 1941

*CHOCOLATE SHAKE (061318)	HMV B 9252, Vi 27531
*I GOT IT BAD AND THAT AIN'T GOOD (061319)	HMV B 9252, Vi 27531

Hollywood, July 2, 1941

CLEMENTINE (061338)	HMV B 9273, Vi 27700
†THE BROWNSKIN GAL (061339)	Vi 27517
†JUMP FOR JOY (061340)	HMV B 9314, Vi 27517
MOON OVER CUBA (061341)	HMV B 9268, Vi 27587

Hollywood, September 26, 1941

FIVE O'CLOCK DRAG (061684)	HMV B 9273, Vi 27700
*ROCKS IN MY BED (061685)	HMV B 9362, Vi 27639
BLI-BLIP (061686) (Ray Nance, *Vocal*)	HMV B 9362, Vi 27639
CHELSEA BRIDGE (061687)	Unissued

Hollywood, December 2, 1941

Alvin Raglin, Jr. *(Bass)* in place of Jimmy Blanton.

RAINCHECK (061941)	HMV B 9305, Vi 27880
WHAT GOOD WOULD IT DO ? (061942)	HMV B 9309, Vi 27740
†I DON'T KNOW WHAT KIND OF BLUES I GOT (061943)	HMV B 9277, Vi 27804
CHELSEA BRIDGE (061944)	HMV B 9309, Vi 27740

Chicago, January 21, 1942

Ray Nance doubling on *Violin* on last two sides.

PERDIDO (070682)	HMV B 9305, Vi 27880
THE " C " JAM BLUES (070683)	HMV B 9292, Vi 27856
MOON MIST (070684)	HMV B 9292, Vi 27856

New York City, February 26, 1942

WHAT AM I HERE FOR ? (071890)	HMV B 9415, Vi 20-1598
I DON'T MIND (071891)	HMV B 9415, Vi 20-1598
SOMEONE (071892)	Vi 20-1584

Hollywood, June 26, 1942

†MY LITTLE BROWN BOOK (072437)	Vi 20-1584
MAIN STEM (ALTITUDE) (072438)	HMV B 9386, Vi 20-1556
JOHNNY COME LATELY (072439)	HMV B 9423, Vi 20-1556

Chicago, July 28, 1942

Chauncy Haughton, *Tenor Saxophone*, for Barney Bigard.

*HAYFOOT, STRAWFOOT (074781)	HMV B 9324, Vi 20-1505
SENTIMENTAL LADY (074782)	Vi 20-1528
A SLIP OF THE LIP (074783) (Ray Nance, *Vocal*)	Vi 20-1528
SHERMAN SHUFFLE (074784)	HMV B 9324, Vi 20-1505

DUKE ELLINGTON UNITS

BARNEY BIGARD AND HIS ORCHESTRA

Cootie Williams, *Trumpet;* Juna Tizol, *Trombone;* Barney Bigard, *Clarinet;* Harry Carney, *Baritone Sax;* Duke Ellington, *Piano;* Fred Guy, *Guitar;* Billy Taylor, *Bass;* Sonny Greer, *Drums.*

December 19, 1936

CARAVAN (LO 373)	Va 515, Vo 3809[1]
STOMPY JONES (LO 374)	Va 515, Vo 3809[1]
CLOUDS IN MY HEART (LO 371)	Va 525, Vo 3813[1]
FROLIC SAM (LO 372)	Va 525, Vo 3813[1]

April 29, 1937

Rex Stewart, *Trumpet*, in place of Cootie Williams.

FOUR AND ONE HALF STREET (M 434)	Va 564, Vo 3820[1]
LAMENT FOR A LOST LOVE (M 433)	Va 564, Vo 3820[1]
JAZZ A LA CARTE (M 436)	Va 655, Vo 3842[1]
DEMI-TASSE (M 435)	Va 655, Vo 3842[1]

June 16, 1937

GET IT SOUTHERN STYLE (M 525) (Sue Mitchell, *Vocal*)	Va 596, Vo 3828
IF YOU'RE EVER IN MY ARMS AGAIN (M 528) (Sue Mitchell, *Vocal*)	Va 596, Vo 3828
MOONLIGHT FIESTA (M 526)	Va 626, Vo 3834
SPONGE CAKE AND SPINACH (M 527)	Va 626, Vo 3834

January 19, 1938

DRUMMERS DELIGHT (M 724)	Vo 3985
IF I THOUGHT YOU CARED (M 725)	Vo 3985

1939

BARNEY'S GOIN' EASY (I'M CHECKIN' OUT, GOOM-BYE) (WM 1036)	Vo 5378[1]
MINUET IN BLUES (WM 1117)	Vo 5378[1]
LOST IN TWO FLATS (WM 1118)	Vo 5422[1]
EARLY MORNIN' (WM 1118)	Vo 5422[1]
MARDI GRAS MADNESS (WM 1141)	Vo 5595[1]
WATCH THE BIRDIE (WM 1142)	Vo 5595[1]
JUST ANOTHER DREAM (WM 1037)	Ok 5663
HONEY HUSH (WM 1119)	Ok 5663

BARNEY BIGARD AND HIS ORCHESTRA

Ray Nance, *Trumpet;* Juan Tizol, *Trombone;* Barney Bigard, *Clarinet;* Ben Webster, *Tenor Sax;* Duke Ellington, *Piano;* Jimmy Blanton, *Bass;* Sonny Greer, *Drums.*

Chicago, November 11, 1940

CHARLIE THE CHULO (053621)	HMV B 9185, Bb 10981
A LULL AT DAWN (053623)	HMV B 9185, Bb 10981
LAMENT FOR A JAVANETTE (053622)	HMV B 9215, Bb 11098
READY EDDY (053624)	HMV B 9215, Bb 11098

Hollywood, September 29, 1941

Harry Carney, *Baritone, Sax* in place of Ben Webster and J. Bryant, *Bass,* in place of Jimmy Blanton.

BROWN SUEDE (061688)	Bb 11581
" C " BLUES (061690)	HMV B 9314, Bb 11581
NOIR BLUE (061689)	Unissued
JUNE (061691)	Unissued

JOHNNY HODGES AND HIS ORCHESTRA

Cootie Williams, *Trumpet;* Johnny Hodges, Otto Hardwick, *Alto Saxes;* Barney Bigard, *Clarinet;* Harry Carney, *Baritone Sax;* Duke Ellington, *Piano;* Fred Guy, *Guitar;* Hayes Alvis, *Bass;* Sonny Greer, *Drums;* Mary McHugh,* *Vocal.*

1937

FOOLIN' MYSELF (21186)	Va 576, Vo 3771
YOU'LL NEVER GO TO HEAVEN (21188)	Va 576, Vo 3771
*A SAILBOAT IN THE MOONLIGHT (21187)	Va 586, Vo 3773
*MY DAY	Vo 3948
*SILVER MOON AND GOLDEN SANDS	Vo 3948

[1]Also issued on the OKeh label with the same number as the Vocalion issue.

Cootie Williams, *Trumpet;* Lawrence Brown, *Trombone;* Johnny Hodges, *Alto and Soprano Saxes;* Harry Carney, *Baritone Sax;* Duke Ellington, *Piano;* Billy Taylor, *Bass;* Sonny Greer, *Drums.*

1938

IF YOU WERE IN MY PLACE (M 794)	Vo 4046
I LET A SONG GO OUT OF MY HEART (M 795)	Vo 4046
RENDEZVOUS WITH RHYTHM (M 796)	Vo 4115
JEEP'S BLUES (M 793)	Vo 4115
EMPTY BALLROOM BLUES (M 854)	Vo 4213
YOU WALKED OUT OF THE PICTURE (M 852)	Vo 4213
LOST IN MEDITATION (M 855)	Vo 4242
PYRAMID (M 853)	Vo 4242
A BLUES SERENADE (M 872)	Vo 4309
JITTERBUG'S LULLABY (M 875)	Vo 4309
KRUM ELBOW BLUES (M 890)	Vo 4351
THERE'S SOMETHING ABOUT AN OLD LOVE (M 888)	Vo 4351
*PRELUDE TO A KISS (M 887)	Vo 4386
THE JEEP IS JUMPIN' (M 889)	Vo 4386
LOVE IN SWINGTIME (M 873)	Vo 4335
SWINGIN' IN THE DELL (M 874)	Vo 4335
HODGE PODGE (M 951)	Vo 4573
WANDERLUST (M 953)	Vo 4573
I'M IN ANOTHER WORLD (M 950)	Vo 4622
DANCING ON THE STARS (M 952)	Vo 4622
LIKE A SHIP IN THE NIGHT (M 974) (Jean Eldridge, *Vocal*)	Vo 4710
SWINGIN' ON THE CAMPUS (M 976)	Vo 4710
DOOJI WOOJI (M 977)	Vo 4849
MISSISSIPPI DREAMBOAT (M 975) (Jean Eldridge, *Vocal*)	Vo 4849
YOU CAN COUNT ON ME (WM 1028)	Vo 4917
KITCHEN MECHANIC'S DAY (WM 1026)	Vo 4917
DANCE OF THE GOON (WM 1003)	Vo 4941
HOME TOWN BLUES (WM 1029)	Vo 4941
THE RABBIT'S JUMP (WM 1072)	Vo 5100[1]
RENT PARTY BLUES (WM 1002)	Vo 5100[1]
SAVOY STRUT (WM 1001)	Vo 5170[1]
GOOD GAL BLUES (WM 1004)	Vo 5170[1]
TRULY WONDERFUL (WM 1074)	Vo 5330
MY HEART JUMPED OVER THE MOON (WM 1027)	Vo 5330
DREAM BLUES (WM 1075)	Vo 5353[1]
I KNOW WHAT YOU DO (WM 1097)	Vo 5353[1]
TIRED SOCKS (WM 1099)	Vo 5533[1]
SKUNK HOLLOW BLUES (WM 1096)	Vo 5533[1]

[1]Also issued on the OKeh label with the same number as the Vocalion issue.

YOUR LOVE HAS FADED (WM 1098)   Vo 5940[1]
MOON ROMANCE (WM 1073)   Vo 5940[1]

JOHNNY HODGES AND HIS ORCHESTRA

Cootie Williams, *Trumpet;* Lawrence Brown, *Trombone;* Johnny
Hodges, *Alto Sax;* Harry Carney, *Baritone Sax;* Duke Ellington,
Piano; Jimmy Blanton, *Bass;* Sonny Greer, *Drums.*

Chicago, November 2, 1940

DAY DREAM (053603)   HMV B 9184, Bb 11021
JUNIOR HOP (053606)   HMV B 9184, Bb 11021
GOOD QUEEN BESS (053604)   HMV B 9229, Bb 11117
THAT'S THE BLUES OLD MAN (053605)   HMV B 9229, Bb 11117

Hollywood, July 3, 1941

Ray Nance *(Trumpet)* in place of Cootie Williams.

SQUATTY ROO (061346)   HMV B 9283, Bb 11447
THINGS AIN'T WHAT THEY USED TO BE   HMV B 9283, Bb 11447
   (061348)
PASSION FLOWER (061347)   Bb 30-0817
GOING OUT THE BACK WAY (061349)   HMV B 9423, Bb 30-0817

REX STEWART AND HIS 52ND STREET STOMPERS

Rex Stewart, *Trumpet;* Lawrence Brown, *Trombone;* Johnny
Hodges, *Alto and Soprano Saxes;* Harry Carney, *Baritone Sax;* Duke
Ellington, *Piano;* Ceelle Burke, *Electric Guitar;* Billy Taylor, *Bass;*
Sonny Greer, *Drums.*   1937

REXATIOUS (B 4369)   Va 517, Vo 3810
LAZY MAN'S SHUFFLE (B 4370) .   Va 517, Vo 3810

Rex Stewart, Freddy Jenkins, *Trumpets;* Johnny Hodges, *Alto
Sax;* Harry Carney, *Baritone Sax;* Duke Ellington, *Piano;* Brick
Fleagle, *Guitar;* Jack Maisel, *Drums.*

TEA AND TRUMPETS (M 552)   Va 618, Vo 3831
THE BACK ROOM ROMP (M 549)   Va 618, Vo 3831
LOVE IN MY HEART (SWING BABY SWING) (M 550) Va 664, Vo 3844
SUGAR HILL SHIM SHAM (M 551)   Va 664, Vo 3844

Rex Stewart, *Trumpet;* Joe Nanton, *Trombone;* Barney Bigard,
Clarinet; Duke Ellington, *Piano;* Billy Taylor, *Bass;* Sonny Greer,
Drums.   March 20. 1939

" FAT STUFF " SERENADE (WM 996)   Vo 5448[1]
I'LL COME BACK FOR MORE (WM 995)   Vo 5448[1]
SAN JUAN HILL (WM 994)   Vo 5510[1]

[1]Also issued on the OKeh label with the same number as the Vocalion issue.

REX STEWART AND HIS ORCHESTRA

Rex Stewart, *Cornet;* Lawrence Brown, *Trombone;* Ben Webster, *Tenor Sax;* Harry Carney, *Baritone Sax;* Duke Ellington, *Piano;* Jimmy Blanton, *Bass;* Sonny Greer, *Drums.*

Chicago, November 2, 1940

WITHOUT A SONG (053607)	HMV B 9208, Bb 10946
MY SUNDAY GAL (053608)	Bb 10946
MOBILE BAY (053609)	HMV B 9208, Bb 11057
LINGER AWHILE (053610)	Bb 11057

Hollywood, June 3, 1941

SOME SATURDAY (061342)	HMV B 9260, Bb 11258
SUBTLE SLOUGH (061343)	HMV B 9260, Bb 11258
MENELIK (THE LION OF JUDAH) (061344)	Unissued
POOR BUBBER (061345)	Unissued

COOTIE WILLIAMS AND HIS RUG CUTTERS

Cootie Williams, *Trumpet;* Joe Nanton, *Trombone;* Johnny Hodges, *Alto and Soprano Saxes;* Harry Carney, *Baritone Sax;* Duke Ellington, *Piano;* Fred Guy, *Guitar;* Hayes Alvis, *Bass;* Sonny Greer, *Drums.* March 8, 1937

DOWNTOWN UPROAR (M 186)	Va 527, Vo 3814
BLUE REVERIE (M 188)	Va 527, Vo 3814
DIGA DIGA DOO (M 187)	Va 555, Vo 3818
I CAN'T BELIEVE THAT YOU'RE IN LOVE WITH ME (M 185)	Va 555, Vo 3818

Cootie Williams, *Trumpet;* Juan Tizol, *Trombone;* Barney Bigard, *Clarinet;* Otto Hardwick, *Alto Sax;* Harry Carney, *Baritone Sax;* Duke Ellington, *Piano;* Billy Taylor, *Bass;* Sonny Greer, *Drums;* Jerry Kruger,* *Vocal.*

October 26, 1937

I CAN'T GIVE YOU ANYTHING BUT LOVE (M 672)	Vo 3890
*WATCHING (M 670)	Vo 3890
JUBILESTA (M 669)	Vo 3922
PIGEONS AND PEPPERS (M 671)	Vo 3922

Cootie Williams, *Trumpet;* Lawrence Brown, *Trombone;* Johnny Hodges, *Alto and Soprano Saxes;* Otto Hardwick, *Alto Sax;* Harry Carney, *Baritone Sax;* Duke Ellington, *Piano;* Fred Guy, *Guitar;* Billy Taylor, *Bass;* Sonny Greer, *Drums.*

1938

ECHOES OF HARLEM (M 729)	Vo 3960
LOST IN MEDITATION (M 726)	Vo 3960

Barney Bigard, *Tenor Sax*, added.

SWINGTIME IN HONOLULU (M 802)	Vo 4061
CARNIVAL IN CAROLINE (M 803)	Vo 4061
OL' MAN RIVER (M 804) (Jerry Kruger, *Vocal*)	Vo 4086
A LESSON IN " C " (M 801) (Jerry Kruger, *Vocal*)	Vo 4086

Same personnel with the exception of Fred Guy.

BLUES IN THE EVENING (M 877)	Vo 4324
SHARPIE (M 878)	Vo 4324
SWING PAN ALLEY (879)	Vo 4425
CHASIN' CHIPPIES (M 876)	Vo 4425
DELTA MOOD (M 954)	Vo 4574
THE BOYS FROM HARLEM (955)	Vo 4574
MOBILE BLUES (M 956)	Vo 4636
GAL-AVANTIN' (M 957)	Vo 4636

Cootie Williams, *Trumpet;* Lawrence Brown, *Trombone;* Johnny Hodges, *Alto and Soprano Saxes;* Otto Hardwick, *Alto Sax;* Harry Carney, *Baritone Sax;* Duke Ellington, *Piano;* Billy Taylor, *Bass;* Sonny Greer, *Drums.*

1939

AIN'T THE GRAVY GOOD (M 984) (Cootie Williams, *Vocal*)	Vo 4726
BOUDOIR BENNY (M 983)	Vo 4726
BLACK BEAUTY (WM 1045)	Vo 4958
NIGHT SONG (WM 1042)	Vo 4958
BEAUTIFUL ROMANCE (M 982)	Vo 5411
SHE'S GONE (M 985) (Cootie Williams, *Vocal*)	Vo 5411

Cootie Williams, *Trumpet;* Lawrence Brown, *Trombone;* Johnny Hodges, *Alto and Soprano Saxes;* Barney Bigard, *Tenor Sax;* Harry Carney, *Baritone Sax;* Duke Ellington, *Piano;* Jimmy Blanton, *Bass;* Sonny Greer, *Drums.*

BLUES A POPPIN' (WM 1043)	Vo 5618[1]
BLACK BUTTERFLY (WM 1143)	Vo 5618[1]
DRY LONG SO (WM 1144)	Vo 5690[1]
GIVE IT UP (WM 1146)	Vo 5690[1]
TOP AND BOTTOM (WM 1044)	Vo 6336[1]
TOASTED PICKLE (WM 1145)	Vo 6336[1]

[1]Also issued on the OKeh label with the same number as the Vocalion issue.

RECORDS MADE AFTER THE AFM RECORDING BAN
(AUGUST, 1942, TO NOVEMBER, 1944)

DUKE ELLINGTON AND HIS FAMOUS ORCHESTRA

Rex Stewart, *Cornet;* Ray Nance, Taft Jordan, Shelton Hemphill, William Anderson, *Trumpets;* Lawrence Brown, Claude Jones, Joe Nanton, *Trombones;* Johnny Hodges, *Alto and Soprano Saxes;* Otto Hardwick, *Alto Sax;* Al Sears, *Tenor Sax;* Jimmy Hamilton, *Tenor Sax and Clarinet;* Harry Carney, *Baritone Sax and Clarinet;* Duke Ellington, *Piano;* Fred Guy, *Guitar;* Alvin Raglin, Jr., *Bass;* Sonny Greer, *Drums.* *Joya Sherrill, †Kay Davis, ‡Marie Ellington,. § Albert Hibbler, *Vocals.*

New York City, December 1, 1944

† §I AIN'T GOT NOTHIN' BUT THE BLUES	HMV B 9427, Vi 20-1623
*I DIDN'T KNOW ABOUT YOU	Vi 20-1623
*I'M BEGINNING TO SEE THE LIGHT	HMV B 9427, Vi 20-1618
§DON'T YOU KNOW I CARE	Vi 20-1618

New York City, December 11, 1944

BLACK, BROWN AND BEIGE :

WORK SONG	HMV C 3504, Vi 28-0400-A
COME SUNDAY	HMV C 3504, Vi 28-0401-A

New York City, December 12, 1944

BLACK, BROWN AND BEIGE :

*THE BLUES	HMV C 3505, Vi 28-0401-B
THREE DANCES	HMV C 3505, Vi 28-0400-B

New York City, January 4, 1945

CARNEGIE BLUES	HMV B 9448, Vi 20-1644
*MY HEART SINGS	Vi 20-1644
MOOD TO BE WOO'D	HMV B 9448, Vi 20-1670
BLUE CELLOPHANE	Unissued

New York City, April 26, 1945

*KISSING BUG	Vi 20-1670

New York City, May 1, 1945

*EV'RYTHING BUT YOU	Vi 20-1697
RIFF STACCATO (Ray Nance, *Vocal*)	Vi 20-1697

New York City, May 10, 1945

PRELUDE TO A KISS	Unissued

New York City, May 11, 1945

BLACK AND TAN FANTASY	Unissued
CARAVAN	Unissued
MOOD INDIGO	Unissued

New York City, May 14, 1945

Same personnel, with Bob Haggart in place of Alvin Raglin, Jr., *Bass.*

IN A SENTIMENTAL MOOD	Unissued
SOPHISTICATED LADY	Unissued
*†‡IT DON'T MEAN A THING	Unissued
TONIGHT I SHALL SLEEP (Tommy Dorsey, *Trombone*, added)	Vi 45-0002

New York City, May 15, 1945

Same personnel, with Sid Weiss in place of Alvin Raglin, Jr., *Bass.*

*†‡§SOLITUDE	Unissued
*I LET A SONG GO OUT OF MY HEART	Unissued

New York City, May 16, 1945

Previous orchestral personnel.

BLACK BEAUTY	Unissued
§EV'RY HOUR ON THE HOUR	Vi 20-1718

Duke Ellington, *Piano*, and rhythm.

FRANKIE AND JOHNNY	Unissued
JUMPIN' ROOM ONLY	Unissued

New York City, July 24, 1945

Previous orchestral personnel.

PERFUME SUITE :	
BALCONY SERENADE	Unissued
§STRANGE FEELING	Unissued

New York City, July 30, 1945

PERFUME SUITE :	
DANCERS IN LOVE	Unissued
COLORATURA	Unissued
TIME'S A-WASTIN'	Vi 20-1718

New York City, October 8, 1945

Same personnel, with Sidney Catlett in place of Sonny Greer, *Drums.*

*TELL YA WHAT I'M GONNA DO	Vi 20-1748
*COME TO BABY, DO	Vi 20-1748

ABBREVIATIONS USED IN THIS DISCOGRAPHY

Records.

Ba	Banner
Bb	Bluebird
Br	Brunswick
Br E	English Brunswick
Br F	French Brunswick
Ca	Cameo
Co	Columbia
Co E	English Columbia
De	Decca
De E	English Decca
Di	Diva
Ge	Gennett
Ha	Harmony
HMV	His Master's Voice
HOW	Hit of the Week
Ma	Master
Me	Meletone
OK	Okeh
Or	Oriole
Pat	Pathe
Pa E	English Parlophone
Pe	Perfect
Re	Regal
Ro	Romeo
Va	Variety
Ve	Velvetone
Vo	Vocalion
Vo E	English Vocalion
Vi	Victor

INDEX